VOLUME EDITOR

DALE JACQUETTE is Senior Professorial Chair in Theoretical Philosophy at the University of Bern, Switzerland. His many previous works include *Wittgenstein's Thought in Transition* (1998), *Ontology* (2002), *David Hume's Critique of Infinity* (2001), and *The Philosophy of Schopenhauer* (2005). He has edited the *Blackwell Companion to Philosophical Logic* (2002), the *Cambridge Companion to Brentano* (2004), and the Elsevier volume on *Philosophy of Logic* (2006) in the Handbook of the Philosophy of Science series.

SERIES EDITOR

FRITZ ALLHOFF is an Assistant Professor in the Philosophy Department at Western Michigan University, as well as a Senior Research Fellow at the Australian National University's Centre for Applied Philosophy and Public Ethics. In addition to editing the *Philosophy for Everyone* series, Allhoff is the volume editor or co-editor for several titles, including *Wine & Philosophy* (Wiley-Blackwell, 2007), *Whiskey & Philosophy* (with Marcus P. Adams, Wiley, 2009), and *Food & Philosophy* (with Dave Monroe, Wiley-Blackwell, 2007).

PHILOSOPHY FOR EVERYONE

Series editor: Fritz Allhoff

Not so much a subject matter, philosophy is a way of thinking. Thinking not just about the Big Questions, but about little ones too. This series invites everyone to ponder things they care about, big or small, significant, serious … or just curious.

Edited by Dale Jacquette

CANNABIS

PHILOSOPHY FOR EVERYONE

What Were We Just Talking About?

Foreword by Richard Cusick

A John Wiley & Sons, Ltd., Publication

This edition first published 2010

© 2010 Blackwell Publishing Ltd except for editorial material and organization

© 2010 Dale Jacquette

Blackwell Publishing was acquired by John Wiley & Sons in February 2007. Blackwell's publishing program has been merged with Wiley's global Scientific, Technical, and Medical business to form Wiley-Blackwell.

Registered Office
John Wiley & Sons Ltd, The Atrium, Southern Gate, Chichester, West Sussex, PO19 8SQ, United Kingdom

Editorial Offices
350 Main Street, Malden, MA 02148-5020, USA
9600 Garsington Road, Oxford, OX4 2DQ, UK
The Atrium, Southern Gate, Chichester, West Sussex, PO19 8SQ, UK

For details of our global editorial offices, for customer services, and for information about how to apply for permission to reuse the copyright material in this book please see our website at www.wiley.com/wiley-blackwell.

The right of Dale Jacquette to be identified as the author of the editorial material in this work has been asserted in accordance with the UK Copyright, Designs and Patents Act 1988.

Library of Congress Cataloging-in-Publication Data

Cannabis – philosophy for everyone: what were we just talking about? / edited by Dale Jacquette.
    p.   cm. — (Philosophy for everyone)
    Includes bibliographical references.
    ISBN 978-1-4051-9967-4 (pbk.: alk. paper) 1. Marijuana.   2. Cannabis.
I. Jacquette, Dale.   II. Title: Cannabis – philosophy for everyone.
    HV5822.M3C285 2010
    362.29′5—dc22

                                                    2010004706

A catalogue record for this book is available from the British Library.

Set in 10/12.5pt Plantin by SPi Publisher Services, Pondicherry, India
Printed in Singapore

1   2010

For Ed Rosenthal,
pioneer and
political lightning rod

If the words "life, liberty, and the pursuit of happiness"
don't include the right to experiment with your own
consciousness, then the Declaration of Independence
isn't worth the hemp it was written on.

Terence McKenna
Live in New York
The Music Faucet
June 20, 1993

CONTENTS

FOREWORD

Three men come up against a locked door. The first man is drunk out of his mind. The second man is tripping wildly on LSD, and the third man is stoned on really good marijuana.

The first man says, "Let's knock down the Goddamn door!"

The second man says, "Let's float through the keyhole . . ."

And the third man says, "Let's sit down and wait for someone to show up with the key."

After nearly a century of American marijuana prohibition – the first US anti-cannabis law passed in Utah in 1915 – it's beginning to look as if someone is finally about to show up with the key.

In 2010 there are an unprecedented forty-plus marijuana law reform bills pending in twenty-three states. These encompass a wide range of reform including proposals for medical marijuana, decriminalization, and legalization. In January New Jersey became the fourteenth state to legalize the medical use of cannabis and full legalization will be included on the California ballot in November.

These are heady days indeed. Hyperbolic prohibitionists insist we stand on the high precipice of increased psychosis, and that the meta-phorical door is really a gateway to a hard drug hell. Proponents of marijuana law reform oraculate a more positive future filled with fiber, fuel, and fun, of miracle medicine and good vibrations. I suspect the upcoming reality will be far more nuanced than either side is willing to admit. The truth is no one knows what's going to happen if and when marijuana finally becomes legal in the United States.

Will use rise? Will prices drop? Will madness or laughter prevail? Certainly, over 800,000 American arrests will fall off the radar and that can't be a bad thing. Medical patients will stop worrying about getting busted for medicine, which in itself will have a palliative effect. But will my teenage daughter be more or less likely to take up smoking pot after criminal sanctions disappear? I don't know the answer but I am bedeviled by the question.

Certainly, I worry more about other demons. I tell her that if she takes up hard drugs she may very well die because those vile pursuits have killed so many good people. I tell her to be very careful of spirits – of wine, whisky, and beer – because those habits very nearly killed me when I was young and perhaps the propensity lies nestled in her genes. I tell her that if she smokes cigarettes "I might kill you myself just for being that stupid," and then I smile (and we'll see how that works out). My many warnings regarding weed, however, are much less straightforward and far more faceted because I don't want to be a hypocrite and because that conversation is necessarily more . . . philosophical.

I believe that marijuana is not for children and as the associate publisher of *High Times* magazine I know something about the subject. I think it should be an honorable widespread activity among responsible adults – like sex or driving a car. I tell my young daughter that she could undoubtedly switch on the engine, put it in gear, and might even get someplace; but without that necessary judgment that comes with experience she might very well cause a terrible accident along the way that will hurt her or hurt someone else.

Then I warn her about driving.

I tell her of the Bashilange: in the nineteenth century, at the time of the dissolution of the great Luba Empire in Central Africa, a number of smaller kingdoms emerged. The Baluba chief, Kalamba-Moukengee, subjugated neighboring tribes at gunpoint and, struggling to unify his new confederation, ordered all the ancient fetishes to be burned in public, and in their place instituted the Bantu custom of smoking hemp to reincarnate the soul. The Baluba men gathered around the fire in the center of the village each night and solemnly smoked cannabis from a huge calabash, and a tribal offender was publicly punished by being forced to smoke hemp until he lost consciousness.

A tribal faction within this new coalition, the aggressive Bashilange led by Moamba Mputt, established the *Ben-Riamba* cult – the so-called "Sons of Hemp" – who quickly put down their spears and foreswore their warlike ways. The Sons of Hemp quickly gained many followers. The Bashilange became less violent, began to treat with other tribes, and made more laws. The land of the hemp smokers along the banks of the Lulua River began to be called *Lubuku*, which is translated as "Friendship," and the partisans of *riamba* were widely known as "Friends" and greeted each other with the Bashilangen word for life (*Moio!*).

It's a pretty tale as far as it goes, but not all was perfect in paradise. Bashilangen women were not allowed to smoke hemp and were consigned to work in the fields, keep the house, and raise the children, while the men made cloth, went hunting or, for the most part, smoked hemp and talked "with incredible fluency."

I urge my daughter and our readers to remember the Bashilange.

The homespun philosopher Yogi Berra (who knew something about baseball) famously observed that "It ain't over 'till it's over," which reminds us that anything can happen. It's possible I suppose that marijuana reform could be repealed instead of marijuana law, but I have my doubts because we've mitigated the hype and because Americans can no longer afford to ignore the billions of dollars in tax revenue that marijuana law reform will provide. While I personally believe that legalizing cannabis would encourage a more civilized society, I also recognize that reasonable people can disagree. That's why this book is so timely and important. There are overblown claims on both sides of the equation and we need to have the more disciplined discourse that philosophy provides. Philosophy, at its best, is the art of reason tempered by the science of thought, and our conversations regarding cannabis need to be more reasonable, more thoughtful, and more civilized – now more than ever. This book is a good place to start. We stand before a locked door or a dangerous precipice – you are free to choose your own metaphor – but whichever you prefer, one thing seems clear. We are about to turn the key or take the jump.

Before we do, let's think about that.

❦ RICHARD CUSICK

PREFACE

This book came about as part of a larger effort to relate contemporary philosophical discourse directly to the interests and concerns of persons outside the tweedy world of professional academic philosophy. No doubt philosophy and the world outside its ivy towers can each benefit from a little positive interaction. But why cannabis? Why weed versus tweed?

Cannabis use is widespread and increasing in worldwide popularity. It is estimated that approximately one out of three Americans has tried or uses marijuana with some frequency. Elsewhere in many parts of the world the percentages of active regular cannabis enjoyment are equally impressive. Cannabis consumption levels are therefore sufficiently noteworthy to draw philosophical attention at the very least as a social phenomenon, and the use, effects, and contemporary prohibition of cannabis raise intriguing philosophical questions.

No doubt it says something interesting about America in the twenty-first century that there exist laws against marijuana, and that so many people continue to risk violating the law for the sake of getting high. The two facts together arguably bespeak a dominant trend in the United States, for a hip and hedonistic part of the population to challenge the Puritanism latent within the culture that goes hand in glove with a severe and often joyless work ethic that seems to have rooted itself into the American grain even after the Puritans themselves had long gone from this earth. The plain fact is that, thus far, not enough responsible adult Americans, even if they smoke pot, have organized themselves politically with any degree of success to revoke the present-day draconian anti-cannabis laws.

Some laggards may reason that pot smoking should remain illegal because, after all, you can still always get it, while in the meantime we should be cautious until we better understand what social impact cannabis legalization might have, say, for the world our children will inherit. Will all of North America start to look like Amsterdam's red light district? Surely not, although some parts of North America could do worse. Nor should we overlook the fact that the Netherlands has friendly non-menacing coffeeshops elsewhere in Amsterdam and all over the country for casual cannabis purchase and use on the premises or at home by responsible, gainfully employed, tax-paying adults, and that the rest of the country does not at all look like Amsterdam's red light district, whatever your opinion of its aesthetics.

Still, what would it be like for the children? We must never cease to ask such questions, it seems, but instead shape all our social policy around the imperative of offering a better future for our eventually ungrateful progeny. What will their world be like if cannabis becomes more freely available potentially in every neighborhood? Even if good models of controlled dispensing are followed, it is axiomatic that cannabis is going to be more freely available if it is legalized than if it were kept illegal. After all, we do not know what it will do to our way of life for cannabis to become no more inaccessible to responsible adults than a visit to the corner liquor store. Things are hard enough as they are, this reasonable-sounding reckoning continues, so let us continue to support or in any case not get active to defeat anti-marijuana laws, and keep things more or less as they are, even if we personally like to smoke and continue to sneak one ourselves from time to time.

This line of argument is no doubt partly to blame for the snail's pace of progress toward cannabis legalization. For all its appearance of good logic, such thinking is nevertheless seriously flawed in one important respect. Parents and other concerned community members need to wonder in practical terms, first, what the probabilities are that their children will someday experiment with and perhaps even come regularly to use cannabis. If the adults in question have also at least experimented with marijuana, then they might understand the attraction, and recognize that their children at some point are more than likely at least to try marijuana for the sake of getting high. If it seems more than likely than not that this will occur, then, secondly, the same responsible-for-our-children's-future adults need to ask themselves whether they would also prefer to have these same children when they're grown up go to jail some day for getting caught holding a little joint. If that does not seem like a good thing, then it appears that persons concerned about the future of today's youth do not have a strong argument for a conservative stance against relaxing marijuana prohibition.

Cannabis laws are currently in flux, which is arguably a good sign. As I write these words, Mexico has just legalized possession of small amounts of a surprising list of drugs that includes cannabis, and Argentina has ruled that, although its sale is still illegal there, it is unconstitutional to imprison anyone for possession of cannabis. It is indeed and ought to be recognized everywhere that it is unconstitutional to prosecute the possession and use of a little noble bud. The cannabis reform movement has been slower to hit a responsive chord with legislators in the United States, but there are already many places today where you will not suffer more than paying a fine if caught with a personal use amount of cannabis, whatever that means according to local ordinance or state law. Still, why should anyone have to pay a fine, as though they were doing something wrong beyond breaking an astoundingly stupid law? If the only wrong you do is break the − . . . my apologies, not *stupid*, but, let's say, this time, possibly well-intentioned although not impressively competent or morally justifiable, and sometimes even more stupidly enforced . . . − law, then you are being prohibited from exercising what ought to be among the sacred freedoms included as a right of responsible and otherwise law-abiding persons. The pursuit of individually defined happiness that does not harm others, promised by the American Declaration of Independence and its counterpart social contracts for citizens in many places around the globe, ought to stub out antiquated cannabis prohibition legislation like a spent roach.

Why is marijuana prohibition tolerated? Here, undoubtedly, we run smack up against part of the mystery that is twenty-first century America. Why, in the past, was slavery tolerated? Why was alcohol prohibition tolerated? Why is same-sex marriage so emotionally resisted by a heterosexual majority? What's it to them, anyway, and how does it hurt them, if gay and lesbian couples want to tie the knot? Why is the virtually unlimited availability of firearms with all the harm they cause put up with today as a sane and historically accurate interpretation of the Constitution's Second Amendment to the Bill of Rights? NPR (National Public Radio) reported just this afternoon as I was sunning on the terrace that the number of bullets sold across the counter in the United States in 2008 was enough to provide every living man, woman, and child in the country with no less than 33 bullets. With a currently estimated population of 305 million souls, that's an astonishing 10,065,000,000 rounds of ammunition beyond military and police requisitions, purchased in just one year. It makes a person wonder, are there really that many deer and pheasant still running around uncooked? I myself don't have any of these bullets, nor does my partner, or most people I know, so some greedy individuals are regularly using or stockpiling considerably more than their allotted 33.

Guns and bullets, despite all the damage they cause when people fly off the handle, you can legally buy. A dime of reefer to kick back with nothing else on the burner and get into some Beethoven, Brubeck, or Beck, a Rembrandt exhibit from years ago in a glossy museum catalogue or reruns of *The Honeymooners*, no. America, like other countries, simply has these quirks. Federal law currently prohibits the purchase, sale, or use of cannabis, even in those states like California that have meaningfully relaxed state and local anti-marijuana legislation. If you use in California, you probably do not risk municipal or California state prosecution, although in theory at least you could still be in trouble with the Feds. So far, the Federal authorities have primarily targeted entrepreneurial medical cannabis dispensaries operating without full legal local approval, but there is no reason why the government in the future could not choose to enforce the Federal anti-cannabis laws at the lowest levels of buyers, sellers, and users. If California or any other state will not enact or enforce subordinate cannabis prohibition laws, then in principle the Federal government might decide that it needs to do so. As things stand today, this would be perfectly legal. In most places in the US, it's unfortunately true that you can still get into a lot of trouble with the law trying to cop a little high.

Nor is cannabis use a particularly new thing. Samir S. Patel reports the following discovery in the March/April 2009 issue of *Archaeology* magazine: "At first archaeologists guessed the two pounds of green plant material, buried with a Caucasian man 2,700 years ago in Turpan, was coriander. Tests revealed the truth – it was cannabis, the oldest-known marijuana stash. Lab work also established that it would have been potent stuff, though it is unknown whether it was used for medicinal or religious purposes." Dope has accordingly been around for a long time and its effects have been understood and appreciated for millennia. It is a sign of the times that the cautious author of this prestigious publication considers only that the Chinese cannabis might have been used for either medicinal or religious purposes. If we read between the lines it is nevertheless not hard to imagine that the owner sent to the afterlife with a lid of good shit in his tomb might have used it primarily for recreational purposes, as is still done today, for the same morally respectable purpose of getting airborne. It also suggests that cannabis was sufficiently available in abundance in the distant Asian past to be considered a desirable grave good.

Leaving the trail of cannabis along ancient trade routes aside, what attitude should contemporary philosophy take toward cannabis? Like other phenomena related to popular culture, philosophy has an opportunity if not an obligation to consider these matters carefully and with all its conceptual analytic tools. There are many philosophical questions raised by the use of cannabis for medicinal, religious ceremonial or sacramental, not to mention for fun and purely recreational, purposes. What is it to get high? How does cannabis alter straight patterns of perception, judgment, and reasoning? Is it morally wrong to use cannabis? Is it morally wrong for legislators and law enforcement officials to prohibit cannabis sale, possession, and use? Can philosophy help us to understand the psychological, phenomenological, ethical, and social implications of cannabis intoxication? Can cannabis, as some users believe, constitute an ally in artistic creativity or in the philosophical pursuit of wisdom?

The essays collected in this book are intended to provide a lively philosophical look at the problems of marijuana use and abuse. The reader should expect many different answers, not always in harmony. It is an essential part of philosophical understanding to collect conflicting arguments relevant to a topic, and to sort through them all carefully and critically, looking for enlightenment in spite of disagreements among the experts, and concerning precisely those matters about which they disagree. We should no more anticipate consensus between writers with philosophical interests reflecting on the nature, cognitive effects, and moral and legal status of marijuana than we would in any other field. Therein lies the philosophical intrigue and whatever philosophical insight we can reasonably hope to attain about this popular and increasingly appreciated but socially still very controversial drug.

I am grateful to Fritz Allhoff for inviting me to edit this volume for his new Wiley-Blackwell series, Philosophy for Everyone, and to Jeff Dean, philosophy editor at the press, for nursing me through some of my early moments of editorial denial. I thank the authors for their superb contributions, and the production team at Wiley-Blackwell for helping to bring this volume to completion with such flair. I am indebted above all to my wife Tina for her encouragement, and for sharing with me all these years her invaluable anecdotal perspective on the vagaries of herbal aviation.

Dale Jacquette
Sydney, Australia

INTRODUCTION
What is Cannabis and How Can We Get Some?

Are You Anywhere?

Cannabis is a psychoactive product of a naturally occurring plant belonging to two main species, *sativa* and *indica*. Cannabis is ingested primarily for the sake of the effects of the active THC (tetrahydrocannabinol) it contains, liberated from the dried resin-bearing plant flower buds and leaves under carbonizing heat for absorption into the bloodstream. There it finds its way like spawning salmon to the grateful brain, where special cannabinoid receptors have evolved in several mammalian animal species, including our own, in parallel with the weed's botanical evolution over millions of years. We, human beings and pot, were biologically made for each other.

The effects of cannabis are varied and variously reported. They depend to a large extent on the kind and strength of the drug, how and how much of it is ingested, psychological and other physiological, as well as circumstantial environmental, factors affecting the experience. Users talk about getting *stoned* or *high*, terms that are sometimes used interchangeably, sometimes distinguished phenomenologically, and sometimes associated respectively with cannabis indica versus cannabis sativa. Words fail, though much ink has been spilled, trying to describe what it is like to get high or stoned, or even, for that matter, what burning marijuana smells like. What, to recall Thomas Nagel's famous philosophical conundrum about the nature of consciousness and the impenetrability of alien subjectivities, is it like to be a bat? What is it like to be high? What is it like to be a bat high?

Descriptions of the drug's effects include mild euphoria, a sense of wellbeing, intensely concentrated attention punctuated by occasional distractions from immediate tasks and disturbances of short-term memory, increased libido or enhanced pleasure in carnal pursuits, including an elevated appetite, a peculiar sensitivity to the humor and absurdity in situations that are otherwise underappreciated when straight, and sometimes remarkably vivid paranoia. It used to be parlance for knowledgeable cannabis users to ask, "Are you anywhere?" meaning simply, in the code language to which persons pursuing an illegal activity are sometimes driven or naturally inclined, "Do you smoke pot?" The implication is that otherwise you are figuratively nowhere. Nowheresville is perhaps the original archaic idiom, back in the day when all hip guys wanted to have a goatee and everyone owned a pair of bongos, daddy-o.

Spark up a thumb of white widow, then, a Jack Herer hybrid, super skunk, Shiva Shanti, or haze. Imagine the cluster bud of baby-sized leaves and stamens at the top of the plant when it was harvested, oozing with rich red cannabinoid-laden resin and gorgeous feathery yellow tops as seen in head shop magazines and hydroponics calendars. Reflect on the fact high, if you will, that such a beautiful flower can be burned and the vapors open up your mind to new ideas, and you can quickly find yourself deeply enmeshed in conceptual subtleties and endlessly absorbing unexpected chains of association that might keep you philosophically entertained for about as long as it should take you to read this book. The main thing of philosophical interest about cannabis is its effect on thought, altering one's state of consciousness in what are usually pleasurable, sometimes surprisingly vibrant and rewarding ways. If users are right, then cannabis can take us outside our normal modes of experiencing the world, and amplify subjective reactions to prevailing conditions both within and beyond the mind.

That, in a gleaming bong bowl, may convey some sense of what cannabis is, for readers entirely new to the drug. Verbal description is nevertheless no substitute for trying and reflecting on first-hand acquaintance with cannabis. This, however, is not lightly to be recommended, because the answer to our second question – How can we get some? – is, unfortunately, almost everywhere in the world at the present time, by breaking the law and risking the brunt of some potentially very unpleasant forensic consequences. The publicized threat of such penalties is supposed to

DALE JACQUETTE

dissuade people from using marijuana, and perhaps in another thousand years or two, when there are more people in jail than on the street looking for harmless kicks, it might actually start to work. Accordingly, today, I can candidly give anyone who's interested in experimenting one very good reason not to smoke marijuana: it's illegal. Contrariwise, after much deliberation, I cannot offer even one good reason why it should be illegal.

Dormroom Confessions of a Casual Cannabiphile

Let me wax a little autobiographical, then, and briefly recall some of my own first cannabis experiences. Reflection takes me back to my Midwestern US college days in the early 1970s, when an evening's lecture by a psychology professor was announced as: "Auditory Masking, or Hearing Simple Sounds Stoned." Could a person actually get degree credit for this? I wondered. Well, no. But it was better than the sepulcher of library stacks for an evening's entertainment. Back then, researchers in cognitive studies, pharmacology, and medicine could still easily obtain government grants for collecting data on cannabis-drugged students. These days my impression is that governmental controls have clamped down rather stridently. I remember on the occasion in question that they had to turn people away at the door.

As a student, I appreciated the occasional free institutionally sanctioned high, which I considered indeed to be not only manna from heaven, but a legitimate part of my education. My problem was that I was too cheap, and, actually, I didn't have any money, to buy my own stuff. I was leery of buying from strangers on the boulevard, and I didn't have a clue how to score unless the stuff presented itself miraculously to me, as often enough it did. What this typically amounted to in practice was sponging dope off my friend, Steve Rosenberg. Steve is a good guy and in those days was and probably still is an excellent air hockey player, straight or high, although I sometimes kept him busy. As a general thing, however, he did not have very good smoke. It was many years later through a series of accidents that I discovered what cannabis at its best can and should be like. By that time, I had developed a preference for *majoun*, a substance made of roasted cannabis dissolved in heated butter, and featured as the star ingredient in a variety of confectionaries. These include the legendary space cake of Amsterdam, and the notorious, too easily underestimated, party pot brownies, to be absorbed into the bloodstream more slowly but also more powerfully through the stomach than by capillaries in the lungs. Or made into the quaint little green pastilles that lyrically stimulated Charles Baudelaire.

What I remember more lucidly about smoking dope back in the golden days of my bacheloriate were the occasional "smoke-downs" in my dorm. I think then that everybody was getting high on a regular basis, and I was the innocent with respect to whatever my more urbane contemporaries were up to, trying against my better judgment sometimes to get with the program, usually struggling more than just a couple of years behind the curve.

A smoke-down, I learned, not wanting to overlook an opportunity to socialize with my dorm mates, was when you sit around in a big circle on the floor of an activity room and pass a bong loaded up with grass, or, in the case of the first one I went to, hashish. From Turkey, as it turns out, courtesy of one of the dorm directors, a stunning, impressively statuesque female African-American senior. You had to take a hit when the bong circulated round the group, or you had to leave the circle. This event, bear in mind, was announced with xeroxed notebook-sized pages scotch-taped to the glass dorm doors. In some sense it had the dorm's approval and, by implication, that of the college. You didn't want to leave the circle because you were meeting people and they played excellent music, there was free food going around on trays, and it was not something you could explain to your mom (not my mom, anyway), or anybody else who wasn't there. It was something unusual and it was genuinely fun.

The circle by design becomes progressively smaller whenever somebody decides that they've had enough. This implies that your turn becomes increasingly more frequent, and soon you realize that you too, virtual cannabis virgin that you are, have now inhaled rather more than you need to get the idea, and that it may now be time to enjoy the rest of this exhilarating feeling by yourself, out walking in the cool night air. If only you can manage to unwrap your legs from one another and stand up gracefully with some confidence in front of your peers without ruining your pathetic social life for the foreseeable future, without having to consider transferring schools. Complicated movement, allowing sheer muscle memory to take over instead of conscious direction, turns out not to be as difficult as anticipated, although you can easily become over-amazed at your sudden unexpected locomotory abilities. You may want to make the world slow down, or to slow yourself down, experience all the nuances of this otherwise inconsequential transaction, and share with people around you the wonder of finding your shoes, feeling for the first time just how properly they fit, and being able to walk a few steps to the toilet, where it seems to take an eternity to pee. Some brilliant jazz guitar by Joe Pass or Herb Ellis over the headphones, and then it's bedtime. In the morning, beyond a few selective droll memories, it's as though it all never happened. And yet you have been transformed. Now you know that your mind can seek out another quite interesting place with an interesting new outlook. That was a vintage college smoke-down, unmolested by the police and in some sense supported by the dorm with dorm facilities and funding. I doubt that there are many institutions in the United States today that still condone quite such a literal application of the concept of higher learning.

The other incident I remember as though it were yesterday took place in a so-called physics for poets class. We had a great but as far as I could tell completely square physics teacher who taught a watered-down concepts of physics course for persons innocent or scared to death of mathematics. The professor did brilliant demonstrations to show us the forces of physics at work, word of mouth about which was one of the things that had attracted me to the lectures. One day the professor was explaining the properties of a number of inert gasses, all sealed in large glass tubes with copper contact wires protruding. These he hooked up one by one to a dry cell battery in order to excite the gasses in each cylinder, producing an impressive bright color as electricity passed through. In a completely darkened room we sat in the little lecture ampitheater, where each gas had its chance to shine with a touch of the battery to its electrodes. There was appreciative polite applause such as normally followed a successful experiment. The professor must have thought he had finished the presentation at that point, because he started putting his equipment away and was going for the light switch, when a student's lazy gravelly voice called out from the pitch dark: 'Wait . . . do *argon* again.' An immediate silence fell, a pregnant pause interrupted at first only by audible intakes of breath, and then a chirping from the audience as more people joined the chorus: "Yeah. Do argon," "Do argon, man."

That, in retrospect, was the exact moment when I realized that large numbers of my classmates were probably having a different college experience than I had previously essayed, and were certainly enjoying more of a particular kind of fun than I had otherwise imagined. Was I overlooking the obvious here? Could there yet be something of wit in this *marijuana*?

Don't Bogart that Inference

Almost anyone interested in cannabis is likely to find the following essays fascinating, even without much background or prior interest in philosophy. On the other hand, I suspect that many persons interested in philosophy, especially professionals in the field, will not automatically be interested in exploring cannabis as a philosophical topic, and their lack of prior interest might prevent them from picking up this book or reading even as far as this.

Which would be a pity, because, as I have indicated, thinkers working in almost any major philosophical subdiscipline should be interested in cannabis-related issues of phenomenology, philosophical psychology and philosophy of mind, epistemology, ethics, philosophy of law, and social policy. Smoking cannabis might not offer philosophically minded persons a special chemical avenue of profound and penetrating insight, so that trying to do philosophy high is unlikely if ever to produce fruitful results. There is nevertheless much to reflect on philosophically about getting high, where *qualia* meets theory, and about the *Realpolitik* of contemporary cannabis prohibition. If we are concerned that cannabis can only cloud our thinking and make fine-grained philosophical analysis and sharp logical distinctions and inferences more difficult if not practically impossible, then the important step is to recognize that we do not need to do philosophy while high in order to profit from the effect of cannabis on philosophical thinking when we are straight once again and settling back into serious work.

The authors of the following essays present interesting scientific and philosophical arguments. They interpret facts and recommend values relevant to some of the philosophical and social policy problems surrounding cannabis. The contributors hail from diverse regional backgrounds, including the US, Canada, Finland, New Zealand, South Africa, and, in my case, as the result of a recent professional relocation, Switzerland. The significance of the authors' home countries lies not in their offering a wide range of cultural coverage, since any of the essays in principle, many of them scientific, could just as easily have been written anywhere in the world. The importance of their participation in the present volume consists rather in demonstrating that interest in cannabis and the relation of cannabis to philosophy is international.

The opening essay, "A Cannabis Odyssey" by Lester Grinspoon, describes Grinspoon's personal and professional journey toward an

DALE JACQUETTE

understanding and appreciation of the medicinal, recreational, and self-enhancement virtues of marijuana. Well known as the distinguished Harvard University Medical School author of such milestone cannabis studies as *Marihuana Reconsidered*, *Marijuana: The Forbidden Medicine*, and numerous medical, pharmacological, and psychiatric findings appearing in scientific publications, Grinspoon takes aim against what he calls cannabinophobia, the fear or hatred of weed based on popular mis-understandings. He lends moral support as well as clinical medical opinion to relaxing the grip of cannabis prohibition.

Next is G. T. Roche, "Seeing Snakes: On Delusion, Knowledge, and the Drug Experience." Roche raises interesting questions about the real effect and truth or exaggeration of anecdotal reports of so-called mind-expanding drugs like cannabis. Roche wonders whether, as William James, Aldous Huxley, Timothy Leary, and others have claimed, such substances "allow us to see beyond the horizon of ordinary perception – that is, see things as they really are?" Even if drugs like nitrous oxide, mescaline, or LSD could allow one's understanding to penetrate the phenomenal appearance of things that some philosophers talk about and grasp reality in the raw, there is no reason according to Roche to suppose that cannabis could ever do so. Looking at the more extensive literature for these powerful drugs enables Roche to draw some valuable analogies about the recognized psychological effects of cannabis. Roche concludes that much of the psychedelic literature is conspicuous for its mystical language and a certain irresponsible worldview advocacy. He looks to scientific evidence instead for social policy guidance concerning drugs like cannabis.

Andrew D. Hathaway and Justin Sharpley, in "The Cannabis Experience: An Analysis of 'Flow'," begin with recent physiological research on cannabinoids and their neural receptors, and explore some of the potential medical benefits of marijuana. The experience of "flow" under cannabis intoxication is described within this general framework in terms of William James's nineteenth-century work in psychology and philosophy of mind, relating the discussion also to elements of Eastern religious mysticism. Flow is something like being caught up in a movement of attention and activity in which time loses some of its meaning as the subject concentrates on particular tasks to the exclusion of surrounding circumstances. To be in flow or in the flow is to be actively participating with this movement in the moment, which exists to begin with, of course, in the subject's mind. Hathaway quotes himself from an earlier source to explain more precisely what he means by flow as gaining a perspective on the movement of events in time in which one wants to participate, for enjoyment of the passing world or more active creative purposes. With solid psychological and sociological data in hand, Hathaway and Sharpley conclude that cannabis has practical and scientific relevance to understanding the experience of flow for cannabis users. The authors endorse cannabis qualifiedly as beneficial for optimizing the experience of consciousness in flow, by which in turn they offer to explain anecdotal accounts of marijuana as consciousness-expanding.

The difficulties of trying to communicate what being intoxicated on cannabis is like are considered by Michael Montagne in his study, "Buzz, High, and Stoned: Metaphor, Meaning, and the Cannabis Experience." Calling upon a tradition of literary descriptions of hashish ingestion, especially among nineteenth-century artists and intellectuals, Montagne proposes to bring conceptual clarity to some of the language in which the sensation of being spaced on cannabis is anecdotally and generally metaphorically expressed. Montagne invokes the writings of Théophile Gautier, Baudelaire, and Bayard Taylor, among others, gathering a wide selection of classical responses to the problem of putting into words what it feels like to get buzzed, stoned, or high. Turning then to more colloquial expressions surrounding cannabis use, Montagne identifies trends in song lyrics and other popular sources of more compact and possibly deliberately obscure linguistic formulations of what it is to be hopped up or laid back on cannabis. Although Montagne does not explore the suggestion, it appears as though the more the novelty of cannabis wears off among those writers inclined to record their impressions of its effects, the more obvious the futility of trying to give voice to the experience becomes. Attempts at description shrink to a minimum, to be replaced by codes and slang that either mean something evocative to another user, or pass by the square noncognoscenti whom as previously noted jazz age hipsters said were nowhere. Montagne's detailed analysis points toward ways in which cannabis can be more fully enjoyed, avoiding brain fog in favor of more meaningful psychically enriching experiences with the drug.

Charles Taliaferro and Michel Le Gall discuss spiritual aspects of cannabis use in quests for religious insight in their essay, "The Great Escape." Evaluating cannabis from a religious and philosophical perspective, Taliaferro and Le Gall consider the question of whether cannabis can open special doors to eternal truths. Or, in keeping with Plato's objections to the subversive effects of poetry and drama, whether dope serves only as another source of falsehood and superficial mere appearance. Are the insights that cannabis and other drug users sometimes report generally correct or illusory? Referring to classical drug literature and romantic traditions in poetry, Taliaferro and Le Gall further consider such related objections to using drugs for spiritual enhancement as the claim that mind-expanding substances like cannabis can involve as part of their downside a loss of freedom and self-determination. As a price to be paid for bright temporary flashes of often deceptive intuitions they may seem to be injurious to the search for spiritual enlightenment. Turning then to some standard religious objections to cannabis and reconciling the history of its reception worldwide, the authors draw useful comparisons with consecrated attitudes toward alcohol and caffeine consumption in different major historical monotheistic religions, Christianity, Judaism, and Islam. Taliaferro and Le Gall conclude that, despite these considerations, chemically altered states of mind can be philosophically defended as beneficial in potentially enlarging the moral imagination.

A psychoanalytic perspective on cannabis use is offered by Brian R. Clack in "Cannabis and the Human Condition: 'Something of the Kind is Indispensable'." Clack raises the important question of why so many people choose to get high on cannabis, given the costs and potential legal risks with all their implications, along with the problem for cannabis smokers of inhaling clouds of iffy substances. Why we like to get high, if we do, is a topic that if satisfactorily addressed would go a long distance toward understanding cannabis culture from the subjective side of things, from the perspective of what it is that is found attractive about being high. It is an issue with possible consequences for social policy matters of cannabis tolerance or prohibition and enforcement. Clack delves into reasons owing originally to Sigmund Freud and Arthur Schopenhauer for regarding life pessimistically, for the sake of coping with profound existential unhappiness and its psychiatric causes and effects that some drug users might experience. Freud's writings especially provide a background to Clack's discussion of the rationales for drug use, emphasizing Freud's own drug experimentation and addiction to cocaine. Existence itself, if Clack is right, or a certain awareness of the human condition, might necessitate the use of drugs like cannabis for the sake of relieving the conflicted psyche through temporary escapism, making something of the kind, some sort of chemical release valve, indispensable.

The theme of poetic reactions to cannabis is taken up in Tommi Kakko's essay, "Hallucinatory Terror: The World of the Hashish Eater." Kakko focuses especially on Fitz Hugh Ludlow's classic, *The Hashish Eater: Being Passages From the Life of a Pythagorean*, and Thomas De Quincey's *Confessions of an English Opium Eater*, along with more recent drug use narratives by such authors as William S. Burroughs. The metaphysical imaginations of poets seem sometimes to have been enhanced or in any case distinctively influenced by their later encounters with cannabis. Situating Ludlow in his cultural, literary, and philosophical context, with special emphasis on his relation to David Hume's empiricism in the eighteenth-century Scottish Enlightenment and the later German philosopher Immanuel Kant's critical idealism and transcendentalism as background to the experience of hashish experimentation, Kakko highlights a very important early source on habitual cannabis experience. He seeks in particular on this foundation to understand what may seem from today's perspective to be Ludlow's floridly embellished reports of cannabis-induced hallucination and sensory distortions.

The question of whether cannabis enhances creativity, especially in the arts, but with an eye toward all areas of human endeavor, is critically examined by Ryan E. Holt and James C. Kaufman in "Marijuana and Creativity." The idea that cannabis might contribute to creativity is often reported by marijuana users in the enthusiasm that accompanies a good high, psychologically certain in those moments that an idea has occurred to them as a result of smoking pot that otherwise would never or at most only improbably have dawned on their straight minds. Otherwise, what are all those improvisational jazz musicians, painters and other artists, poets and writers and other intellectuals talking about? But is it so? What does the actual scientific evidence suggest? Holt and Kaufman rely on careful psychological studies involving double-blind controlled cognitive experiments with cannabis and placebos being offered to subjects, who then complete a number of specially designed creativity-measuring problem-solving tasks. Locating their conclusions in a historical context of general creativity research, the authors consider tests of cognitive problem-solving ability as determined by efforts to arrive at divergent answers to open-ended questions. Subjected then to multiple criteria intended to reveal comparative levels of creativity, the significance of such data is first established for straight consciousness, and then applied to psychological subjects high on cannabis. Performance levels of cannabis users in creativity experiments are compared with subjects given placebos, and their implications are considered for evidence as to whether or not cannabis use actually contributes to creativity as measured by contemporary psychological science, or is purely or partly a myth. The answer at which Holt and Kaufman arrive from the scientific evidence they consider is that creativity does not seem to be enhanced by actual cannabis intoxication as opposed to an individual's expecting to get high.

Dale Jacquette, in "Navigating Creative Inner Space on the Innocent Pleasures of Hashish," bridges topics in several of the book's major divisions on phenomenology, belief in the creative and spiritual potential of cannabis, and the moral, legal, and social implications of contemporary cannabis prohibition. He coins the expression "creative inner space" to represent what many persons in the arts have described as a kind of cannabis-induced elevated field of play in which new ideas experimentally appear. Jacquette is skeptical of some of these anecdotal claims, but allows that artists, musicians, and intellectuals who believe that cannabis is an aid to creativity might produce more interesting work as a result of ingesting cannabis. He notes that cannabis need not promote creativity while the subject is high, when distractions are rife and attention is sometimes powerfully focused and at other times strays, in order to have a positive effect on the subject's creative thought processes. A supporting analogy is perhaps between promoting creativity by means of cannabis and reading. We expect that reading can positively affect creativity, but we generally do not expect that its effect will be immediate while the person is actually reading, but, possibly, only later and cumulatively. Similarly for cannabis, whose positive effects on creativity need be no less real for not occurring simultaneously with the incidence of getting off. This topic leads naturally to Jacquette's discussion of the moral and especially legal aspects of contemporary cannabis prohibition. If cannabis is relatively harmless in all the ways that medical and sociological scientific evidence suggest, if it assists in obscure ways the creativity of valuable minds and artistic talents in society, and if people flock to it despite the legal risks, then society may have an obligation not to punish its use.

Mark Thorsby, in his essay "Cannabis and the Culture of Alienation," considers some interesting social manifestations of cannabis use. Inspired by Zen Buddhism and the writings of Karl Marx, among other sources, Thorsby presents a psychological social perspective on the pleasures of cannabis. Drawing on personal experience as an art instructor, he cites examples of seeing familiar things in unfamiliar ways as a way of unlocking the difficulties students sometimes encounter in elementary art courses. Thorsby thereby illustrates his positive sense of the value of cannabis, not in seeking respite from life's troubles, but rather more positively in enhancing the experience of consciousness and creativity. Appealing to Plato, Marx, Zen, Erich Fromm, and others, Thorsby finally paints a neo-Marxist account of alienation in modern social life. He suggests that cannabis and the altered ways of seeing and thinking it encourages might contribute to an edifying critique of the self-alienating conditions of contemporary culture, and thereby help promote a more salutary kind of healing and resolution of society's contradictions and their impact on the individual.

The question as to why cannabis has become such a popular drug is investigated by Tuomas E. Tahko in his essay "Reefer Madness: Cannabis, the Individual, and Public Policy." The illegality of cannabis and the exposure of risk to users trying to acquire the substance increases the mystery as to why people continue to smoke marijuana in spite of its potential dangers. Among these are to be included the criminal contacts to be taken into consideration when looking at what it means to score weed for most cannabis users under prohibition worldwide today. The user is made a criminal buying the drug illegally from questionable unregulated dealers with no guarantee of quality, purity, or potency, of fair weight or competitive price, or of legal repercussions. Turning then to health-related issues in cannabis consumption, Tahko argues that the potential health risks of smoking pot appear to be outweighed by the potential health benefits. Tahko is nevertheless concerned about the possibility of cannabis addiction. Despite the fact that cannabis has been shown not to be physiologically addictive in the manner of nicotine, opiates, prescription medicines – especially pain killers – and alcohol, cannabis and its subtle pleasures have been said to insinuate a kind of psychological addiction in the lives of certain users. Again, Tahko does not think that the quasi-addictive potential of cannabis for some users justifies prohibition, but tries to assess the moral permissibility of cannabis tolerance and its likely personal and societal consequences from an objective philosophical standpoint, considering the arguments pro and con in their strongest formulations.

Whether drugs can be easily distinguished as hard or soft is the topic of the final essay in this section of the volume, Brian Penrose's "Soft vs. Hard: Why Drugs are Not Like Eggs." The hackneyed distinction between hard and soft drugs, with cannabis in its various forms generally being classified as soft, is challenged by Penrose. In this specimen of philosophical conceptual analysis of essential concepts relating to our understanding of cannabis, Penrose explodes the myth of there being any unifying characteristics of so-called hard or soft drugs. Contrary to prevailing practice, he is skeptical of the distinction in both theory and clinical and forensic practice, and he illustrates his misgivings very powerfully by means of plausible counterexamples. He shows that any effort to cash out the distinction between hard and soft drugs does not succeed insofar as it (a) places cannabis unequivocally on the side of soft rather than hard drugs, and (b) locates such substances as cocaine, crack cocaine, heroin, and crystal metham-phetamine on the side of hard drugs. We cannot make scientifically defensible progress applying the hard-soft drug distinction to these substances, let alone for even more gray area drugs such as LSD, psilocybin mushrooms, mescaline, peyote, ecstasy (XTC), and the like, or, for that matter, alcohol, nicotine, caffeine, uppers, downers, and all the rest. Penrose's essay serves as a pointed philosophical reminder that we should not take the conceptual schemes entrenched in ordinary discourse for granted.

The title says it all, but Jack Green Musselman, Russ Frohardt, and D. G. Lynch's essay, "'Smoking Pot Doesn't Hurt Anyone But Me!' Why Adults Should be Allowed to Consume Cannabis," does considerably more than rehearse the standard libertarian moral-philosophical argument for the moral permissibility of smoking pot, provided that no one else suffers wrong in the process. Developing a variation of John Stuart Mill's classic utilitarian position, the authors present an imaginative but believable fictional scenario of a morally responsible occasional recreational pot smoker. They examine in detail the question of whether any moral objection can reasonably be laid at the idealized cannabis user's door. Musselman, Frohardt, and Lynch argue that there seems to be no decisive moral, scientific health-related, or social policy objections to responsible cannabis use. Referring to recent scientific studies, psychological and sociological, against a backdrop of the history of cannabis prohibition, the authors find good reasons for relaxing anti-marijuana legislation and enforcement. They maintain that, realistically speaking, people enjoy the effects of cannabis and want to use some kinds of drugs regardless of the law, that prohibition has been a dismal failure as a deterrent, and that it has contributed to an absurdly inflated prison population in many places where anti-marijuana laws are still vigorously enforced. With all the social pain produced by cannabis prohibition, weighed against the miniscule social harm cannabis causes, especially when compared with unprohibited but also controlled substances like alcohol and tobacco, not to mention overlooked economic opportunities under cannabis prohibition, it appears that if anything it is the anti-marijuana laws that are morally unjustified, at least on the sort of consequentialist ethical principles championed by Mill. The authors finally project a balanced commonsensical advocacy of cannabis tolerance under the law. They base their judgment on an interpretation of the history of anti-cannabis legislation and the latest pharmacological, psychological, and sociological science related to cannabis. The potential harmfulness of cannabis in their view is vastly outbalanced by its potential for several categories of good, including but not limited to the medical, psychic or spiritual, and social. There are good reasons for cannabis law reform, no good reasons for sustaining the status quo of cannabis prohibition, and hence no moral justification for the continuation of anti-marijuana prosecution.

In an eloquent moral indictment of cannabis prohibition and pleas for its repeal, Mitch Earleywine's "Pot Politics: Prohibition and Morality" makes an impassioned case for the moral permissibility of using cannabis and the immorality or at best highly questionable morality of cannabis prohibition. The issue for Earleywine is multi-faceted. It involves at least the scientific and clinical anecdotal and social data about cannabis ingestion and its effects, and the attendant risks and rewards in all relevant categories. Ultimately, the morality of cannabis use and the conspicuous lack of moral justification for cannabis prohibition comes down to a matter of the moral right of responsible adults to experiment with and even to choose regularly to consume such psychoactive substances as cannabis, provided that they can do so in socially responsible ways. This seems to entail using cannabis only when through lack of pressing commitments one can afford the luxury of getting high. Earleywine's well-informed discussion, from the standpoint of his familiarity with the relevant facts and current state of political play, reflected also in his dedicated cannabis activism, makes his lucidly rational assessment of the immorality of cannabis prohibition on many counts especially valuable in the present discussion.

An extension of moral justification not merely for the right to use cannabis but for cannabis use itself is made by Theodore Schick, Jr., in "Cannabis and the Good Life: Needs, Capabilities, and Human Flourishing." Schick argues persuasively that cannabis use and its toleration under the law can be morally justified as contributing to the happiness resulting from gratifying the natural desire to flourish of curious dynamic human agents. To flourish, in simplest terms, is to be all that one can potentially be, to develop one's talents and capacities to the fullest extent possible. Adapting moral considerations about the basic human right to flourish from recent philosophical proposals by Amartya Sen and Martha Nussbaum, Schick applies the concept to the two principal questions of cannabis ethics, the morality of using and the morality of prohibition. He concludes that it is unjust to prohibit responsible adults from experiencing the sort of human flourishing that can come about in several ways as a result of indulging in cannabis-induced highs. If cannabis as a drug of choice contributes to the expansion of human capabilities when a user rides the psychic waves of cannabis intoxication, then it can rightly be judged as enhancing the user's personal flourishing, thus securing in one stroke both the morality of cannabis use and immorality of cannabis prohibition.

Michael Funke, in "Weakness of Will: The Cannabis Connection," considers the question of what the ancient Greek moral philosophers called *akrasia* or weakness of will. Weakness of will in the face of the temptations posed by cannabis adds another important dimension to the general philosophical topic of the morality of cannabis use and prohibition. Does cannabis have the potential of weakening the moral resolve to limit its use? Or, for that matter, to undertake other morally obligatory actions? What, in any event, can philosophy come to learn about weakness of will when the will after habitual use enters a kind of psychological if not physiological cannabis addiction or dependence? It can be a legitimate moral objection to marijuana and its social and legal tolerance if its regular use, as is sometimes said, deprives the user of sufficient motivation to act in accord with more important moral obligations, and thus increasingly to neglect acquired moral duties for the sake of getting wrecked. The moral challenge here is to think of cannabis as itself a substance that inherently robs a regular long-term user of the moral will to meet independent responsibilities. Up to now we have spoken blithely about cannabis use by morally responsible adults. What now if cannabis itself can undermine a user's capacity for morally responsible decision and action by instilling or magnifying a preexistent weakness of moral will? The problem of weakness of will in light of cannabis use is thereby directly related to the anticannabis argument that cannabis is a gateway drug that leads cannabis users to graduate to such harder substances as cocaine, heroine, and crystal meth. Funke concedes that cannabis might constitute a gateway drug in this limited sense, but does not believe that this possibility alone justifies cannabis prohibition. On the contrary, Funke maintains that cannabis prohibition is among the factors that lead persons who would otherwise be satisfied with an occasional cannabis high to use the drug more frequently and to move on to harder and harder drugs.

Roll Another One, Like the Other One

I offer in closing, for the sake primarily of its sociological interest, the following brief list of synonyms for cannabis or specific kinds of cannabis. Some terms in the list have been harvested from the United States Drug Enforcement Agency (DEA), and I would like to think that many of these terms may have been invented on the spot by subjects who knew they were under surveillance and wanted to have a little joke at the gullible investigators' expense. I promise, in any case, on my word of honor, that I did not make up any of these terms, but offer them for the sake of philosophical reflection on the widespread popularization of cannabis and the subculture it represents. What does it mean for something illegal that grows wild in fields to have so many nicknames? The list, itself suggestive rather than exhaustive, includes but undoubtedly is not limited to the ensuing incomplete compilation of amazing street names. Have you heard of these?

Ace, Afgani, African black, airplane, Alice B. Toklas, ash, ashes, assassin of youth, astroturf, atshitshi, Aunt Mary, B-40, babysitter, bamba, bambalacha, bammies, bammy, bar, bash, basuco, bc, beedies, beefy, belyando, bhang, billies, bob, black, black bart, black ganga, black gungi, black mo, black moat, black mote, blanket, blax, blaze, block, blonde, blow, blue de hue, blue sage, blue sky blond, blunt, bo, bo-bo, boo, bobo bush, bohd, bomber, boo boo bama, boom, broccoli, brown, bud, buds, buddah, bullyon, burnie, bush, butter, butter flower, cali, cam [Cambodia] trip, cam red, canamo, canappa, cavite all star, cesd, cest, charas, charge, cheeba, cheebs, cheeo, chemo, chiba chiba, chief, chira, choof, chop, chronic, chunky, churus, citrol, clickums, climb, cochornis, colas, coli, coliflor tostao, Colorado cocktail, Columbus black, cones, cosa, crazy weed, cripple, crying weed, cryptonie, culican, CS, dagga, dank, dawamesk, dew, diambista, diesel, dimba, ding, dinkie dow, ditch, ditch weed, djamba, dody, doja, domestic, dom jem, Don Juan, Dona Juanita, donk, doob, doobee, dooby, dope, droz, duby, dubbe, doradilla, draf, draf weed, drag weed, dry high, duff, durong, duros, earth, el Gallo ("the rooster"), endo, esra, Fallbrook redhair, fatty, feeling, fine stuff, finger, finger lid, fir, firewood, flower tops, fraho, frajo, fu, fuma D'Angola, gage, gange, gangster, ganj, ganoobies smoke, gash, gasper, gauge, gauge butt, Ghana, giggle smoke, giggle weed, goblet of jam, gold star, golden, golden leaf, gong, gonj, goody-goody, goof butt, googe, gorge, grass, grasshopper, grata, green, green goddess, greeter, greta, griefo, griefs, grifa, griff, griffa, griffo, gunga, gunge, gungeon, gunion, gungun, gunja, gyve, haircut, hanhich, harsh, has, Hawaiian, hay, hay butt, herer, herb, herbs, hocus, hooch, hooter, hydro, Indian boy, Indian hay, indica, Indo, indoor, instaga, instagu, j, jay, Jamaican red hair, jane, jive, jolly green, joy stick, joy smoke, Juan Valdez, Juanita, juja, ju-ju, kabak, kaff, kalakit, kali, Kansas grass, Kate Bush, Kawaii electric, kaya, kb, kee, keef, key, KGB (Killer Green Bud), khayf, ki, kick stick, kief, kif, kiff, killer, kilter, kind, king bud, kona gold, krippy, kumba, LL, Lakbay diva, laughing grass, laughing weed, leaf, leak, leno, LG (Lime Green), lid, light stuff, lima, little smoke, llesca, loaf, lobo, loco, loco weed, log, loose shank, lubage, m, macaroni, machinery, macon, maconha, mafu, magic smoke, Manhattan silver, mari, marijuana, marimba, Mary, Mary and Johnny, Mary Ann, maryJ, Mary Jane, Mary Jonas, Mary Warner, Mary Weaver, Maui wauie, Meg, megg, meggie, mersh, messorole, mexi, mighty mezz, mj, mo, modams, mohasky, mohasty, monk, monte, mooca, moocah, mooster, moota, mootie, mootos, mor a grifa, mota, moto, mother, mu, muggie, muggle, muggles, muta, mutah, mutha, m&m, majoun, mj, mull (Australian), my friend, nigra, Northern lights, nuggets, number, OJ, outdoor, PR (Panama Red), pack, pakaloco, pakalolo, panatela, pasto, pat, philly blunts, pin, plan (Russian), plumbing, pocket rocket, pod, poke, pot, potlikker, potten bush, pretendica, pretendo, punk, queen anne's lace, ragweed, railroad, railroad weed, rainy day woman, rangood, rasta reed, red dirt, red cross, red seal, reefer, righteous, righteous bush, rip, roach, roacha, rocky, root, rope, rose marie, rough stuff, rubia, ruderalis, rugs, salad, salt and pepper, Santa Marta, sasfras, sativa, schwagg, scissors, scrub, seeds, sen, sensi, ses, sess, sezz, shake, shee-et, shit, shotgun, siddi, sinse, sinsemilla, skunk, skunkweed, smoke, snop, splim, splif, spliff, square makerel, stack, stems, stick, sticky icky, stoney, stoney weed, straw, sugar weed, swag, sweet lucy, shwag, super skunk, taima, takkouri, tea, tea-weed, tex-mex, texas tea, thirteen, thumb, toke, tops, torch, trauma, tree, trees, triple A, trupence bag, Tustin, twist, twistum, unotque, viper's weed, wake and bake, weed, whackatabacka, wacky-backy, wheat, white Russian, white-haired lady, widow, yeh, yellow submarine, yen pop, yerba, yerhia, yesca, yesco, Zacatecas purple, zambi, zay, zol.

PART I

CANNABIS PHENOMENOLOGY

This giddy cheer, poignant or languid by turns, this uneasy joy, this insecurity, this permutation of the malady, generally lasts but for a short time. Soon the links that bind your ideas become so frail, the threat that ties your conceptions so tenuous, that only your accomplices understand you. And here again you cannot be completely certain; perhaps they only think they understand you, and the illusion is reciprocal. These outbursts of loud cries and laughter, which resemble explosions, seem like true madness, or at least like the ravings of a madman, to all those who are not similarly intoxicated. Likewise will wisdom, good sense, and the logical thoughts of the sober, prudent observer, delight and amuse you like a particular form of dementia.

Charles Baudelaire, *The Poem of Hashish*,
Artificial Paradises, 1860

CHAPTER I

A CANNABIS ODYSSEY

 This is my account of how I, as a young instructor in psychiatry, veered, without realizing it, from my tenure track at Harvard Medical School when I began to study marijuana in 1967. Upset by the growing use of this dangerous drug by young people who were ignoring the government's warnings about its toxicity, I decided to review the science on which these warnings were based. Much to my surprise, I discovered that I had been brainwashed, as had most other people, by an almost ubiquitous cannabis catechism which was based primarily on fear, not science.

Both because of my fascination with the depth and ubiquity of this misunderstanding as well as my growing interest in the psychopharmacological properties of marijuana, I began to devote a significant fraction of my time to learning more about it, and in 1971 I published a book, *Marihuana Reconsidered*, in which I asserted that marijuana was far less dangerous than either alcohol or tobacco and that there was no psychopharmacological effect of the drug which justified the annual arrest of 300,000 (now almost 900,000) mostly young people in the United States.[1]

While this book touched on the subject of the nineteenth-century use of cannabis as a medicine, it was only after my oldest son, who had been stricken by a grave illness in 1967, discovered in 1971 how miraculously useful it was symptomatically to him, that I began to explore the clinical and scientific evidence of its usefulness as a medicine. In 1993 I published the first edition of *Marijuana, the Forbidden Medicine*, in which I made the claim that marijuana would eventually be recognized as a wonder drug because of its virtual lack of toxicity, its medical versatility, and its potential, once free of the prohibition tariff, to be much less expensive than the conventional drugs it will replace.[2]

In the meantime, in 1973, I began to use marijuana, and have been doing so for 36 years. I now believe that there are three overlapping categories of marijuana use: recreation, medicine, and personal enhancement. Because most people have at least a glimmer of understanding of its use recreationally and a growing appreciation of its usefulness as a medicine, I will emphasize my personal use and the way it buttressed my belief that it can be used to enhance personal experience and understanding.

Every age has its peculiar folly, and if Charles Mackay, the author of the nineteenth-century classic, *Extraordinary Popular Delusions and the Madness of Crowds*, were alive today, he would surely see "cannabinophobia" as a popular delusion along with the "tulipmania" and "witch hunts" of earlier ages. I believe that we are now at the cusp of this particular popular delusion, which to date has been responsible for the arrest of over 20 million US citizens. I also believe that future historians will look at this epoch and recognize it as another instance of the "madness of crowds." Millions of marijuana users have already arrived at this understanding, but for some of us enlightenment came later than we would have wished.

In every life there occur seminal events that modify the seemingly established probable trajectory of one's personal history. For me, there have been four. The first three were, in order of importance, the extraordinary good fortune of meeting the woman I married, the gift of children, and the decision to go to medical school. The fourth was my improbable encounter with cannabis, an event that divided my life into two eras: the before cannabis era, and the cannabis era (my son David refers to these phases of my life as BC and AD for before cannabis and after dope). My cannabis era began to unfold in 1967. As the senior author of a book which would summarize the results of our seven-year study of schizophrenia, I found myself with what I estimated would be two to three relatively free months before my co-authors would finish their chapters. Because I had become concerned that so many young people were using the terribly dangerous drug marijuana, I decided to use the time to review the scientific literature so that I could write a reasonably objective and scientifically sound paper on the harmfulness of this substance. Young people were ignoring the warnings of the government, but perhaps some would seriously consider a well-documented review of the available data. So I began my systematic review of the medical and scientific literature bearing on the toxicity – mental and physical – of marijuana. It never occurred to me then that there were other dimensions of this drug that warranted exploration.

During my initial foray into this literature I discovered, to my astonishment, that I had to seriously question what I believed I knew about cannabis. As I began to appreciate that what I thought I understood was largely based on myths, old and new, I realized how little my training in science and medicine had protected me against this misinformation. I had become not just a victim of a disinformation campaign, but because I was a physician, one of its agents as well. Believing that I should share my skepticism about the established understanding of marijuana, I wrote a long paper that was published in the now-defunct *International Journal of Psychiatry*; a shorter version was published as the lead article in the December 1969 issue of *Scientific American*. In these papers I questioned whether the almost ubiquitous belief that marijuana was an exceedingly harmful drug was supported by substantial data to be found in the scientific and medical literature. While there was little notice of the paper published in the psychiatric journal, there was much interest in the *Scientific American* article.

Within a week of the appearance of the article, I received a visit from the associate director of the Harvard University Press, who suggested that I consider writing a book on marijuana. I found the idea both attractive and daunting. The subject was worthy of a book-length exposition, and I would have a reason to deepen my exploration of this fascinating and harmful misunderstanding. And there was another reason, perhaps the most compelling of all. The one aspect of my work that interested my 12-year-old son Danny was my study of marijuana. His illness began in July of 1967, just about the time I had decided to learn about the dangers of marijuana. He was diagnosed with acute lymphocytic leukemia, and his prognosis was, of course, guarded. He was both excited and pleased when I told him that I had decided to write a book on marijuana.

A few weeks later I learned that the Board of Syndics of the Harvard University Press had rejected the book proposal as too controversial. Until that moment I was unaware of the existence of this board, which must approve every book published by the press. An image of the Rembrandt painting "Syndics of the Cloth Guild" came to mind: a group of serious-looking, longhaired men sitting around a table, exuding caution and conservatism. I was disappointed but not surprised that they rejected this proposal; it was the first instance of academic resistance to my work in this area. I could have signed on immediately with a trade publisher that offered the prospect of selling more books. But I believed that a conservative, prestigious press would lend more credibility to a book that promised to be quite controversial. The director of the press was undaunted; he believed that he could persuade the Syndics to reverse their decision. And so he did.

It turned out to be a much bigger project than I had anticipated. I found that I had more than the medical and scientific literature to review. Because so much of the misinformation and myths about this drug had their origins in the gaudy writings of the French Romantic literary movement, I felt compelled to examine the works of Théophile Gautier, Charles Baudelaire, and other members of Le Club des Haschischins, as well as those of Bayard Taylor and Fitz Hugh Ludlow. It was fascinating to learn that much of the mythology about cannabis that was being promulgated by the US government had its origins in these writings. It is difficult to imagine that Harry Anslinger (our first drug czar) was directly familiar with these nineteenth-century authors, but clearly some of their hyperbolic descriptions of the cannabis experience, largely products of effusive imagination under the influence of copious amounts of hashish, are echoed almost a century later in the "teachings" of Harry Anslinger.

I had come to understand that marijuana was not addicting in the usual, rather vague understanding of that word, but I certainly got hooked on learning about it. I was fascinated by my growing understanding of how little I actually knew about this drug, and even more so by the many false beliefs I had held with such conviction. It soon dawned on me that I, like most other Americans, had been brainwashed, that I was a part of this madness of the crowd. And the more I learned about cannabis, the more it seemed to be capable of providing experiences which would be worth exploring personally sometime in the future. In the meantime, I felt like an explorer sailing an inaccurately and inadequately mapped ocean. Where earlier cartographers had found many shoals, I found few; where others found barren and dangerous islands, I saw lands that looked increasingly interesting as I drew closer. The clearer the view, the greater the temptation to land and make a direct exploration, but I reminded myself that the point of this trip was to chart the ledges and shoals, not to explore forbidden lands to look for riches. Long before I decided to land, more than a year after the publication of *Marihuana Reconsidered* in 1971, it had become inescapably clear that while marijuana was not harmless, its harmfulness lay not so much in any inherent psychopharmacological property of the drug but in the social and legal consequences of our firmly held misbeliefs.

After the publication of *Marihuana Reconsidered*, I was often asked about my personal experience with cannabis. Some questioners were skeptical when I replied that I had never used it: "What, you wrote a book about marijuana and you have never experienced it!" The implication was that inexperience would invalidate my claim to expertise. I would defensively respond, "I have written a book on schizophrenia and I have never experienced that." It was not until some years later that I realized that there was validity to this criticism of my lack of personal experience with cannabis. Especially in the later phases of this research and writing, I had flirted with the idea of trying marijuana, not because I believed at that time that it would inform my work, but because it appeared to be such an interesting experience. I decided against it out of fear that it would compromise my goal of producing as objective a statement as I could. Of course, the further I pursued the subject the more I realized how difficult, if not impossible, it would be to produce a truly neutral and objective statement. But I was not about to add to this difficulty by personally exploring marijuana at this time, even though the temptation to do so became greater as I learned more about it.

I had another reason for postponing personal experience with cannabis. If the book were successful, I expected to be called as an expert witness before legislative committees and in courtrooms. I correctly anticipated that some of my interrogators would want to know whether I had ever used cannabis, and I wanted to be able to deny it so as to preserve at least the appearance of objectivity. In the beginning I did not believe this question unfair. It seemed to me to be no different from other questions about my credentials. But I soon learned that when it was asked, it was almost always put by a legislator, lawyer, judge, or media person who was hostile to the suggestion that cannabis might not be as harmful as he firmly believed. It became increasingly clear that the question was asked, not in the spirit of learning more about the context of my understanding of this drug, but rather in the hope that I would answer affirmatively and that this would discredit my testimony. More than a year after the publication of the book I was testifying before a legislative committee when a senator who had already revealed his hostility asked, "Doctor, have you ever used marijuana?" Perhaps because

I was irritated by the hostility reflected in his previous questions and his sneering tone of voice, I replied, "Senator, I will be glad to answer that question if you will first tell me whether if I answer your question affirmatively, you will consider me a more or less credible witness?" The senator, visibly upset by my response, angrily told me that I was being impertinent and left the hearing room. That was the moment that I decided that the time had come.

Later that week Betsy and I went to a party in Cambridge where we knew that some guests would be smoking marijuana. Ever since a review of *Marihuana Reconsidered* had appeared on the front page of the *New York Times Book Review* (under the banner, "The best dope on pot so far") people had been offering my wife and me marijuana, and we had been politely and often a little apologetically declining it. Those guests who knew of our previously resolute abstemiousness were surprised when we decided to join them. We were cautious, as cannabis-naïve people should be, as we inhaled our first tokes ever. Shortly afterward, my first and only unpleasant cannabis experience began. A lit joint was passed around a small circle and we took turns inhaling big, noisy puffs and holding them in for a few seconds. One by one the others said they had had enough and waved off the passing joint; they were high, or at least claimed to be. I asked Betsy, "Do you feel anything?"

"Not a thing!"

"Neither do I."

We were disappointed. We had been looking forward to this initiation for several years. I had come to expect so much from the experience, from the magical possibilities of this subtly altered state of consciousness – and now nothing! I began to wonder: Was this all there was to it? Was my acceptance of the claims of cannabis aficionados just as naïve as my earlier belief in the propaganda disseminated by the Harry Anslinger truth squad and its descendants? Could it be true that all I had accomplished in over three years of intensive research was to swing the pendulum of my gullibility from one extreme to the other? Soon my disappointment gave way to a palpable level of anxiety. Was it possible that I had spent all this time studying what must be for some people an enormously persuasive placebo? Would not the author of a book that took as a basic premise that marijuana is a real drug be considered fraudulent? I tried to reassure myself. I reminded myself that I had, after all, carefully explained to the reader that many if not most people do not get high the first time they use marijuana.

At that time I believed that the anxiety I experienced that night was generated by a precipitous loss of confidence in my newly arrived-at understanding of cannabis, an unshakable belief that after more than three years of hard work, I had gotten it wrong and as a consequence had misled a lot of people – certainly sufficient grounds for a good dose of anxiety. It was not until much later, both chronologically and in my experience with "stoned thinking," that I began to question that explanation. It occurred to me only years later while I was smoking cannabis that I might have actually achieved a high that first night, an "anxiety high," not the kind I had expected. This was certainly not impossible; a small percentage of people who use cannabis for the first time experience some degree of anxiety. There are even a few people who always get anxious when they use marijuana. Among the Rastafarians of Jamaica, these folks are considered slightly deviant, but are understandably excused with the expression, "He don't have a head for ganja!"

This was not a problem with my head, for a week or so later we smoked cannabis, and again neither Betsy nor I noticed any change in our states of consciousness that would even remotely suggest that we were high. Thankfully, however, I was not the least bit anxious this time – only disappointed again. Finally, on our third attempt, we were able to reach the promised high. Our awareness of having at last crossed the threshold arrived gradually. The first thing I noticed, within a few minutes of smoking, was the music; it was *Sgt. Pepper's Lonely Hearts Club Band*. This music was not unfamiliar to me, as it was a favorite of my children, who constantly filled the house with the sound of the Beatles, the Grateful Dead, and other popular rock bands of the time. They frequently urged me to get my "head out of classical music and try listening to rock." It was impossible not to listen to rock when they were growing up, but it was possible for me, as it was for many parents of my generation, not to hear it. On that evening I did "hear" it. It was for me a rhythmic implosion, a fascinating new musical experience! It was the opening of new musical vistas, which I have with the help of my sons continued to explore to this very day. A year later, I related this story to John Lennon and Yoko Ono, with whom I was having dinner. (I was to appear the next day as an expert witness at the Immigration and Naturalization Service hearings that Attorney General John Mitchell had engineered as a way of getting them out of the country on marijuana charges after they became involved in anti-Vietnam War activities.) I told John of this experience and how cannabis appeared to make it possible for me to "hear" his music for the first time in much the same way that Allen Ginsberg reported that he had "seen" Cézanne for the first time when he purposely smoked cannabis before setting out for the Museum of Modern Art. John was quick to reply that I had experienced only one facet of what marijuana could do for music, that he thought it could be very helpful for composing and making music as well as listening to it.

In my next recollection of that evening, Betsy and I and another couple were standing in the kitchen in a tight circle, each of us in turn taking bites out of a Napoleon. There was much hilarity as each bite forced the viscous material between the layers to move laterally and threaten to drip on the floor. It seemed a riotous way to share a Napoleon. But the most memorable part of the kitchen experience was the taste of the Napoleon. None of us had ever, "in our whole lives," eaten such an exquisite Napoleon! "Mary, where in the world did you find these Napoleons?" "Oh, I've had their Napoleons before and they never tasted like this!" It was gradually dawning on me that something unusual was happening; could it be that we were experiencing our first cannabis high?

We drove home very cautiously. In fact, one of the observations I made on the way home was how comfortable I, an habitual turnpike left-laner, was in the right-hand lane with all those cars zipping past me. It seemed like a very long time before we arrived home. Not that we were in a rush – the ride was very pleasant. Time passed even more slowly between our arrival and our going to bed, but once we did, we knew with certainty that we had finally been able to achieve a marijuana high. And that marked the beginning of the experiential facet of my cannabis era, a development that furthered my education about the many uses of this remarkable drug.

I was 44 years old in1972 when I experienced this first marijuana high. Because I have found it both so useful and benign I have used it ever since. I have used it as a recreational drug, as a medicine, and as an enhancer of some capacities. Almost everyone knows something of its usefulness as a recreational substance, growing numbers of people are becoming familiar with its medical utility, but only practiced cannabis users appreciate some of the other ways in which it can be useful. It has been so useful to me that I cannot help but wonder how much difference it would have made had I begun to use it at a younger age. Because it has been so helpful in arriving at some important decisions and understandings, it is tempting to think that it might have helped me to avoid some "before cannabis era" bad decisions. In fact, now, when I have an important problem to solve or decision to make, I invariably avail myself of the opportunity to think about it both stoned and straight.

I cannot possibly convey the breadth of things it helps me to appreciate, to think about, to gain new insights into. But I would like to share several not too personal instances. For example, let me tell you about the worst career choice I have ever made; it was my decision to apply to the Boston Psychoanalytic Institute as a candidate for training in psychoanalysis. I began this training, which was enormously costly in both time and money, in 1960, and graduated seven years later. Although I developed considerable skepticism about certain facets of psychoanalytic theory during training, it was not sufficient to dull the enthusiasm with which I began treating patients psychoanalytically in 1967 (coincidentally, the same year I began to study cannabis). It was not until about the mid 1970s that my emerging skepticism about the therapeutic effectiveness of psychoanalysis began to get uncomfortable. This discomfort was catalyzed by cannabis. On those evenings when I smoke marijuana, it provides, among other things, an invitation to review significant ideas, events, and interactions of the day; my work with patients is invariably on that agenda. This cannabis review-of-the-day is almost always self-critical, often harshly so, and the parameters within which the critique occurs are inexplicably enlarged. My psychotherapy patients, patients who sat opposite me and who could share eye contact and free verbal exchange, always appeared to be making better progress than my psychoanalytic patients. I was generally satisfied with my work with the former, and invariably at first impatient and later unhappy with the lack of progress made by patients on the couch. There is little doubt that it was the cumulative effect of these stoned self-critiques that finally, in 1980, compelled me to make the decision not to accept any new psychoanalytic patients. The subsequent decision to resign from the Boston Psychoanalytic Institute was very difficult, a little like deciding to get a divorce after more than a decade of marriage. But I have no doubt that it was the only way I could deal with this growing discomfort and rectify what was now clearly seen as a mistake. Some of my former psychoanalyst colleagues might believe, among other things, that I had merely traded my involvement in what I considered a macro-delusional system for immersion in an inverse micro-version. Such a possibility notwithstanding, I am indebted to cannabis for the help it provided me in achieving the clarity necessary to arrive at this most difficult decision.

Cannabis can also be used as a catalyst to the generation of new ideas. Experienced cannabis users know that under its influence new ideas flow more readily than they do in the straight state. They also understand that some are good and others are bad ideas; sorting them out is best done while straight. In the absence of an agenda, the ideas are generated randomly or as close or distant associations to conversation, reading, or some perceptual experience. It is sometimes worthwhile to have a stoned go at trying to solve a particular problem. An illustration comes to mind. In 1980, during my tenure as Chairperson of the Scientific Program Committee of the American Psychiatric Association (APA), I "invented" and then edited the first three volumes of the *Annual Review of Psychiatry*, a large book which is still published yearly by the APA. Mindful of how much money this annual publication was earning for the APA, the chief off our sub-department of psychiatry asked me to put my "thinking-cap" on and come up with a way for the Harvard Department of Psychiatry to supplement its shrinking budget. Taking his request seriously, I smoked that night for the express purpose of trying to generate relevant ideas. Within days, at a meeting in the Dean's office, it was agreed that the idea I arrived at that evening would be pursued – the publication of a monthly mental health letter. The first edition of *The Harvard Mental Health Letter* appeared in July 1984 and it soon achieved considerable success as an esteemed mental health publication and a steady source of income to the Harvard Medical School Department of Psychiatry. Would the idea have come or come as easily in a straight state? Maybe.

All through the seemingly endless heated discourse on cannabis in this country over the last four decades, little has been said or written about its many uses. The overwhelming preponderance of funding, research, writing, political activity, and legislation has been centered on the question of its harmfulness. The 65-year-old debate, which has relatively recently included discussion of its usefulness and safety as a medicine, has never been concerned with its non-medicinal uses; it is always limited to the question of how harmful it is and how a society should deal with the harm it is alleged to cause. It is estimated that 100 million Americans have used cannabis and more than 10 million use it regularly. They use it in the face of risks that range from opprobrium to imprisonment. From the time I began my studies of marijuana, 20 million citizens of this country have been arrested for marijuana offenses. The number of annual marijuana arrests is increasing, and in 2007 over 872,000 people were arrested on marijuana charges, 90 percent of them for possession. Because the government allows confiscation of property in drug cases, many have lost valued possessions ranging from automobiles to homes. Most have to undertake expensive legal defenses and some have served or will serve time in prison. Unless we are prepared to believe that all these people are driven by uncontrollable "Reefer Madness" craving, we must conclude that they find something in the experience attractive and useful. And yet there is very little open exploration of these uses, with the growing exception of its value as a medicine. Even here, government officials want to mute the discussion out of a fear expressed by the chief of the Public Health Service when in 1992 he discontinued the only legal avenue to medicinal marijuana: "If it is perceived that the Public Health Service is going around giving marijuana to folks, there would be a perception that this stuff can't be so bad . . . it gives a bad signal."[3] The government has, until very recently, refused to acknowledge that cannabis has any value, even medicinal, but there are millions of citizens who have discovered through their own experience that it has a large variety of uses they consider valuable and that the health costs are minimal.

This large population of marijuana users is a subculture, one that has been present in this country since the 1960s. Three decades ago it was an open, vocal, active, and articulate culture on and off campus. Today, it is silent and largely hidden because most users, understandably, do not want to stand up and be counted. They have more than the law to fear. Urine testing is now a fact of life in corporate America; a positive test result can lead, at the very least, to a stint in a "drug treatment" program, and at most, to the loss of a job, career destruction, even imprisonment. Users are very mindful of this minefield, and most find ways around it. Even more pervasive and in some ways more pernicious is the stigmatization attached to cannabis use. Young people often experience little of this, at least among their friends. But as they grow older and move into increasingly responsible and visible positions they become much more guarded. Many believe, correctly, that colleagues would regard them as deviant if they knew. This stigmatization is abetted by the media, which have created and perpetrated a stereotyped image of "potheads" as young, hirsute, slovenly dressed ne'er-do-wells or disreputable, irresponsible, and socially marginal hedonists who use marijuana only to hang out and party. One reason for the fierce resistance to marijuana is the fear that it will somehow taint middle-class society with the "pothead" culture.

There is no denying that many, especially young people, use marijuana primarily for "partying and hanging out" in the same way that many more use beer. And most non-users, until they become aware of its medical value, believe that smoking to party and hang out pretty much defines the limits of its usefulness. This stereotype is powerful, and reactions ranging from puzzlement to outrage greet claims that this party drug could be useful as medicine or for any other purposes. People who make claims about its usefulness run the risk of being derided as vestigial hippies. Under these circumstances it is not surprising that most people who use cannabis do so behind drawn curtains, alone or with others who share some appreciation of its value.

It is unfortunate that those who, from personal experience, are aware of its usefulness are so reluctant to be public about it. I believe it would be good for the country if more people in business, academic, and professional worlds were known to be marijuana users. The government has been able to pursue its policies of persecution and prosecution largely because of the widespread false belief that cannabis smokers are either irresponsible and socially marginal people or adolescents who "experiment," learn their lesson, and abandon all use of the drug. That lie is unfortunately perpetuated when those who know better remain silent. It's time to let the truth come out. Just as the gay and lesbian out-of-the-closet movement has done so much to decrease the level of homophobia in this country, when the many people of substance and accomplishment who use cannabis "come out" it will contribute much to the diminution of cannabinophobia.

Not many well-known people are identified as users of cannabis. A few politicians have been outed by their enemies (one went so far as to claim that he did not inhale), and some would-be political appointments have failed because of a history of marijuana use. Occasionally a screen star, musician, or professional athlete is arrested for possession. Aside from Allen Ginsberg, Bill Maher, some popular musicians, and a few notables from the Beat and hippie movements, few people in the public eye have voluntarily acknowledged cannabis use. Except for one well-known scientist, the physicist Richard Feynman, academics have been most cautious. Feynman, by courageously acknowledging his ongoing use of marijuana, won the respect and appreciation of many and the enmity of others. Fear of "coming out" is, of course, not without foundation. As long as the present stereotyped understanding of marijuana use and its effects continues to prevail, anyone who acknowledges using it will risk being taken less seriously from then on. It is thought that potheads could not possibly be considered mature, serious, responsible, and credible. Yet only those who actually use cannabis can teach us how useful it is.

There was a time not so long ago when it was generally assumed that any use of marijuana was "merely recreational." This was certainly true at the time I wrote *Marihuana Reconsidered*. The chapter on marijuana as medicine ("The Place of Cannabis and Medicine") was concerned with past (nineteenth- and early twentieth-century) and potential uses; there was no overt and little covert use of cannabis as a medicine at that time.

Now, there are many thousands of patients who use cannabis medicinally. And as the ranks of these patients grow, so does the number of people who observe for themselves how relatively benign this substance is. Seventy-four percent of Americans presently believe that cannabis should be made available as a medicine; very few people would have held this belief in 1971. Currently, it is generally thought that there are two generic categories of marijuana use: recreational and medical. But in fact many uses do not fit into these categories without stretching their boundaries to the point of distortion; they fall into a third category, one that is more diverse and for that reason difficult to label. It includes such disparate uses as the magnification of pleasure in a host of activities ranging from dining to sex, the increased ability to hear music and see works of art, and the ways in which it appears to catalyze new ideas, insights, and creativity, to name a few. Furthermore, at its edges, which are fuzzy, there is some conflation with both medicine and recreation. Yet, the preponderance of these uses falls into this broad and distinctive third category that I call enhancement. This is the class of uses which is generally the least appreciated or understood by non-cannabis users. It is also the case that some people who use or who have used marijuana may not be aware of some – if not most – of the enhancement possibilities.

One category of cannabis utility that we have studied is its usefulness as a medicine. Because there is not at this time a systematic clinical literature on the medicinal uses of cannabis, James B. Bakalar and I asked patients to share their experiences with cannabis as a medicine for our book, *Marihuana: The Forbidden Medicine*. We supplemented these anecdotal patient accounts with our own clinical experience and what we could glean from the medical literature. Anecdotal evidence is not as persuasive as that from double-blind placebo-controlled studies, the more scientifically sound modern medical approach to the safety and efficacy of new therapeutics. As the results of such studies become available we may be compelled to modify our estimate of the clinical usefulness of cannabis. At this time, however, it is difficult to imagine that future studies will subtract much from the clinical experience-driven perception that cannabis is a remarkably versatile medicine with relatively little toxicity.

It is my intention to roughly follow the same format in the Uses of Marijuana Project (www.marijuana-uses.com). While I will attempt to illuminate the various uses of cannabis through literary accounts and by sharing some of my own experiences, the prime source of what I hope will be a fairly comprehensive understanding of the uses of this versatile drug will come from contemporary users. Some will identify themselves; others will prefer to remain anonymous for reasons that have already been noted. Either way, I hope to present enough information about the witness to put his or her account into a meaningful context. Unlike medicinal use, which will eventually be fitted with scientific costume, an understanding of those uses which fall into the category of enhancement will probably always be based on anecdotal accounts; it is unlikely that marijuana's capacity for the enhancement of sexual pleasure, for example, will ever be the subject of a modern scientific (double-blind placebo-controlled) study. However, if this ethnographic method is successful, we should be able to provide a reasonably proximate picture of the varieties and value of cannabis use in contemporary society. And in so doing, we cannabis users can make a significant contribution to the demise of cannabinophobia, one of our age's most damaging popular delusions.

NOTES

1 Lester Grinspoon, *Marihuana Reconsidered* (Cambridge, MA: Harvard University Press, 1971).
2 Lester Grinspoon, *Marijuana, the Forbidden Medicine* (New Haven: Yale University Press, 1993, 1997).
3 Lester Grinspoon and J. B. Bakalar, *Marijuana: The Forbidden Medicine*, 2nd edn. (New Haven: Yale University Press, 1997), p. 22.

LESTER GRINSPOON

G. T. ROCHE[1]

CHAPTER 2

SEEING SNAKES

On Delusion, Knowledge, and the Drug Experience

Were such things here as we do speak about?
Or have we eaten on the insane root
That takes the reason prisoner?
William Shakespeare, *Macbeth*,
Act I Scene III

Chemical Revelations?

Advocates of psychedelic drugs argue that they can induce experiences that are of great spiritual and philosophical value, and that they have the potential to "expand consciousness." But can drugs, as William James (1842–1910), Aldous Huxley (1894–1963), and Timothy Leary (1920–96) argue, allow us to see beyond the horizon of ordinary perception – that is, see things as they really are? To put the philosophical question more generally, can an artificial change (by the means of drugs, electrical stimuli, or psychosurgery) to the brain – to the mind's material foundations – reveal *knowledge* through the resulting experience? And could such a change actually provide an authentic religious experience, or rather, knowledge of what it is like to have an authentic religious experience? Or are such claims of instant enlightenment merely a mystical facade?

There is no doubt that some substances (such as nicotine and caffeine) can stimulate the mind and enhance concentration. It is also possible that a handful of philosophers have been *imaginatively* inspired by their drug experiences. Yet many philosophers would find the claim of knowledge acquired through a drug experience deeply implausible, for two reasons.

First, the psychedelics disrupt mental processing, making it impossible, in the words of Immanuel Kant (commenting on intoxicants) for one's mind to order "sense representations by laws of experience."[2] Likewise, Michel Foucault (who had himself allegedly experimented with LSD) is scathing of the "fortunetellers" who ascribe to the drug revelatory powers, given that drugs "have nothing at all to do with truth and falsity."[3] Further, if any intoxicating substances induce experiences that are similar to religious ecstasies, suggests Bertrand Russell, so much for religious ecstasies: we "can make no distinction between the man who eats little and sees heaven and the man who drinks much and sees snakes. Each is in an abnormal physical condition, and therefore has abnormal perceptions."[4] Given the widely reported relationship between abnormal mental states and religious ecstasy, this objection is not easily dismissed. It has also been noted that there are a number of commonalities between the psychedelic drug experience and schizophrenia, in particular thought disorder, paranoia, delusion, and depersonalization. As we do not typically think of schizophrenia as granting access to otherwise inaccessible knowledge, it seems unlikely that drugs that may mimic schizophrenia (Dimethyltryptamine [DMT], LSD, cannabis) could do this either. The only knowledge that the drug experience could provide, according to this view, is of what certain mental anomalies must feel like.

Secondly, to hold some claim to be knowledge, rather than being merely a strongly held belief, we need some justification for it. The claims (like the claims of mathematicians or scientists that are considered knowledge) made by the users of psychedelic drugs of their revelations must be shown to have a source that has proven to be reliable in the past. As such, even if a psychedelic drug user were to make some drug-inspired claim about the world which was later verified by some other means, we would *still* not be able to say that she had therefore provided knowledge: the drug experience would still need to be shown to be a reliable source of a number of such independently verifiable claims. Were it to be shown that the drug experience could provide such knowledge, the implications would be serious. As Catholic philosopher Raphael Waters points out, "if the drugs reveal more of reality than would otherwise be available to the knower, we must call into question the knowledge that we already possess. For it is obvious that the dependability of our powers of knowing external reality would become questionable."[5]

The Veil of Maya and the Reducing Valve

In response, advocates of psychedelic substances argue that the drugs are *not* mere intoxicants. Merely because unusual states of consciousness are derived through artificial means, argue William James and G. S. Spinks, it does not follow that the resulting insights or experiences are invalidated: the end-product is to be judged, rather than the means. As James writes in *The Varieties of Religious Experience*, mystic states of awareness, obtained by whatever means,

> offer us *hypotheses*, hypotheses which we may voluntarily ignore, but which as thinkers we cannot possibly upset. The supernaturalism and optimism to which they would persuade us may, interpreted in one way or another, be after all the truest of insights into the meaning of this life.[6]

James also emphasizes the profoundly philosophical nature of the insights he gained following his nitrous oxide experiments, remarking that the drug gave him a new appreciation of Hegel:

> Looking back on my own experiences, they all converge towards a kind of insight to which I cannot help ascribing some metaphysical significance. The keynote of it is invariably a reconciliation. It is as if the opposites of the world, whose contradictoriness and conflict make all our difficulties and troubles, were melted into unity. . . . I feel as if it must mean something, something like what the hegelian [*sic*] philosophy means, if one could only lay hold of it more clearly. Those who have ears to hear, let them hear; to me the living sense of its reality only comes in the artificial mystic state of mind.[7]

Later psychedelicists likewise explicitly reject the primacy of rational thought over intuition, and would agree with James's assertion that "the existence of mystical states absolutely overthrows the pretension of non-mystical states to be the sole and ultimate dictators of what we may believe."[8] Rather than rejecting the drug experience because it leads to irrational thoughts, the psychedelicists typically hold that the insights of the drug experience reveal reason's limits.

Four general approaches have been proposed to support this view. Firstly, Gerald Heard (1889–1971) and others have argued that the psychedelics provide insights that are intelligible within an intuitive paradigm, as opposed to that of "analytic" thought.[9] Charles T. Tart suggests a computer analogy to illustrate this principle. Just as a computer can run different programs, argues Tart, the human mind can be put in an alternate state of consciousness in order to better appreciate different aspects of reality, from the perspective of (what Tart terms) "state-specific sciences."[10] Similarly, Heard describes the mind as having several "focal lengths." He notes the methods of meditation used by such thinkers as René Descartes (1596–1650), who would write as thoughts came to him while half asleep, William Harvey (1578–1657), discoverer of the mechanism of the circulation of blood, who would meditate in a coal mine, and the mathematician Henri Poincaré (1854–1912), who was acutely aware that many of his ideas came to him as the result of intuition, rather than through conscious intellectual labor. LSD is proposed by Heard as providing a more direct route to the subliminal faculties of mind and their creative powers, through bypassing the "critical filter" of ordinary, waking consciousness. Andrew Weil and James Kellenberger have also noted the relationship between altered states of consciousness and creative genius.

A related approach is the "reducing-valve" model proposed by the philosopher Charlie Dunbar Broad (1887–1971) and psychiatrist John Raymond Smythies (b. 1922), popularized by Aldous Huxley and adapted from the theory of mind proposed by French philosopher Henri Bergson (1859–1941). According to this view, in ordinary consciousness we do not see reality in an unadulterated way. Rather, the mind continuously filters out extraneous thoughts and perceptions, allowing only that which is useful to us to reach conscious awareness. Further, as Bergson notes, our mind is constantly composing reality through arranging and interpreting sensed phenomena in the light of our prior memories. For Huxley, psychedelic drugs "open the valves" of perception, allowing us to see the world in its true splendor, just as the great artists and mystics could. No longer yoked to the mundane needs of ordinary existence, advocates of the psychedelics also hold that intellectual and perceptual powers become greatly enhanced; that the user of LSD or mescaline will "reach philosophic conclusions of rare profundity";[11] that their eyes will "seem to become a microscope through which the mind delves deeper and deeper into the intricately dancing texture of our world."[12] Huxley also holds that psychedelic drugs can break through linguistic and cultural conditioning. As the excessively rational Western concepts of ordinary consciousness rob reality of its "native thinghood,"[13] reasons Huxley, the psychedelics are necessary "solvents for liquefying the sludgy stickiness of an anachronistic state of mind."[14] In a similar vein, Walter Houston

Clark suggests that the psychedelics improve one's morality by revealing the "unity of all peoples and all things."[15]

Thirdly, it has been suggested that, under the effects of psychedelics, one may become directly conscious of entities, objects, or principles that are described by natural science but are invisible to ordinary awareness. Leary and Ralph Metzner write of directly experiencing DNA, for example. Watts writes of an immediate sensorial understanding of Einstein's mass-energy equivalence. And Rick Strassman suggests that DMT allows one to see dark matter. This would suggest (it is implied) that what is perceived is objectively real, rather than being merely delusional. The case is perhaps most strongly made by Susan Blackmore, who, echoing the reducing-valve model, suggests that ordinary consciousness is not ideally suited to science or philosophy. With reference to the common psychedelic experience of becoming "one with the universe," Blackmore argues that this view "fits far better with a scientific understanding of the world than our normal dualist view. . . . We really *are* one with the universe. This means that the psychedelic sense of self may actually be truer than the dualist view."[16]

Fourthly, psychedelicists and their precursors note the long history of psychoactive substances used in mystery cults or religious practices; rites allegedly perfected and practiced over centuries to pierce through the illusory barrier of ordinary consciousness (the veil of Maya, as it is termed in Hindu philosophy), and to bring about union with absolute reality. In *The Birth of Tragedy* Friedrich Nietzsche (1844–1900) writes of ancient Dionysian rituals in exactly these terms, noting that their participants used "narcotic potions" to attain oneness with both one's fellow man and with Nature:

> Now that the gospel of universal harmony is sounded, each individual becomes not only reconciled to his fellow but actually at one with him – as though the veil of Maya had been torn apart and there remained only shreds floating before the vision of mystical Oneness.[17]

Carl A. P. Ruck (b. 1935), Albert Hofmann (1906–2008), and R. Gordon Wasson (1898–1986) have further explored the relationship between ancient Greek religion and philosophy and the use of psychoactive drugs. Wasson and Hofmann hypothesize that the rites of the Eleusinian Mystery cult of ancient Greece incorporated a beverage that contained rye ergot (*Claviceps purpurea*), a hallucinogenic fungus. In keeping with Nietzsche's description above, Hofmann suggests that this substance was used to attain a mystic "experience of totality."[18] Further, it has been suggested that such drug use may have inspired the philosophies of Plato and Aristotle, given that both had written favorably of their experiences of the Eleusinian Mysteries.

The Insane Root

The case for drug-induced enlightenment is problematic, for a number of reasons. Firstly, the assumptions of Leary, Wasson, Watts, and other representative psychedelicists are loaded with a considerable amount of mystical baggage, suggesting that the "psychedelic revelation" is not complementary to the achievements of logic or physics (as Blackmore or Tart suggest) but explicitly *contradicted* by them. This irrationalism is found in the originators of the psychedelic view. Broad's seemingly scientific description of the "reducing valve," adopted unmodified by Huxley, is underpinned by the problematic assumption that each person "is at each moment capable of remembering all that has ever happened to him and of perceiving everything that is happening everywhere *in the universe*."[19] Such claims of drug-given omniscience and even supernatural powers appear in much of the psychedelic literature since Huxley, and could be said to be a defining trait of the genre. Psychedelic drugs have inspired in their advocates beliefs in extrasensory perception, the power to communicate telepathically with extra-terrestrials (or with psilocybin mushrooms, which Terence McKenna believes *are* sentient extra-terrestrials), time travel, and the ability to foresee the end of the world. Advocates have also asserted that the drug experience grants access to ancestral or prehistoric memories that are (according to Leary and others) encoded in DNA, reveals that the soul is immortal, or that it has lived through past lives. Equally beyond parody are the theories that have been inspired by the psychedelic experience (in the absence of evidence, or even any *concern* with the need of evidence): the view, for example, that human language originated as a result of psilocybin ingestion, that psychoactive drugs caused the defining leap in the evolution of human intelligence or language, could further stimulate human evolution, or will eventually replace philosophical analysis. In each of the cases cited above, the drug experience *itself* is presented as the key justification of these views.

In the absence of any evidence that ESP phenomena are real, we could be forgiven for taking claims of having experienced first hand such phenomena to be delusional. The same could perhaps be said of many of the other drug-inspired claims about the real world noted above. Blackmore's suggestion that with hallucinogens one can experience first hand "cosmic oneness" is also problematic. Although psychedelics are known for inducing the *feeling* that "all is one," it is doubtful that anyone could *literally* experience a real "loss of ego" or "fusion," as there is still an ego – an experiencing subject – that observes the event. The division of subject and object is built into the very concept of experience, regardless of how things might feel at the time. Further, many psychedelic experiences inspire the opposite, *dualist* view: people on drugs may have the sense that they are entirely separate from their bodies.

Claims of moral or existential enlightenment under the effects of psychedelics are also questionable. Where a philosophy of life is expressed, psychedelicists can come across as merely flippant, somewhat undermining James's suggestion that the drug experience could provide some answer to the Great Question. McKenna states that the purpose of life is a "good party"[20] and Watts asserts that all the pain and suffering in the universe "are simply extreme forms of play," adding that "there isn't anything in the whole universe to be afraid of because it doesn't happen to anyone!"[21] Concerning moral enlightenment, for Huxley and Leary psychedelic drugs actually seem to *suspend* the moral sense. For Huxley, the mescaline had delivered him from "the world of selves, of time, of moral judgments and utilitarian considerations," adding that the mescaline user "sees no reason for doing anything in particular and finds most of the causes for which, at ordinary times, he was prepared to act and suffer, profoundly uninteresting."[22] For Leary, likewise, virtue and morality following LSD enlightenment are revealed to be just "part of [the] old con game."[23] Even cannabis has the capacity to temporarily suspend moral sensibility, according to C. R. Marshall's 1897 post-trip account: "I was devoid of feeling, fearless of death, and even insensible to the feelings of others: if the friend by my side had died I think I should [*sic*] have laughed."[24] None of these accounts, of course, demonstrate that psychedelics can *make* someone immoral, even temporarily, but they undermine any straightforward case for drug-inspired *moral* wisdom (assuming of course that moral wisdom is not the realization that morality *is* a myth).

Further, the association of altered states of awareness and scientific insight is not compelling; only a handful of historical cases are given of this relationship, and none of those cited involve drug use. Rather, they all involve highly learned researchers who were ready for inspiration when it came to them, whether when wide awake or half-asleep. Lester Grinspoon and James B. Bakalar suggest that an important distinction has been missed in this analogy – "withdrawing reason's watcher at the gates" through some meditative technique may well work for some, but this is a far cry from the radical distortion of cognitive processing that the psychedelics induce.[25]

Also problematic is the association between the Eleusinian Mysteries – hence, the origins of Greek thought – and psychoactive drugs. While it is true, as Carl A. P. Ruck notes, that the hallucinogenic properties of rye ergot were well known in the classical world, its very toxicity also made it a potent chemical weapon, on account of the horrific visions it could induce, and because it made one's limbs turn black and then fall off. Nor is there much evidence that rye ergot was ever used ritualistically, despite its use for millennia in obstetrics. Further, experimental trials of rye ergot suggest that its visionary potential is limited: even a barely psychedelic dose is toxic enough to cause painful leg cramps.

Other suggestions as to the intoxicated origins of Greek philosophy are not much better supported. Yet *even if* drug use could be associated with the insights of a particular great philosopher (Plotinus' use of opium, for example), this still would not constitute *philosophical* insight as such; that is, the fruit of systematic intellectual labor. Nor does it show that any such particular insight counts as knowledge. Such evidence would simply show that early Greek philosophy had not entirely distinguished itself from mysticism.

Finally, the psychedelicists' case against ordinary logic and conceptions of reality is essentially rhetorical. James gives us nothing but his word to support his assertion that nitrous oxide inhalation grants "illuminations, revelations, full of significance and importance" that "carry with them a curious sense of authority."[26] The same is true of later writers. Watts contrasts, for example, "pedestrian consciousness" against "multidimensional superconsciousness," Huxley similarly dismisses "rationalistic philosophy" as "bumptious," and Leary dismisses the ordinary worldview as a "system of paranoid delusions."[27] Similar dismissals in defense of psychedelic "truth' are given by McKenna and Gottfried Benn. Others have proposed a new category of "knowledge" to account for the holding of beliefs that have no other basis than the drug experience. Walter N. Pahnke (1931–71), for example, defines the "known" as something that is "intuitively felt to be authoritative, requires no proof at a rational level, and produces an inward feeling of intuitive truth" – thereby dissolving the distinction between knowledge and delusion.[28]

The psychedelicists are essentially proclaiming that their own, drug-inspired worldview is a better guide to reality than the combined efforts

🍁

of all scientists and philosophers, in fact the worldview of anyone whose thinking has not been permanently modified by a psychedelic drug. Yet the reasoning offered to support this claim is correspondingly outrageous. Leary insists that one must use the drugs themselves to assess the claims of their powers, yet rejects out of hand the testimony of those who have tried psychedelic drugs and remained unconvinced. Watts even attempts to seize the moral high ground, comparing the refusal to accept the psychedelic doctrine with racist bigotry.

As Sidney Cohen notes, there is no *doubt* in the accounts given by the psychedelicists; no acknowledgment of the need to account for one's views. As Benjamin Paul Blood (1832–1919) puts it, referring to the inhalation of nitrous oxide, the "anaesthetic revelation" is "the satisfaction of philosophy."[29] The psychedelicists's view – Watts makes this very clear – is that philosophical questioning simply dissolves in the blinding light of the Experience; explanations "are just another form of complexity."[30] As such, it does not seem implausible to suggest that a sufficiently large dose of some hallucinogen could simply silence the philosophical muse.

Whether due to a gross overvaluing of an intense aesthetic experience (as suggested by Robert A. Oakes), a profound drug-induced suggestibility, or a well-researched capacity of the psychedelic drugs to *impair* cognition, perception, and concentration, their revelatory powers are clearly exaggerated. Given these facts, the real question is perhaps "what knowledge is only accessible to the individual through chemically degrading one's capacity for rational thought?" If one simply assumes that the acquisition of knowledge (that is, sound understanding that something is true) requires rational thought, the question is absurd. Watts, Leary, and Huxley all write of the insight acquired through the psychedelic experience as a *direct apprehension* of some deep truth, rather than through *intellectual* insight. Without an argument as to how such a direct, drug-induced experience can warrant such certainty, Watts, Leary, and Huxley are essentially appealing to their own authority.

The Peacock in the Mirror

The discussion above, perhaps, demystifies the issue over the psychedelic drugs, yet there still remains the issue of "psychedelic spirituality." Advocates of psychedelic drugs argue that they can induce mystic states of consciousness of spiritual value, and give two reasons for this view.

The first argument is that the drug experience *feels* mystical or religious, in particular to those qualified to make a judgment: religious people. One famous study supporting this claim is the so-called Good Friday Experiment, in which Pahnke gave psilocybin to ten Protestant divinity students at Boston University in 1962 (another ten were given a placebo). Most of those who were given psilocybin reported having a deeply religious experience. Secondly, Huxley, Watts, and Leary have noted striking parallels between the psychedelic drug experience and classic accounts of mystic experience, both Christian and Buddhist. Both types of experience, it is observed, produce a profound feeling of "oneness," or the sense that one is encountering a "great presence" or the "ground of being."[31] Watts and Leary have also noted the similarities between the LSD experience and the state of *satori* that is attained in Zen meditation.

However, for some religious skeptics, this association between the drug state and mysticism may well be trivial. The psychedelic drugs are known to inspire uncanny experiences and non-rational beliefs, and religious experiences tend towards, by definition, that which goes beyond what can be scientifically or logically verified. To note the similarity between the two types of experience simply compares (for the religious skeptic) two different but equally delusional worldviews. As for the Pahnke experiment, it is only natural that religious people who accept the possibility of a divine encounter through drugs will interpret the drug experience to be authentically religious. Indeed, for a skeptic, the similarities of drug states and religious states could simply reinforce the association of religious belief and neurosis. Psychedelic drugs also raise the possibility that any given exotic, paranormal experience, unless corroborated by a number of witnesses to the same, objectively verifiable event, is potentially the work of non-divine intervention.

Yet it would be fallacious to assume that all unusual states of awareness are cut from the same cloth, and one does not need to be a religious skeptic to suspect that there is something wrong with the case for psychedelically induced religious experience.

First is the lack of fit with religious tradition. The association made between psychedelics and Buddhism is questionable, and not merely because one of the five key precepts of Buddhism is abstinence from intoxicating substances that may cloud thinking. It is true that hallucinogens may give a sense of timelessness and "oneness with the universe" that roughly corresponds with some Buddhist accounts of absolute reality, but the similarity may be superficial. Buddhist writings emphasize that meditation requires steady, focused concentration and *emptying* thought of all content, suggesting that psychedelic drugs would simply get in the way. Critics have also questioned the accuracy of the accounts of Buddhism given by both Watts and Leary. Further, as the Catholic thinker R. C. Zaehner (1913–74) notes, a number of mystic traditions are incompatible with the psychedelic experience, given their assumption that God is unknowable to the intellect and hence cannot be perceived.

There are also serious problems with associating the psychedelic experience with Christianity. Unlike an authentic mystic union, the psychedelic experience arguably does not lead to a religious transformation of character. It has also been remarked that the drug experience is simply too hedonistic, or too amusing; the traditional means of attaining a mystic union (with Jesus, Christians argue) requires a necessarily difficult and painful process.

There are also differences between biblical accounts of divine encounters and those reported by people suffering hallucinations. Whereas schizophrenics, epileptics, and people on drugs often describe encounters with God or angels face to face, Otto Doerr and Óscar Velásquez note that the angels described in the Torah and New Testament conceal their identity, which is only made apparent after they have left the scene. Further, note Doerr and Velásquez, the God of the Torah never appears to humans directly (Exodus 33:20).

These arguments may appear to some as being culturally chauvinistic, given that some Central American Christian groups actually use hallucinogens in their traditional rites. The debate also hinges on assertions that are perhaps impossible to verify, given that they require some independently verifiable criteria of authenticity (that is, proof that God exists and that the drug experience gives a true experience of God's existence). For all we know, one could argue, God *does* exist, *and* no one tradition has the complete picture. But there is no escaping the strangeness of the assertion that one could attain an experience of the Divine Presence through a drug, or for that matter by any physical means at all. Put simply, no omniscient being, by definition, could be summoned by whatever worldly means against her or his will. To suggest otherwise seems more in keeping with those South American shamanistic traditions that hold that supernatural forces can be summoned through ritualistic use of hallucinogens.

Further, the case for psychedelic spirituality is open to the charge of sample bias: many recorded psychedelic experiences are not merely unpleasant, but positively Lovecraftian, and there is at least one case of LSD *reducing* the religious belief of a subject. One of Strassman's DMT research subjects went through the hallucinated experience of being raped by a crocodile; another hallucinated that "insectoids" simultaneously had sex with and ate him.[32] Jean-Paul Sartre (1905–80), following a horrific mescaline experience in February 1935, had a persistent hallucination of a lobster stalking him days later, and both Henri Michaux (1899–1984) and Stanisław Witkiewicz (1885–1939) (again on mescaline) reported perverse, nightmarish visions. Huxley's suggestion that such non-"Beatific" experiences are somehow due to a lack of spiritual preparation only begs the question.

For those who wish to retain the concept of the drug-induced religious experience, but without retaining the idea of God or gods, these arguments may all seem beside the point, and some have taken exactly this approach. But the outcome of this view scarcely qualifies as a concept of religion. Leary explicitly defines religion as the practice of achieving states of ecstasy; for Huxley, religions are merely failed attempts to escape reality, and should be replaced with "chemical vacations from intolerable selfhood and repulsive surroundings."[33]

As Zaehner notes, Huxley and Leary are essentially promoting "an extension of soulless technology to the soul itself."[34] Whereas Leary and others insist on the *transcendental* nature of the drug experience, its very possibility simply reinforces the view that our very minds are embodied in the world, and are thereby *controllable* (consider Leary's proposal to use LSD to "cure" homosexuality or suppress criminality, for example). Psychedelic drugs demonstrate just how thin the ice of reason actually is, and how easily the very citadel of the mind can be stormed. The use of psychoactive agents as tools of war or coercion in fact goes back centuries, and the experimental use of psychedelics by the Nazis (mescaline, at Dachau), the CIA, and other agencies is now well known. The great pharmacologist Louis Lewin (1850–1929) notes that the uses of drugs for psychological control and for ritual use need not be distinct: datura and other psychotropic drugs have long been used "by religious fanatics, clairvoyants, miracle-workers, magicians, priests, and impostors" in the course of religious ceremonies.[35] We already know of at least one cult leader who has used LSD as a tool of psychological control over their followers (Shoko Asahara, responsible for the 1995 sarin attack on the Tokyo subway system). The very characteristics of the psychedelic drugs that have led to their mystical veneration – the power to disrupt cognition and attention, to warp perception, to leave the subject wide open for new ideas and beliefs, to flood consciousness with imagery of stultifying beauty – make them and more purpose-specific substances (such as the chemical weapon Agent BZ) potent incapacitating agents. The idea that involuntary ingestion of such a substance could lead to union with a benevolent and omniscient God is absurd, yet the psychedelic doctrine cannot rule this possibility out.

How to account for the attribution of divinity with something so potentially dangerous? It may be that the drug simply triggers a deep intuition that the very beautiful must be divine. If so, the irony is profound. As some researchers have suggested, the intense aesthetic experience created by psychedelic drugs is perhaps brought about by their ability to disclose to consciousness the mind's normally occulted machinery of perception, hence the geometric patterns and fantastic architectural forms that are often reported by psychedelics users (temporal lobe epilepsy and delirium tremens can cause similar visions). According to this view, a feedback loop of sorts is established between the conscious mind and mental processes: the very evolved machinery of perception that makes aesthetic pleasure possible breaks through into the theatre of consciousness, creating seemingly preternatural visions. To borrow Charles Baudelaire's metaphor of hashish as being a mirror of the natural, rather than the divine, the "psychedelic mystic" is like an unwittingly resplendent peacock that mistakes its own reflection in the mirror for something else.

NOTES

1   Many thanks to James Stewart, Raphael Waters, Daavid Stein, and Andrew Trigg for valuable comments on an earlier version of this essay. Thanks also to Chris J. Mathews, Ruth Lionberger, Charles Laurier, Robert Wicks, Andrew Jones, Aaron Davidson and, again, James Stewart, for recommending and providing literature.
2   Immanuel Kant, *Anthropology from a Pragmatic Point of View*, trans. Mary J. Gregor (The Hague: Martinus Nijhoff, 1974), p. 46.
3   Michel Foucault, "Theatrum Philosophicum," in *Language, Counter-Memory, Practice: Selected Essays and Interviews*, ed. Donald F. Bouchard, trans. Donald F. Bouchard and Sherry Simon (Ithaca: Cornell University Press, 1977), pp. 165–98.
4   Bertrand Russell, *Religion and Science* (Oxford: Oxford University Press, 1935), p. 188.
5   Raphael Waters, "Some Epistemological Questions Concerning the Non-Medical Use of Drugs," *Revue de l'université d'Ottawa* 45 (1975): 518–40.
6   William James, *The Varieties of Religious Experience: A Study in Human Nature* (Glasgow: Collins, 1962), p. 412.

7   Ibid., p. 374.

8   Ibid., p. 411.

9   Gerald Heard, "Can This Drug Enlarge Man's Mind?" *Psychedelic Review* 1 1 (1963): 7–17.

10 Charles T. Tart, "States of Consciousness and State-Specific Sciences," *Science* 176 (1972): 1203–10.

11 P. G Stafford and B. H. Golightly, *LSD In Action* (London: Sidgwick and Jackson, 1969), p. 38.

12 Alan Watts, *The Joyous Cosmology* (New York: Vintage, 1965), p. xix; see also p. 26.

13 Aldous Huxley, *The Doors of Perception and Heaven and Hell* (New York: Perennial/Harper Collins, 1990), p. 92.

14 Aldous Huxley, "Culture and the Individual," in David Solomon (ed.) *LSD: The Consciousness-Expanding Drug* (New York: G. P. Putnam's Sons, 1968), pp. 38–48.

15 Walter Houston Clark, "Ethics and LSD," *Journal of Psychoactive Drugs* 17, 4 (1985): 229–34.

16 Helen Phillips, Graham Lawton, and Susan Blackmore, "The Intoxication Instinct," *New Scientist* 184, 2473 (November 13, 2004): 32–41 (italics added).

17 Friedrich Nietzsche, *The Birth of Tragedy*, in *The Birth of Tragedy and The Genealogy of Morals* trans. Francis Golffing (New York: Anchor Books/ Random House, 1956), pp. 22–3.

18 Albert Hofmann, "The Message of the Eleusinian Mysteries for Today's World," trans. Jonathan Ott, in Robert Forte (ed.) *Entheogens and the Future of Religion* (San Francisco: Council on Spiritual Practices, 1997), pp. 31–9.

19 Cited in Huxley, *Doors of Perception*, p. 22 (italics mine).

20 Terence McKenna, *The Archaic Revival: Speculations on Psychedelic Mushrooms, the Amazon, Virtual Reality, UFOs, Evolution, Shamanism, the Rebirth of the Goddess, and the End of History* (New York: Harper Collins, 1991), p. 210.

21 Watts, *The Joyous Cosmology*, p. 78.

22 Huxley, *Doors of Perception*, pp. 25, 36.

23 Timothy Leary, *The Politics of Ecstasy* (London: Paladin, 1973), p. 223.

24 C. R. Marshall, "The Active Principle of Indian Hemp: A Preliminary Communication," *The Lancet* (January 23, 1897): 235–8.

25 Lester Grinspoon and James B. Bakalar, *Psychedelic Drugs Reconsidered* (New York: Basic Books, 1979), p. 266.

26 James, *Varieties of Religious Experience*, p. 367.

27 Watts, *The Joyous Cosmology*, p. 89; Huxley, *Doors of Perception*, p. 126; Timothy Leary, "How to Change Behavior," in David Solomon (ed.) *LSD: The Consciousness-Expanding Drug* (New York: G. P. Putnam's Sons, 1968), pp. 103–18.

28 Walter N. Pahnke, "Drugs and Mysticism," in Bernard Aaronson and Humphry Osmond (eds.) *Psychedelics: The Uses and Implications of Hallucinogenic Drugs* (New York: Anchor Books, 1970), pp. 145–65.

29 Benjamin Paul Blood and Alfred Tennyson, "The Anaesthetic Revelation: A Brief Explanation by its Discoverer, and a Remarkable Letter from Alfred Tennyson," *New York Times* (December 6, 1874).

30 Watts, *The Joyous Cosmology*, p. 78.

31 Watts, *The Joyous Cosmology*, pp. 10–19; Timothy Leary, Ralph Metzner, and Richard Alpert, *The Psychedelic Experience: A Manual Based on the Tibetan Book of the Dead* (New York: Citadel Press/Kensington Publishing, 1992), p. 30; Huxley, *Doors of Perception*, p. 56.

32 Rick Strassman, *DMT: The Spirit Molecule: A Doctor's Revolutionary Research into the Biology of Near-Death and Mystical Experiences* (Rochester: Park Street Press, 2001), pp. 206, 252.

33 Ibid., pp. 64, 155.

34 R. C. Zaehner, *Zen, Drugs and Mysticism* (Lanham: University Press of America, 1989), p. 84.

35 Louis Lewin, *Phantastica, Narcotic and Stimulating Drugs, Their Use and Abuse*, trans. P. H. A. Wirth (London: Routledge and Kegan Paul, 1964), pp. 134–5.

ANDREW D. HATHAWAY AND JUSTIN SHARPLEY

CHAPTER 3

THE CANNABIS EXPERIENCE

An Analysis of "Flow"

Introduction

Cannabis sativa/indica and related species, also widely known as marijuana, is subjectively experienced and understood by users in terms departing widely from the classification schema denoting common properties of psychoactive drugs (e.g., stimulant, depressant, hallucinogen, etc.). There is an extensive literature on cannabis effects that documents the influence of dosage, set and setting, and other variations in its use. There is also an array of contributions on essential properties of altered conscious states. This chapter emphasizes the experience of people who self-medicate with cannabis for a wide range of conditions. A recurring theme among the benefits it brings them is a sense of *flow*, wellbeing, or harmonious existence described in other literature, but interestingly rarely with respect to cannabis or other substance use. Transpersonal and positive psychology and Eastern spiritual traditions are considered for their insights for better understanding the experience of flow.

Despite its widespread use today, our modern understanding of cannabis is steeped in years of reefer madness, drug war, propaganda, plain lies, and mistruths. A lengthy history of cultural ambivalence to drug use is found in Western popular and scholarly depictions and in the early lurid intensive explorations of cannabis experience by literary figures. The "artificial paradise" of Baudelaire's (ca. 1860) description exemplifies a sense of fascination and aversion to pursuing altered conscious states. Heroic portions of hashish consumed in Paris by "Hashish Club" notables like Dumas, Baudelaire, and Hugo led to fantastic visions and dramatic flights of fancy producing an extension of the self "in all directions," "wonderful debauchery," and feelings of benevolence. Nonetheless, this God-like state invoked a heavy payment in lethargy and discomfort once the intoxication ended and more troubling surrender of the will to substance use.

The rapturous heights attained, for Baudelaire,[1] were an affliction marked by equal lows and an intense habituation on failure to achieve the high without the use of drugs. Compared with more enduring states of mind achieved by mystics and poets through hard work and meditation, chemically induced states of consciousness were deemed practically and morally inferior. Ingesting massive doses of hashish is thus discouraged for all but the most curious experimental users. But what of the more moderate contemporary user in pursuit of artificial paradise with drugs? Another literature suggests intoxication is adaptive, a universal drive or instinct like avoiding pain or hunger, and pursuit of happiness or pleasure.[2] Unlike these sensations, which are end points in themselves, intoxicants are rather tools or triggers to transcendence that satisfy the urge for stimulation, relaxation, or alleviation of unpleasant mental states.

New research on cannabinoids and cannabinoid receptors offers physiological support for the suggestion that the use of cannabis may be beneficial in maintaining homeostasis, equilibrium, or balance. Cannabinoids coordinate large systems that support the cardiovascular, endocrine, digestive, excretory, and musculo-skeletal functions of the body, among others. The use of cannabis, for Melamede,[3] equates to harm reduction. Cannabinoids, in his view, are neuroprotective agents, preventing cell death and dysfunction, or neurodegeneration, as found with Multiple Sclerosis, for example, among other progressively debilitating autoimmune diseases. In light of its foregoing larger regulatory function, endocannabinoid deficiency might also help explain why cannabis appears to be so helpful for some people.[4] Biomedical advances in this area may one day validate our ancient admiration and allow for fuller recognition of the value of this plant.

The present exploration of its benefit to users is grounded in the personal experience of people who use cannabis as medicine for the relief of symptoms of a wide variety of chronic health conditions. The connection between physical and mental health and healing is a common observation, in addition to frustration with allopathic medicine and the ineffective treatment they received from their physicians.[5] There are other commonalities of interest in this study considering the wide range of medical conditions and variety of symptoms reported by respondents. To preface our analysis of flow as a recurring benefit or feature of their cannabis experience, we begin with William James's phenomenology of consciousness and related literature informing this discussion.

Investigating Consciousness and Consciousness Expansion

Consciousness, for James,[6] is a stream that ebbs and flows, with elements like images and meaning that combine in forming a coherent albeit "pulsing" stream of thought. Unlike other elements, like wind or fire, the water metaphor for consciousness is supported by phenomena that are described as "streaming" in the physical world as well.[7] This theme is found again in Taoist teachings which develop the personal and social transformative potential of expanding consciousness with reference to flow. Literally, the "proper way or path," Tao is described as "a patterned flow of the universe" and "deeper harmony, a moving point of equilibrium and balance."[8] A life lived in congruence with the Tao is understood to bring "creative quietude," the *wu wei* – "supreme action" and supreme relaxation – "the precious suppleness, simplicity, and freedom" flowing through us.

Inspired by William James and Taoism among other older Eastern spiritual traditions, the transpersonal perspective in psychology contributes a distinctly East meets West flavor. *Transpersonal psychology* is concerned with understanding transcendent states that go beyond self, consciousness, or being – including causes, effects, and correlates, as well as the disciplines and practices inspired by these phenomena.[9] This movement gained ascendance with interest in the 1960s in the use of psychoactive drugs to attain "nirvana" and other popular conceptions of Eastern spiritualism for seeking greater self-awareness and experience of life. Altered states of consciousness, with or without drug use, through discipline and training such as with meditation, are typically dismissed in *monophasic* Western cultures or pathologized as symptoms of diseases of the mind. These pursuits are more in line with *polyphasic* cultures' acknowledgment of worldviews derived from different states of consciousness as being both legitimate and healthy.[10]

Neglect of altered consciousness in Western science and culture has made the language of clinicians and lawmakers hegemonic, denying all but the destructive consequences of drug taking. Recognizing benefits of drug use as among the pathways to transcendence, improved health, and wellbeing, the transpersonal perspective in psychology contrasts with the emphasis on negatives in scientific discourse and research emphasizing individual pathology. *Positive psychology*, more generally, is likewise overtly humanistic in its concern for the promotion and understanding of "peak experience," autonomy, and wellbeing as subjectively experienced in the lives of individuals.[11] This shift in focus from disease etiology and treatment to understanding mental health as optimal performance puts emphasis on *mindfulness* or practices concerned with clarified perception of the object and awareness of consciousness, surroundings, and personal experience.[12]

Transpersonal and positive psychologists like Maslow[13] and Csíkszentmihályi[14] first popularized transcendent, peak, or optimal experience as subjects for intensive scholarly investigation. Csíkszentmihályi's work on flow provides a working definition and framework highly relevant to cannabis experience.[15] Whereas perceptions of the latter are the focus of this chapter, we will outline preexisting applications of the concept prior to our adaptation and analysis of flow. The flow experience is optimal experience of order in oneself, one's consciousness or psyche. The experience described is marked by several sensations, especially the sense of an ability to balance the challenges at hand with a capacity to meet them. Other common elements are intense concentration of attention, with a clear sense of control of one's actions and what needs to be done from moment to moment (although time may be distorted such that minutes seem like hours or hours seem like minutes). The flow experience is optimal in striking the right balance between one's set of coping skills and challenges, resulting in reduction of over- or understimulation which are typically experienced as anxiety or boredom. Activities are felt to be intrinsically rewarding; irrelevant distractions are excluded, with a perception of immediate feedback about how well the activity is going.

Csíkszentmihályi's work is popular and cited, much like Maslow's, in academic research on motivation and creativity, and for its practical utility in management and business. But whereas flow has been identified with reference to artists, musicians,[16] chess enthusiasts,[17] and athletes,[18] its relevance to drug use has not yet been developed or otherwise suggested, to our knowledge. That is not to say that Western culture is entirely unfamiliar with Tim Leary, among other proselytizers, or so-called "deviant" subcultures that promote the use of drugs. Convention dictates that legal drugs, however, are the only chemicals considered beneficial for our health. Notwithstanding pharmaceutical predominance in mainstream Western understanding of acceptable drug use, it is noteworthy that non-"medical" intoxicants, including alcohol, tobacco, tea, and coffee, have all at one time or another been promoted or encouraged for better health, vitality, or vigour.

The popularity of alcohol as social lubricator has long outstripped its early reputation and employment as a medicinal ingredient or tonic. Whisky, for example, is a word originating in a Gaelic term translated as the "water of life." This designation, likewise, has been applied to distilled spirits – as in the Latin *aqua vitae* – in Europe since the early fourteenth century at least.[19] Tobacco's social history is marked by transformation from banned substance in some eras to valued stimulant in others, or commodity denoting status, style, and sophistication to its status presently as public health pariah. Despite the common method of delivery by smoking, other properties of cannabis are more like tea or coffee in their respective benefits and reported health effects. Known as *kahweh*, "that which stimulates," in Middle Eastern countries, coffee has for centuries been cultivated, lauded, and outlawed in some places for its excitatory properties.[20] By the eighteenth century in Europe coffee houses were popular establishments, attracting merchants, poets, intellectuals, and artists who were drawn by its capacity to stimulate the mind. Coffee's reputation as a stimulant today is as culturally embedded, commoditized, and valued as the use of alcohol for social relaxation.

The coffee plant, like cannabis, has two main cultivated species: *C. canephora* or robusta and *C. arabica*. Arabica is considered the most suitable for drinking. Containing more caffeine than arabica, the robustas are relatively bitter and inferior in flavor, but the plant is hardier and easier to grow.[21] Tea, another ancient beverage with hundreds of varieties, has lower caffeine content and a considerably longer history of use for health and mental stimulation. Respective differences in use and reputation versus coffee are arguably more cultural than chemical in nature. Tea's Far Eastern origin and rituals imbue it with a sense of calm in addition to alertness, as an aid to contemplation restoring harmony and balance. These observations warrant further investigation of the flow experience with reference to cannabis and other "drugs" in common use around the world today.

❦ ANDREW D. HATHAWAY AND JUSTIN SHARPLEY

It is worth repeating here that cannabis cannot be classified the same way as alcohol or coffee, with reference to stimulant, depressant, for example, or other physiological effect. There are important differences between cannabis (the Latin term for preparations made from the hemp plant, such as marijuana and hashish) and stimulants like cocaine, narcotics such as morphine, or sedatives including alcohol and the barbiturates. Most important, tolerance or physiological dependence is considered relatively rare; that is, persons who discontinue use do not typically experience debilitating symptoms of withdrawal. William Burroughs defined cannabis as consciousness-expanding, because (quite unlike narcotic drugs and sedatives) it actually "increases awareness of surroundings and bodily processes" and further "serves as a guide to psychic areas which can then be reentered without it."[22]

The Cannabis Experience

Once I have my day figured out, I can have a toke, go out to the studio and focus on exactly what I have to do for hours and hours. Everything has a flow. *If it doesn't, I'll stop, have a coffee and a toke and go back to work, [asking myself]* now do you have the flow – now is the perspective better?[23]

Invariably in studies of the cannabis experience, users report euphoria or feelings of wellbeing, with some accounts of altered awareness and time perception. Many say it calms them and is useful for relaxing, while others paradoxically describe the drug as being a stimulant for body, mind, or both. Its euphoric properties are experienced in ways that are far from unequivocal, reflecting a variety of motives and effects. A common observation is that users gain a different outlook or perspective which has beneficial outcomes for work or mental health or recreational enjoyment.

To illustrate, creative or artistic work as noted in the quote that prefaces this section may benefit from moderate, strategic use of cannabis by experienced users either on or off the job. Looking at things differently reportedly provided a better understanding of how they fit together, allowing users to see nuances or disregard distractions that might otherwise prevent them from seeing the "big picture." Building on these observations, the present study looks at perceptions and experiences of people who use cannabis to cope with chronic medical conditions.

The study

Respondents were recruited from "compassion clubs" located in Victoria (the Victoria Island Compassionate Society [VICS]), Vancouver (the British Columbia Compassion Club Society [BCCCS]), and Toronto (the Toronto Compassion Centre [TCC] and Cannabis as Living Medicine [CALM]). We are grateful for their kind facilitation of this research. Although still technically illegal, the clubs selected are among the largest, longest serving dispensaries in Canada providing marijuana to about 10,000 members. Membership requires a letter from a family doctor or other medical practitioner certifying that the applicant has a medical condition for which the use of cannabis is helpful.

One-hundred and three respondents were recruited to take part in in-depth interviews about their use of cannabis as medicine. Two-thirds of them were male, and the total sample ranged from 22 to 67 years of age. A wide variety of medical problems were reported, including chronic pain conditions (e.g., fibromyalgia, arthritis, Irritable Bowel Syndrome), anxiety, depression, and other psychological disorders (e.g., addiction, ADHD, Post Traumatic Stress, bipolar). Other common illnesses reported by respondents were HIV/AIDS, Hepatitis C, and neurological disorders such as epilepsy and Multiple Sclerosis. Notwithstanding their diversity in health history and status, all respondents suffered from chronic medical conditions and shared a general discontent with allopathic treatments. Most said pharmaceuticals had worsened their conditions or reported side effects that outweigh any benefits. Using cannabis, however, not only helped their symptoms, but came with other benefits for body, mind, and spirit.

The experience of flow

The essential properties of the two main species (*C. sativa* and *C. indica*) have practical and scientific relevance to better understanding cannabis in terms of flow experience, and its use as medicine for optimizing health. These are not the focus of this chapter, but respondents commonly observed that their experience depended on the type of species or strain that they were using. Higher indicas reportedly are helpful for the body, especially for chronic pain, and for the mind, as well as a means of coping with anxiety and stress. These strains have a calming influence, in other words, on users, as compared to the sativas, which are typically experienced as a stimulation of the senses. A stimulant by definition rouses one to activity, which may also be experienced as a

❧ ANDREW D. HATHAWAY AND JUSTIN SHARPLEY

lifting of the spirits – to help alleviate depression, enhance the appetite, and heighten awareness, energy, or motivation.

People using marijuana have commonly reported a sense of fascination with the world and their surroundings, or alternative perspective that, for many in this study, is a major benefit of using. Some offer similar descriptions as "recreational" consumers, suggesting that this aspect is widely valued among users regardless of their more specific individual motives. The use of cannabis as medicine, put otherwise, has further benefits for mental health, wellbeing, or fulfillment described in other research on marijuana users. To illustrate, consistent with the earlier quotation, additional advantages were noted by respondents that suggest their use of cannabis fosters creativity by facilitating flow experience. For example: "Pot opens up some kind of a *pathway to God* and the outcome is music; without it . . . I just don't have the inspiration" and, likewise, said another:

> Some pot is uplifting . . . it sparks more creative things and I have a lot of hobbies. . . . I think that's important . . . to keep you level headed, just *to balance out your "mind/body/soul."*

People commonly made reference to the physical and mental and spiritual connections in their view of health and healing, and use of cannabis for coping with a medical condition. Chronic pain and mental health conditions, for example, particularly benefit from cannabis affording relaxation, stimulation, or distraction needed to relieve pain or restore a sense of balance: "it makes me feel like getting up and doing something with my life . . . my mobility is better, so then I can get more done. Without it, I just lie in bed in pain all day and I can't move." And:

> A lot of the anxiety I have comes from over-thinking things, over-analyzing everything . . . *it helps your mind drift away and you can focus on the task at the moment*, as opposed to thinking about the past, present and future, and worrying about things.

The experience of flow in terms of harmony or balance was frequently reported by respondents diagnosed with psychological disorders like anxiety, depression, and "bipolar" episodes, marked by dramatic mood swings, as noted in the following examples:

> My mood rotation is so random and rapid that I can have changes from depression to mania on a daily basis . . . when I wake up having that

depressed, I wanna die feeling . . . it just changes your mood – it brightens you up. At the same time, when I'm in one of the mania phases . . . it calms me down and brings me back to normal.

And, as one interviewee stated:

> With pot, my reasoning becomes better, my anger calms down a lot, and it just centers me. I'm no longer swept up in depression as much because I'm able to think it through better. It sounds a little strange but I'm able to think with my soul, where it's this more logical place . . . I might just *be more connected to myself*, more open . . . maybe because I'm not so trapped in fear and anxiety.

Mention of the soul and its connection to wellbeing was commonly encountered in the narratives of persons who use cannabis to cope with chronic mental health conditions. "It calms the anger," for example, said another interviewee; "it makes some other sort of insight come in, or something that makes me . . . count my blessings. I'm alive; I'm breathing the air, you know . . . *I take an inventory on my soul.*"

Discussion

Holistic conceptions of health recognizing the inexorable connection between the body, mind, and spirit are difficult to reconcile with emphasis in Western medicine on scientific knowledge. The alternative philosophies on which these views are founded transcend the definitions of health and diagnosis and disease of conventional medical science. The use of cannabis as medicine is threatening to those who maintain the modern worldview in which experts hold dominion and define what counts as evidence or proof. So-called "anecdotal evidence," such as the foregoing, is dismissed as hearsay because it is untested or lacks the needed expertise to "verify" results. Collective narratives of personal experience, however, were a widely trusted source of medical knowledge up until the very recent past.[24] Respect for lived experience as evidence has waned with the trend of formalism over the last century towards medicine as science, with its emphasis on research as the product of clinicians in experimental laboratories.

Despite an ancient history of use in other cultures, cannabis was only introduced to Western medicine about 150 years ago.[25] Prepared as a tincture in solution with alcohol, it was widely prescribed for pain and as a sedative because doctors deemed it safer, albeit less reliable, than opium and opium derivatives. When barbiturates and aspirin became available these new drugs gained favor over time because their potencies were fixed and doctors could dispense them as a pill. Pharmaceutical solutions to health problems since this era have eclipsed "folk remedies" and relegated them to the margins of society where these options have been outlawed, otherwise defamed, or disregarded. Use of unregulated substances like cannabis, says Dupont,[26] makes no distinction between non-medical and medical consumption, returning us in essence to a time before physicians oversaw addictive and potentially abused drugs. Plant products are inherently unstable, Dupont continues – inferior to scientific medicines which target specific illnesses with closely controlled and measured doses of chemicals with recognized effects.

More to the point perhaps, Dupont and other adversaries of (re)medicalizing cannabis contend that any benefits of smoking marijuana are countered by impairment due to psychoactive effects (and the well-known health risks of inhaling tar from smoke). Most modern medicines are orally administered, he argues, to maintain a given concentration in the blood. Cannabis, by contrast, and other commonly "abused" drugs are administered by smoking (or injection) to "get high," which requires more elevated levels of the drug. The science advanced by Russo, Melamede, and others on the role of cannabis in human physiology is not germane to medicine for anyone accustomed to viewing psychoactive effects as an impairment or detriment of using marijuana. It is simply a "drug" in the wrong category to be endorsed as medicine – or even tolerated – according to the law, in the majority of countries. The shift in power required to change this, and accommodating science, remain in short supply around the world today. Notwithstanding some advances, the plant itself is widely banned, including use for medicine and research.

The "anecdotes" presented here suggest a different worldview, wherein being "high" does not equate to an impairment. Indeed, it is a benefit of using marijuana. Accounts of flow experience included in this chapter demonstrate that cannabis contributes to wellbeing or optimal experience of consciousness for users. Consistent with descriptions found in other applications of the flow experience (e.g., with reference to athletes, artists, or musicians, or otherwise creative individuals), cannabis enhances the ability of users to meet and manage challenges arising from impairment due to chronic physical or mental health conditions. Complementing biomedical, scientific warrants for the use of cannabis as medicine, users experience a state of mind or spiritual connection marked by a sense of harmony, autonomy, empowerment, order, and control over their actions and surroundings. These accounts contribute to the literature describing the cannabis experience, more generally, in terms of consciousness expansion, alteration, or enhancement. This challenges myopic views of substance use as criminal, pathological, or deviant in modern Western culture, and offers a perspective that is founded on authentic experience and "unofficial" knowledge.

NOTES

1   Charles Baudelaire, *Artificial Paradise: On Hashish and Wine as a Means of Expanding Individuality* (New York: Herder and Herder, 1971). See also Fitz H. Ludlow, *The Hasheesh Eater: Being Passages from the Life of a Pythagorean* (New York: Harper Bros, 1857; reprinted New York: Rains, 1903).
2   Ronald Siegel, *Intoxication: Life in Pursuit of Artificial Paradise* (New York: E. P. Dutton, 1989); Andrew Weil, The Natural Mind: A New Way of Looking at Drugs and the Higher Consciousness (Boston: Houghton Mifflin, 1972).
3   Robert Melamede, "Harm Reduction: The Cannabis Paradox," *Harm Reduction Journal* 2, 17 (2005).
4   Ethan Russo, "Clinical Endocannabinoid Deficiency (CECD): Can this Concept Explain Therapeutic Benefits of Cannabis in Migraine, Fibromyalgia, Irritable Bowel Syndrome and other Treatment-Resistant Conditions?" *Neuroendocrinology Letters* 29, 2 (2008): 192–200.
5   Craig Jones and Andrew D. Hathaway, "Marijuana Medicine and Canadian Physicians: Challenges to Meaningful Drug Policy Reform," *Contemporary Justice Review* 11, 2 (2008): 165–75.
6   William James, *The Principles of Psychology* (New York: Dover, 1890).
7   Harry T. Hunt, *On the Nature of Consciousness: Cognitive, Phenomenological, and Transpersonal Perspectives* (New Haven: Yale University Press, 1995).
8   Duane Elgin, "The Tao of Personal and Social Transformation," in Roger Walsh and Francis Vaughan (eds.) *Beyond Ego: Transpersonal Dimensions in Psychology* (Los Angeles: J. P. Tarcher, 1980).
9   Roger Walsh and Francis Vaughan (eds.) *Paths Beyond Ego: The Transpersonal Vision* (Los Angeles: J. P. Tarcher, 1993).
10   Charles D. Laughlin, John McManus, and Eugene G. D'Aquile, *Brain, Symbol, and Experience* (New York: Columbia University Press, 1992).
11   Martin Seligman and Mihaly Csíkszentmihályi, "Positive Psychology: An Introduction," *American Psychologist* 55, 1 (2000): 5–14.
12   Daniel Goleman, "Mental Health in Classical Buddhist Psychology," in Roger Walsh and Francis Vaughan (eds.) *Beyond Ego: Transpersonal Dimensions in Psychology* (Los Angeles, J. P. Tarcher, 1980).

13   Abraham H. Maslow, "Humanistic Science and Transcendent Experience," *Journal of Humanistic Psychology* 5 (1965): 219–27.

14   Mihaly Csíkszentmihályi, "Towards a Psychology of Optimal Experience," in Ladd Wheeler (ed.) *Review of Personality and Social Psychology*, Vol. 2 (Los Angeles: Sage, 1982).

15   Mihaly Csíkszentmihályi, *Flow: The Psychology of Optimal Experience* (New York: Harper and Row, 1990).

16   Richard Parncutt and Gary E. McPherson, *The Science and Psychology of Music Performance: Creative Strategies for Teaching and Learning* (Oxford: Oxford University Press, 2002).

17   Antony Puddephatt, "Chess Playing as Strategic Activity," *Symbolic Interaction* 26, 2 (2003): 263–85.

18   Jeremy Hunter and Mihaly Csíkszentmihályi, "The Phenomenology of Body-Mind: The Contrasting Cases of Flow in Sports and Contemplation," *Anthropology of Consciousness* 11, 3–4 (2000): 5–24.

19   James Ross, *Whisky* (London: Routledge, 1970).

20   Robert S. de Ropp, *Drugs and the Mind* (New York: H. Wolff, 1957).

21   Elin McCoy and John Frederick Walker, *Coffee and Tea* (Redwood City: G. S. Haley, 1998).

22   David Solomon, *The Marijuana Papers* (New York: New American Library, 1966).

23   Andrew D. Hathaway, "Marijuana and Lifestyle: Exploring Tolerable Deviance," *Deviant Behavior* 18, 3 (1997): 213–32.

24   Desmond Manderson, "Formalism and Narrative in Law and Medicine: The Debate over Medical Marijuana Use," *Journal of Drug Issues* 29, 1 (1999): 121–34.

25   Lester Grinspoon, "Whither Medical Marijuana?" *Contemporary Drug Problems* 27, Spring (2000): 3–15.

26   Robert L. Dupont, "Examining the Debate on the Use of Medical Marijuana," Proceedings of the Association of American Physicians 111, 2 (1999): 166–82.

PART II

MARIJUANA AND SPIRITUAL ENLIGHTENMENT

Let's look at Monopoly for a moment. You're spending a quiet evening at home with your wife and another couple. You've all gotten stoned, and someone suggests that you play Monopoly. You bring the Monopoly set down from the closet shelf. It's dusty because four years ago you swore you'd never subject yourself to the extreme boredom one faces when playing Monopoly. Then you blow the dust off the box and open it, and it's a new surge of excitement. It's nostalgia mixed with challenge. You think for a moment of the kid next door who used to win all the time, and who told you filthy and impossible things about girls. You weep openly upon seeing the mustachioed face of the man on the Chance cards, and you revisit the childhood hours you spent on Marvin Gardens and Illinois Avenue. You look with contempt at Baltic Avenue and with wonder at Boardwalk. And then the game begins.

> Jack S. Margolis and Richard Clorfene,
> *A Child's Garden of Grass: The Official*
> *Handbook for Marijuana Users*, 1974

CHAPTER 4

BUZZ, HIGH, AND STONED

Metaphor, Meaning, and the Cannabis Experience

Walter Benjamin, the German literary critic and philosopher, described his first hashish experience in his "Protocols of Drug Experiments: Main Features of My Second Impression of Hashish," January 15, 1928 at 3:30 p.m.:

> Moreover, it is the murky, alien, exotic aspects of the intoxication that remain in my memory, rather than the bright ones.[1]

The cannabis experience is unique compared to most other psychoactive drugs, and it is highly variable, malleable, and tacit in nature. Users' descriptions of their experiences are intensely personal and oftentimes difficult to put into words. Effects portrayed appear to have limited basis in the drug's pharmacological activity. How do users describe and assign meaning to their cannabis experiences?

The cannabis experience is perceived, interpreted, and described metaphorically. Users employ a great variety of metaphors to comprehend and find meaning in their drug experiences. These metaphors allow for communication and exchange of ideas and information about cannabis and its effects. In the 1960s, terminology evolved for this experience that emphasized three words still popular today: buzz, high, and stoned.

Metaphorical Pharmacology of Cannabis

The ancient Greek word for drug is *pharmakon,* and it typically has three distinct meanings: remedy (cure), poison, and (magical) charm. These meanings, as general results from drug use as well as how drugs and their effects are perceived, apply to all pharmacological substances. Cannabis has been regarded in these ways.

For many users in a variety of cultures, it is a remedy imparting medicinal effects, and its health benefits have been known for centuries, from which the medical marijuana movement is an extension of this meaning. Cannabis produces positive, beneficial effects, but it also produces negative, harmful effects. It is considered a poison, the "Devil's weed," an evil, insidious substance that not only destroys lives, it abolishes moral behavior and traditions. It moreover is perceived as a mystical substance given magical, fantastical descriptions and meanings.

Cannabis effects, individual and subjective in nature, challenge interpretation and description by the user, especially when experience with the drug is limited. This language difficulty is well illustrated in Fritz Frankel's "Protocol of April 18, 1931":

> It is a characteristic as well as a regular feature of hashish intoxication that the act of speaking is bound up with a sort of resignation; that from the beginning the intoxicated person has renounced the possibility of speaking about what really moves him; that he applies himself to the expression of something incidental, trifling, in place of the real but unsayable; that not infrequently, when he's speaking, he feels he's become guilty of insincerity; and that – what is remarkable and very much in need of elucidation – the utterance broken off and deflected, as it were, may be far more striking and profound than that which would correspond to the "intended meaning."[2]

Consider the three meanings of *pharmakon* and various metaphorical descriptions in the following accounts of cannabis experiences from the nineteenth and twentieth centuries. Difficulty in expressing the nature and meaning of the experience is manifest; metaphors abound to illustrate effects. Accounts from the nineteenth century refer to hashish typically taken orally, while most twentieth-century accounts usually refer to smoking marijuana. Few people use the word "cannabis" when referring to it as a drug.

French critic, playwright, and novelist Théophile Gautier, in his article "Le Club des Hachichins," for the *Revue des Deux Mondes* (February 1,

1846), wrote of his hashish experience partaken at the club in the famous Hotel Pimodan:

> The water I drank seemed the most exquisite wine, the meat, once in my mouth, became strawberries, the strawberries, meat . . . I abandoned myself to the fantastic effects of the drug . . . the salon was filled with extraordinary figures, such as are found only in the etchings of Callot or the aquatints of Goya. . . . Not all the visions were monstrous or burlesque . . . in this carnival of forms. I myself melted into the objects I regarded . . . I felt my limbs turn to stone. I was a statue in the middle of my body . . . I became mad, delirious. . . . I was overcome with despair, for, in lifting my hand to my skull, I found it open, and I lost consciousness.[3]

Gautier also reported what other hachichins were saying about their experiences: "I'm swimming in ecstasy! I'm in Paradise! I'm plunging into the depths of delight!. . . Today is the day we must die laughing."[4]

Hashish and the horrors of addiction were moralized by French poet Charles Baudelaire, based primarily on his own experiences, in "The Poem of Hashish" (from Les Paradis artificiels, 1860):

> They think of the intoxication caused by hashish as a land of miracles, a huge conjuror's theatre where everything is marvelous and unexpected. This is an ill-formed notion, a complete misunderstanding. . . . Hashish is a disorderly demon. . . . What, after all, is a paradise bought at the price of one's eternal salvation?[5]

He referred to hashish both as happiness and as poison and argued that his descriptions of the evils of hashish should not be seen as exaggerated metaphor. He noted the important influence of user set (state of mind, intentions in using the drug, other obligations and serious thoughts) and setting (music, picturesque surroundings) on the nature and meaning of the hashish experience. He also remarked on the occurrence of synesthesia during the experience: "Sounds clothe themselves in colors, and colors contain music."[6]

Famous American explorer of exotic lands and author of many travel books, Bayard Taylor recounted his "hasheesh" experience in Damascus in The Land of the Saracen (1855):

> the Spirit (demon, shall I not rather say?) of Hasheesh had entire possession of me. I was cast upon the flood of his illusions . . . I suddenly found myself at the foot of the great Pyramid of Cheops.[7]

Fitz Hugh Ludlow, American author of *The Hasheesh Eater; being passages from the life of a Pythagorean* (1857), made reference to Bayard Taylor's account and wrote most famously of his own:

> The moment that I closed my eyes a vision of celestial glory burst upon me. I stood on the silver strand of a translucent boundless lake.[8]

He also mentioned two laws of the hashish operation: first, after the completion of one set of visual effects, fantasia, or dreams, there is a shifting of the action to another set of visual effects entirely different; and second, after the first vision of intense sublimity passes, the next vision is generally of a quiet, relaxing nature.

American jazz musician Mezz Mezzrow wrote of his early marijuana experiences in his autobiography, *Really the Blues* (1946):

> When you first begin smoking it you see things in a wonderful soothing, easygoing new light. All of a sudden the world is stripped of its dirty gray shrouds and becomes one big bellyful of giggles, a spherical laugh, bathed in brilliant, sparkling colors that hit you like a heatwave . . . there's a humorous tickle and great meaning in the least little thing . . . all your pores open like funnels, your nerve-ends stretch their mouths wide, hungry and thirsty for new sights and sounds and sensations; and every sensation, when it comes, is the most exciting one you've ever had. You can't get enough of anything – you want to gobble up the whole goddamned universe just for an appetizer. Them first kicks are a killer, Jim.[9]

The slogan among Mezzrow's group of smokers was *Light up and be somebody*.[10]

With resurgent use of marijuana in 1950s and 1960s countercultures and later mainstream use, these colorfully exotic, extravagant, literarily embellished accounts of hashish and marijuana experiences disappeared in favor of shorter, simpler descriptions that are more vague, tacit, and obscure in nature. That is when the terms "buzz," "high," and "stoned" came into common usage as ways to describe the experience, and it continues today.

> Devil, just come on back if you ever wanna catch a *buzz*. (Travis Meyer's parody song *The Devil Went to Jamaica*, 1998)[11]

> Hits from the bong y'all, gonna get *high*. (Cypress Hill's rap song, *Hits from the Bong*, 1993)[12]

You're *stoned* out of your mind, man." (Wyatt [Peter Fonda] to Billy [Dennis Hopper] when the latter claims to see UFOs after smoking marijuana, in *Easy Rider*, 1969)[13]

Each of these three words, and many others, succinctly describes the cannabis experience. Or do they?

What does it mean when a user says, "I want to catch a buzz," "get high," or "get stoned"? The word "buzz" has limited and singular meaning in reference to cannabis effects, while the experience of being high involves more descriptors; but still, the general meaning seems more commonly accepted among users. It is the experience of being stoned in which descriptions and metaphors truly expand with a variety of meanings. What has become confusing is that besides being major descriptors for the cannabis experience, all three words have been applied differentially to other drug experiences, especially alcohol and stimulants, and many types of non-drug experiences.

Buzz

The buzz state is experienced after one to two hits (inhalations) of cannabis, a low dose. It is of short duration (30–60 minutes), with minimal physical, mental, and social effects. The buzz state is a calming, enjoyable feeling, somewhat lightheaded in nature, with little impact on the user's ability to go about life's business. "Catch a buzz" is an invitation to inhale once or at most twice and sometimes refers to a user taking a hit off someone else's joint, in terms of being available now, so take advantage and get a small dose.

High

The high state comes about for experienced users after smoking half a joint or more (3–6 inhalations), a moderate dose with a longer duration (1–3 hours) of action. Effects are more pronounced and are influenced by user set and setting. This state makes objects and events in the social context seem funnier, with racing, unfocused thoughts, anxiety or paranoia, but in general a good feeling with sensory enhancement. The user becomes more talkative and most physiological effects (red eyes, dry mouth, increased appetite) are evident. The user feels active and lightheaded (more so than the buzz state), with perceived enhancement of usual activities and sensations, but still with an ability to engage in and

FIGURE 4.1   *Stoned Agin!* Copyright © Robert Crumb, used by permission.

appreciate them. Most users say being high entails a feeling of energy and being social. Some users, however, note that the species or strain of cannabis smoked produces different types of effects, usually centered as a head-high versus a body-high. *Sativa* strains produce a head-high (stimulating) and are viewed as an "up" experience, while *indica* strains produce a body-high (sedating) and are viewed more like a "down" experience.

Stoned

The stoned state results from a larger dose than that which produces a high. It might entail smoking a whole joint or continuous use over a period of time. The duration of effects can be many hours, even most of a day. A full range of physical and mental effects are experienced, most prominently sedation, lethargy, sleepiness, a slowing of thought processes or unnatural thought processes that influence thinking, and a dream-like state with random undisciplined thought patterns. The user does not want to move much physically or exert his or her mind on serious or focused thought. Extreme instances of being stoned, involving very high doses, induce states that are difficult to describe in large part due to the pharmacological action of various chemical constituents on the user's perceptual systems, memory, and cognition. The stoned state also has been portrayed in many graphic and symbolic formats – essentially visual metaphors – such as Robert Crumb's famous *Stoned Agin* cartoon.

Are the high state and stoned state different and dose dependent, or synonymous in terms of how the experience is described and understood, or simply related states that occur at different points in time during the experience?

Most users feel there is a big difference between being high and being stoned, with the latter coming from much higher doses. The high is a cerebral state while stoned is a whole body state. When high, the user wants to be active and move around, while when stoned the user wants to stay in one place not doing much, like a rock. For a few users, interestingly, the words high and stoned are interchangeable for the same type of experience.

For some users, it is simply a temporal issue, moving from the high state to the stoned state over time during the same experience from the same dose, usually a more moderate to high dose. They progress from being high, during the first 30–60 minutes of the experience, to being stoned after about 60 minutes. In this explanation, however, it is obvious that a lower dose would get you high but may not get you over time to the next level, of being stoned. Being high versus being stoned, then, is based on the specific effects as perceived by the user.

Some users attribute their high state to use of a *sativa* species of cannabis, while the stoned state is attributed to *indica* species, again with a mind-body difference, or perhaps based on various active constituents and their concentrations in the specific strain they have smoked. Most users typically do not know the specific strain they smoke; but they infer the strain from the effects they experience. The names of different types of cannabis strains thus become an indicator of potential effects. Metaphorical descriptions of the cannabis experience, more so than physical effects, often have less correlation with actual dosing and pharmacological activity.

Synonyms in general for the word "buzz" are hum, noise, thrill, or kick; for the word "high" they include elevated, soaring, peak, and important (e.g., exalted, lofty, prominent); and for the word "stone" they include rock and seed. The word "high" is a classic up metaphor, while the word "stone" implies something heavy and is a down metaphor.

TABLE 4.1   Metaphors and descriptors for the cannabis experience

Buzz	High	Stoned
no related metaphors	mellow	cooking metaphors
	chillin'	explosion or ruin metaphors
	toasty	spatial metaphors
	flying	brain/mind metaphors
	mighty-fine	doper slang metaphors

Metaphor is a bit of language used to describe something new in terms of other things that are more familiar. It sets up a relationship between the known thing and the novel thing so as to make the novel interpretable and understandable. Drug effects are described metaphorically, using words that relate to other more familiar experiences in the user's life to provide meaning and attribution to the drug that was taken.

Metaphors and descriptors for the cannabis experience, gleaned from literary and other user accounts, magazines such as *High Times* and *Cannabis Culture*, and from multiple postings on many websites, are listed in table 4.1. Note there are no related or alternative descriptors *per se* that users employ for the term "buzz." The state of being stoned has by far the greatest number of alternative metaphors and descriptors. They can be grouped into interesting categories, such as cooking metaphors (fried, baked, toasted, cooked, mashed, vegetated); explosion or ruin metaphors (blitzed, blasted, ripped, wrecked, smashed, blazed, leveled, destroyed, blowed, annihilated, plastered, hammered, wasted); spatial area metaphors (floating, zoned, traveling); brain/mind metaphors (dazed and confused, lobotomized, brain-melt, brain-fog, blinded); and doper slang metaphors (dope-faced, cheeched, chonged, monged, munted, blunted, Morley'd, McMashed). Other descriptors that do not fit these categories include couch-locked, shit-faced, fucked (up), and crunked up.

The buzz, high, and stoned states correlate closely with physiological and psychological research on cannabis intoxication over the past one and a half centuries. Effects measured in these studies occur during stages of a distinct experience and are dose dependent.

As reported by French physician Jacques-Joseph Moreau, in the first published scientific study of the cannabis experience, *On Hashish and Mental Alienation* (1845), there are three levels of hashish intoxication with eight distinct phenomena.[14] One dose of hashish produces a sensation of wellbeing but imperceptible physical effects. Increased doses produce physical effects and feelings of restlessness and uneasiness. Considerable doses that he did not define by amount produce strong physical effects and nervous phenomena. Those phenomena (seemingly dose dependent) include a feeling of happiness, excitement and dissociation of ideas, errors of time and space, synesthesia, fixed ideas, changes in emotion, irresistible impulses, and finally illusions and hallucinations. The three levels of cannabis effects, referred to today as being buzzed, high, or stoned, correspond well to the three levels and eight phenomena he identified.

Baudelaire, in his "Poem of Hashish," mentioned three phases of hashish intoxication: "a childish mirth with irrelevant and irresistible hilarity and an initial anxiety followed by a momentary lull; the second phase consists of relaxation, calm, and languor or stupor but mostly in terms of feeling happy; and the third phase presents an acuity of senses, a change in sense of self and hallucinations."[15] Baudelaire's first phase is similar to the high state, the second phase is similar to being very high or stoned, while the third phase also represents aspects of being stoned or again a state beyond being stoned.

Charles Tart's study of cannabis, reported in his book *On Being Stoned: A Psychological Study of Marijuana Intoxication* (1971), uncovered an astonishing and extensive array and variety of effects as experienced and described by users in his study.[16] With as little embellishment as possible, he identified five levels of marijuana intoxication influenced primarily by dose (labels are his): (1) *Just stoned* (a threshold level with barely perceptible effects); (2) *Fairly stoned* (consisting of restlessness); (3) *Strongly stoned* (a quieting, opening, calming, or relaxing state with sensory enhancement, greater sensitivity to others in social setting, and feelings of efficiency, or a centeredness and ability to focus and work well); (4) *Very Strongly stoned* (alterations in perception of space and time, imagery intensified, alterations in memory function, feelings of drifting and inefficiency, and enhanced awareness of internal body processes); and (5) *Maximally stoned* (nausea, dizziness, sleepiness, floating feeling, loss of consciousness).

The cannabis experience, then, is significantly inspired by what users think about the effects, the meanings they hold, and how they are described. The application of meaning to a specific experience entails a struggle to describe what is real but inexpressible, particularly those "murky, alien, exotic aspects," and to comprehend its value and consequence in the user's life.

Cannabis Effects and Meanings Applied

Meaning is essentially how humans interpret and comprehend something, an object, event, phenomenon, or experience. It is viewed as a mental process or activity or a state of behavior and is typically dependent on context and the situation in which the meaning was originally applied. It also is important in attribution of experience to that which produced and fashioned it. If the object, event, or experience is novel, then the human mind labors to determine and apply new meaning, and usually metaphors are employed.

Meanings about a drug such as cannabis and its effects are instrumental in a number of ways: setting expectations of effects to be experienced; perceiving, interpreting, and describing effects; attributing effects (beneficial or adverse) to the drug itself; providing reasons and directing use; and condemning or glorifying the drug and the drug experience. Studies of metaphors and meanings in the context of drug use suggest that meaning is a powerful component in drug-taking behaviors and plays a key role in how a drug, in this case cannabis, is portrayed in any society. As meaning is constructed from a neurochemical basis to language to its depiction in thought and behavior, it is formulated and labeled in specific ways, often metaphorically, in words, images, and symbols. As Fitz Hugh Ludlow realized:

> It is this process of symbolization which, in certain hasheesh states, gives every tree and house, every pebble and leaf, every footprint, feature, and gesture, a significance beyond mere matter or form, which possesses an inconceivable force of tortures or happiness.[17]

These meanings help users better understand the cannabis experience, how it is shaped, what it signifies to them, and how it affects behavior, either for good or bad. Getting high or any level of cannabis intoxication is a learned thing. Users discover how to interpret changes called effects and describe these changes from what they read, from other users, and eventually from their previous experiences.

Effects are modified greatly by user set, setting, and other social pharmacological factors. Research in social pharmacology has shown that both internal and external factors shape and determine the drug experience. A cannabis experience begins with molecules (the species/strain of cannabis with different pharmacologically active components), the dose taken, and route of administration. Expectations of effects, prior to

❦ MICHAEL MONTAGNE

administration, are generated from previous experiences or information and knowledge about the drug. The experience is greatly influenced by user set (prior mood and body state, beliefs, suggestibility, effect sensitivity and tolerance level, personality, perceptual capability, and reason for use), and physical and social setting of use. The user also employs internal and external cues to perceive and define how intoxicated he or she is and whether or not those effects are desirable.

To get an idea of how meaning and metaphor influence behavior, contemplate what is being said by the user and how it regulates his or her specific behavior or change in behavior. Also note in everyday life how the words buzz, high, stoned, and related terms set expectations and structure the user's set and setting. When a user is high or stoned, especially with an unclear reason for use, there is greater likelihood of violating personal limits of use and rules of behavior. Those rules, primarily how much to use and when and where, are dismissed as not being significant (or not well remembered) while intoxicated, so drug use behavior changes and increased use (dose or duration of use) occurs. Many cannabis users tend to consume doses that are excessive, disregard their user set and the setting and rituals of use, ignore tolerance over time, and forget the original reasons for use and what the experience truly means to them.

Sincere attention to how the cannabis experience is perceived and described, and its meaning in relation to how cannabis is used, results in better experiences. If the desire is simply to "wake and bake," then use of cannabis is a serious waste of time. The varieties of cannabis experience are lost on those who overdose or who have vague notions of the effects they wish to achieve. If the cannabis experience is metaphorically one of being stoned, then what is accomplished except "brain-fog" and eventual loss of thought, consciousness, or at least valuable time in one's life? Cannabis experiences that provide relaxation, sensory enhancement, social interaction, and creative inspiration, and that are poignant and pleasurable to describe, should be the aspiration of all enlightened users.

NOTES

1 Walter Benjamin, "Protocols of Drug Experiments: Main Features of My Second Impression of Hashish," in *On Hashish*, ed. Howard Eiland (Cambridge, MA: Belknap Press of Harvard University Press, 2006), p. 23.
2 Fritz Frankel, "Protocol of April 18, 1931," in Walter Benjamin, *On Hashish*, ed. Howard Eiland (Cambridge, MA: Belknap Press of Harvard University Press, 2006), p. 77.

3 Théophile Gautier, "Le Club des Hachichins," in David Ebin (ed.) *The Drug Experience* (New York: Orion Press, 1961), p. 8.

4 Ibid., pp. 9, 11.

5 Baudelaire, "The Poem of Hashish," in David Ebin (ed.) *The Drug Experience* (New York: Orion Press, 1961), pp. 19, 30, 40.

6 Ibid., p. 27.

7 Bayard Taylor, *The Land of the Saracen*, in David Ebin (ed.) *The Drug Experience* (New York: Orion Press, 1961), p. 45.

8 Fitz Hugh Ludlow, in David Ebin (ed.) *The Drug Experience* (New York: Orion Press, 1961), p. 75.

9 Mezz Mezzrow and Bernard Wolfe, *Really the Blues* (New York: Random House, 1946), p. 70.

10 Ibid., p. 71.

11 Lyrics available online at www.themadmusicarchive.com/song_details. aspx?SongID=693 (accessed September 29, 2009).

12 Lyrics available online at www.elyrics.net/read/c/cypress-hill-lyrics/hits-from-the-bong-lyrics.html (accessed September 29, 2009).

13 Scene available online at www.youtube.com/watch?v=73PnAymHAHk (accessed September 29, 2009).

14 Jacques-Joseph Moreau, *Hashish and Mental Illness*, ed. Helene Peters and Gabriel G. Nahas (New York: Raven Press, 1973).

15 Baudelaire, "The Poem of Hashish," pp. 21–2.

16 Charles Tart, *On Being Stoned: A Psychological Study of Marijuana Intoxication* (Palo Alto: Science and Behavior Books, 1971).

17 Ludlow, in *The Drug Experience*, p. 83.

CHAPTER 5

THE GREAT ESCAPE

 It is a widespread popular belief – if not a rationalization – that cannabis may be employed in a healthy, useful way to develop altered states of consciousness, or states of mind that remove us from our ordinary conscious awareness of ourselves and the surrounding world. Is this position defensible? We put aside engaging legal matters concerning cannabis (e.g., would legally permitting cannabis use reduce crimes of violence in the drug trade?) and moral side-effects (e.g., even if the use of cannabis is deemed morally permissible in itself, perhaps it should not be used on moral grounds because of its embedded use in corrupt and unjust practices), and take up instead this general question: When is the stimulation or creation of altered states induced by cannabis healthy and permissible in light of ethical and religious values?

Let us first consider, from a philosophical point of view, some of the reasons why the use of cannabis might be unhealthy and in tension with accepted societal values. Since very few philosophers of recognized standing have addressed the use of cannabis directly, we hope to fill this lacuna by taking up the general concern about the prohibitability of artificially (or chemically) inducing altered states. We then turn to arguments that are in play in religious traditions that may prohibit cannabis use. Any comprehensive evaluation of cannabis must give some attention to religious ethics as, historically, religions have played an important role in the governing of substance use and abuse. Due to limitations of space, we focus on Judaism, Christianity, and Islam. Although investigating Hindu, Buddhist, Confucian, Daoist, and other traditions in relation to cannabis would also be very illuminating, we do not have space for a full tour of the religious ethics of all religions.

Philosophical Prohibitions

There are at least four general philosophical reasons that may lead one to think that using cannabis to produce altered states is not good: the problem of falsehood, the distortion of reason, the undermining of agency, and the loss of freedom or the power of self-determination.

The problem of falsehood

In the first extensive treatment of education and justice in the West, Plato's *Republic*, there is a severe warning against poetry and theatre because of the ways in which poetry and theatre involve mere appearances and falsehood. After all, a play about the Trojan War is not itself a war; nor is the *rhapsode* (or poet), reciting the lines attributed to Achilles by Homer, Achilles. This ancient argument is not limited to classical Greek philosophy. In Great Britain the theatres were closed in the sixteenth century due to controversies aroused by puritans who accused theatres of promoting falsehoods and delighting in the vice of deception.[1] Just as one might think of a hypocrite as a kind of actor, the puritans thought of actors as a kind of hypocrite – persons who are not whom they claim to be. (The term "hypocrisy" is derived from the Greek *hypokrisis*, which means play acting or feigning.)

Some sympathy can be generated for the early Platonic critique if we take seriously the fact that Plato's generation had just survived a devastating war that was built on what some of the philosophers considered sophistry and vanity. After all, the statesman Pericles, who was the aristocratic powerhouse behind Athens' imperial ambitions, was trained by sophists in the art of persuasion, and not by philosophers in the art of loving wisdom. Athens was beaten decisively by Sparta and even faced the very real threat that Sparta would do to Athens what the Athenians

❋   CHARLES TALIAFERRO AND MICHEL LE GALL

had done to a potential Spartan ally – kill all the males of military age (essentially, all males who are not children) and enslave the women. After such trauma, perhaps one can sympathize with a stern insistence on truth-telling.

The distortion of reason

Consider the portrait of reason and passion that we find in Euripides' tragedies, especially *Medea* and the *Bacchae*. In the latter, a group of women are intoxicated by the god Dionysius and led to dismember violently the King of Thebes. In an altered state of mind, the mother of the king actually rips off her son's head and then carries it to Thebes, mistakenly thinking that she is carrying the head of a lion. In *Medea*, a spurned woman takes revenge on her faithless husband by killing his mistress and then killing her two children. Medea, herself as a character, gives voice to the danger of acting on passion or spirit, ungoverned by wisdom or reason. "I know how evilly I am about to act," Medea laments, "but my spirit is stronger than my will to resist, spirit, the greatest cause of the evil for men."[2] Even older than Euripides' plays, the *Iliad* and the *Odyssey* include warnings about altered states brought on by passion (as in the war fervor that took over Diomedes that drove him to strike a goddess).

Some philosophers have been wary of substances that give the appearance of ushering in great insights but ultimately are not helpful. William James's analysis of nitrous oxide might be rearticulated in terms of a case against cannabis. In *The Varieties of Religious Experience*, James writes:

> Nitrous oxide and ether, especially nitrous oxide, when sufficiently diluted with air, stimulate the mystical consciousness in an extraordinary degree. Depth beyond depth of truth seems revealed to the inhaler. This truth fades out, however, or escapes, at the moment of coming to; and if any words remain over in which it seemed to clothe itself, they prove to be the veriest nonsense. Nevertheless, the sense of a profound meaning having been there persists; and I know of more than one person who is persuaded that in the nitrous oxide trance we have a genuine metaphysical revelation.[3]

Insofar as cannabis is akin to nitrous oxide, philosophers have reason to be wary of its seductive Siren affect. And speaking of Sirens . . .

The undermining of agency

Consider the seductive voice of the Sirens (in book 12 of the *Odyssey*, in which Odysseus is nearly done in by "the enchanting sweetness" of the Sirens' song). Insofar as the use of cannabis can seduce us to inaction, there is a further reason to think of it as has having ill-effects. The danger of an induced, seductive, pacific state which threatens all our powers of agency was well addressed by Alfred Lord Tennyson in his classic poem "The Lotus-Eaters." They sing:

> Surely, surely, slumber is more sweet than toil, the shore
> Than labor in the deep mid-ocean, wind and wave and oar;
> O, rest ye, brother mariners, we will not wander more.

Cases abound when opium use has led to lethargy or the atrophy of skills, as one can see most famously in the tragic addiction of the otherwise brilliant Romantic poet (and philosopher) Samuel Coleridge.

Loss of freedom and the power of self-determination

Another philosophical source that may move us to accept the prohibition of using cannabis rests upon the generally recognized value of self-governance or the power of voluntary action. Many of the Stoics lamented the ways in which our nature is impaired when we act in ignorance or under any conditions that cloud our judgments, as well as in states of physical captivity or enslavement. As Epictetus puts the matter: "Zeus has set me free; do you think that he intended his own son to be enslaved?"[4] Philosophers were aware of the ways in which excessive drink could deprive one of reason, as witnessed, for example, by Plato's portrait of a very drunk, disorderly and confused Alcibiades, who stumbles into a party in which the guests are asked to speak of love (*Symposium*). Plato's objections to altered states brought on by poetry were not just about appearances and falsehood; he also worried about the ways in which poetry can weaken or impair one's ability to reason (*Ion*). We can see a warning about excess in pre-philosophical sources like the *Odyssey*, such as in the incident of the boy who drinks too much on the magical island of Circe's, falls off a building and is killed.

Perhaps one of the best, more recent laments about the problem of losing one's freedom in a state of addiction is Thomas De Quincey's *Confessions of an English Opium Eater*. "If opium-eating be a sensual pleasure," writes De Quincy,

❧ CHARLES TALIAFERRO AND MICHEL LE GALL

and if I am bound to confess that I have indulged in it to an excess, not yet recorded of any other man, it is no less true, that I have struggled against this fascinating enthrallment with a religious zeal, and have, at length, accomplished what I never yet heard attributed to any other man – have untwisted, almost to its final links, the accursed chain which fettered me.[5]

Such addiction, whether it be to opium, cannabis, or alcohol, is at odds with the philosophical ideal of free thinking and unimpaired powers to act as a free agent.

There are other philosophical positions that might prohibit cannabis use, though these are mostly indirect. For example, in Plato's dialogue *Crito* there is an argument that one should obey the state even if the state's laws are not fair, thus providing a reason for a person not to use cannabis in a state where it is prohibited even if the use of cannabis itself is deemed healthy, can be used in moderation, and so on. But we will stick to the above reasons as the more serious objections. In brief, the objections amount to the claim that the use of cannabis is escapist: its use makes it more likely one will escape from the truth, and escape or evade the rigor and demands of reason, responsible agency, proper freedom, and self-determination.

Let us briefly consider some religious arguments that might be marshaled against the use of cannabis.

Religious Arguments

What religious arguments can be mustered against cannabis use? As noted earlier, we will have to limit ourselves to Judaism, Christianity, and Islam, owing to limitations of space. In early Jewish and Christian sources there is no reference to cannabis and so we will need to look at possible arguments based on the prohibitions against wine, though matters differ in Islam.

Judaism and Christianity would appear to be very receptive to alcohol use. While there are warnings about being drunk (e.g., Proverbs 20:1, the story of Noah, the prohibition of drinking while serving at a religious meeting, Leviticus 10:9), there are abundant records of the widespread use of wine by patriarchs, monarchs, and Jesus himself. Jesus even turns water into wine in the Gospel of John as his first sign of his seeking to bring about the Kingdom of God. In the Epistle to Timothy (1 Timothy

3:8), church leaders are admonished not to be addicted to wine, but it appears as though a warning about an abuse implies that there is a reasonable, permitted use. Someone who warns you about not being *addicted* to sweets is (other things being equal) implying that eating *some* sweets is acceptable.

Insofar as cannabis is on a par with the use of alcohol, presumably these religions would not prohibit it. Judaism and Christianity have each allowed that there can be persons and periods when the use of wine is not permitted. But for the most part, while these religions and the cultures influenced by them condemn addiction and abuse, they countenance a proper use. This point is brought out in the practice by Christians in the medieval period to engage in sober drinking. "Sober," from the Latin *sobrius*, means sober, moderate, temperate, continent, self-possessed, sensible, prudent, reasonable, cautious. Sober drinking of wine or beer was distinct, then, from drinking to intoxication. Note that even the Rule of St. Benedict allows for wine and beer, since it advocates that the monks drink the "local beverage" in moderation.

At most, we believe that one can find Jewish and Christian sources that suggest that while alcohol use is countenanced, there can be some reasons for thinking that it is a sign of sanctity to abstain. Daniel does not drink wine, for example, and there are Hebrew (Christian Old Testament) figures who take vows to abstain from wine (Jeremiah 35:2). But this call to abstention seems to mark extraordinary rather than ordinary lives and missions or vocations.

Early Islamic law prohibits alcohol on the grounds that intoxicating behavior prevents the faithful Muslim from executing his or her duties towards the nascent community. Interestingly, the Quran first prohibited Muslims from attending prayers while intoxicated (4:43). Subsequent verses maintained that alcohol combines both good and evil, but that the evil exceeds any good to be derived from drinking (2:219). This was the next step in turning people away from consumption of alcohol. Finally, intoxicants and games of chance were labeled "abominations of Satan's handiwork," aimed at diverting people from God and forgetting about prayer. Muslims were therefore ordered to abstain (5:90–91). What is striking about Islamic tradition is that the focus is first and foremost on the individual's legal obligations and not on his or her "altered state" in and of itself or any loss of free agency. Following the logic of this Islamic law, theoretically, a faithful Muslim who can "hold his own" and not suffer the ill-effects of alcohol would be fine as long as they tend to their duties.

❧ CHARLES TALIAFERRO AND MICHEL LE GALL

Not all stimulants, however, met with the ire of the Muslim 'ulama or other religious groups. Coffee is a case in point. A Shadhili Sufi shaykh first encountered coffee-drinking in Ethiopia, where the native fruit grew in the highlands and the beverage made from it was known as *bun*. Unconfirmed traditions say that this Sufi was Abu al- Hasan 'Ali b. 'Umar, who resided for a time at the court of Sa'd al-Din II, a sultan of Southern Ethiopia in the early sixteenth century. Abu al-Hasan subsequently returned to Yemen with the knowledge that the berries promoted the wakefulness and the attentiveness Sufis sought in their devotions. To this day this Shadhili shaykh is regarded as the *wali* (patron saint) of coffee-growers, coffee-house proprietors, and coffee-drinkers, and in Algeria coffee is sometimes called *shadhiliyye* in his honor and in that of the Sufi tariqa to which he belonged.

The Shadhili shaykh and contemporary of Abu al- Hasan 'Ali b. 'Umar, Abu Bakr b. 'Abd Allah al-'Aydarus, was impressed enough by its effects that he composed a *qasida* (classical Arabic poem) in honor of the drink and coffee-drinkers even coined their own term for the euphoria it produced – *muraqaha*. The mystic and theologian Shaikh ibn Isma'il b. 'Alawi of the Yemeni town of al-Shihr maintained that the use of coffee, when imbibed with prayerful intent and devotion, could lead to the experience of *qahwa ma'nawiyya* ("the ideal *qahwa*") and *qahwat al-Sufiyya*, interchangeable terms defined as "the enjoyment that the people of God feel in beholding the hidden mysteries and attaining the wonderful disclosures and the great revelations."

Interestingly, coffee met no legal opposition until it made its way to the heartlands of the Ottoman world. There coffee, although it had clear connections with Sufism and certain strands of coffee-induced spiritual exuberance, was at first unopposed. But as coffee-houses began to spread in Istanbul and the government grew concerned about the milieu of coffee-houses – notably that they attracted crowds and encouraged people to venture from their neighborhoods and make contacts in other quarters during hours when the gates of respective quarters were to be closed – the 'ulama began to muster their arguments against coffee.

By this time there was both a vast spiritual and legal literature which addressed the themes of intoxication. For Sufis, the idea of intoxication was reserved for the benefits of *dhikr*, the spiritual exercise by which one induced a spiritual high by incessantly repeating the name of God. For the 'ulama, the argument against coffee largely steered clear of Sufi conduct and related issues, and instead focused on wine (*khamr*) as a forbidden stimulant. In sum, a very cursory case based entirely on analogy and altogether forgoing any clear distinction between coffee as a stimulant and alcohol as both a stimulant and depressant.

By contrast, cannabis (*hashish*, literally "grass" in Arabic) was a forbidden substance that never gave birth to much literature compared to, say, the vast medieval Abbasid literature which used wine and inebriation as analogous with love and love of God. There is no evidence that the Arabs became familiar with the intoxicating properties of hashish before the ninth century. At that time, they had already conquered Iraq and Syria and swept eastward to the border of Persia and Central Asia and westward through Asia Minor, North Africa, and Spain. In the ninth century, well after the establishment of the Abbasid caliphate in Bagdad, Arab scholars translated the Greek texts of Dioscorides and Galen, and became familiar with the medicinal properties of cannabis. One physician of the early tenth century, Ibn Wahshiyah, warned of possible complications resulting from the use of hashish. In his book *On Poisons* he claimed that the plant extract might cause death when mixed with other drugs. Another physician, the Persian-born al-Razi, counseled against overprescribing cannabis.

Hashish made its way into the Islamic world from the Asian steppes where it had arrived from India in the ninth century. Hashish is invariably linked in Western – and to some extent Islamic – tradition with the story of Hasan-i Sabah, who is familiar to many. He was an Isma'ili leader who in 1090 founded in Persia a radical group known in Sunni Islamic tradition as the *Hashashiyya* (*Hashashiyyin*), or as we know them, the Assassins.

Marco Polo, the Venetian explorer, related how Hasan, "the old man of the mountain," snagged young men and fed them a secret potion in the splendid gardens of his fortress, the Alamut. In this earthly paradise he explained their main activity was to make love to sensuous women. This way Hasan kept his young followers under his spell and was able to send them on dangerous missions to assassinate his opponents. He promised the young men, "Upon your return, my angels shall bear you into paradise." Interestingly, all the great Sufi mystics and saints, such as al-Bistami and al-Ghazzali, rejected the use of psychoactive drugs, which they considered a "diabolic perversion."

That did not prevent the eventual widespread use of the drug among the population of the Middle East, including certain royal households. Nor did it prevent infrequent but multiple efforts to suppress the use of cannabis among the poor who could not afford wine. Interestingly, according to the late professor Franz Rosenthal of Yale University,

CHARLES TALIAFERRO AND MICHEL LE GALL

cannabis was deemed to "generate low social rank (*safalah*) and a bad moral character (*radhalah*)" and "negate the existence of a well ordered society."[6]

The Syrian poet Ibn Rustum al-Isirdi (1222–58) extolled the virtues of wine over hashish:

> Would you by eating grass that is not juicy
> Want to be like a dumb beast without reason?
> Their herb brings shame upon a decent person
> So that he slinks about just like a killer
> Our wine brings honor to the lowly person
> And dignity so none is his master
> Unlike hashish, its qualities are useful
> Speak out! Count and describe wine's many meanings!

The association of cannabis with the lower classes may explain the curtailed literary and philosophic celebration or support of the properties of cannabis. That being said, Muslim doctors did not ignore the potential medical benefits of cannabis. The physician al-Razi (865–925) mentions the use of cannabis leaves as a salve for ear infections and prescribes it as a cure for dandruff and flatulence. He also describes its curative power – when eaten – in cases of epilepsy. Al-Zakarshi (1344–92) remarked that the use of hashish could be considered lawful if consumed "for medical necessity to produce anesthesia for an amputation, and if consumed to quiet hunger," and on the (improbable) condition that the user is immune to the intoxicating effect of hashish. He further noted some of the many negative side-effects or altered states, including reddening of the eye, dryness of mouth, excessive sleeping, and heaviness in the head. Prolonged use was said to dry up the semen (noted by Galen), cut off the desire for sexual intercourse, and curtail reproductive capacity; it also does damage to the intestine, causes a shortage of breath, diminishes vision, and induces depression after initially causing joy. Hashish was further said to produce narcosis, laziness, stupor, weakening sensory perception, and foul breath. In sum, Hashish is mind-changing and personality-changing, can cause insanity in the habitual user, and changes the mind so as to make it absent from reality.

We conclude our survey of religious sources without discovering a forceful reason that would offer clear grounds against cannabis use, though there are religious reasons against the abuse of cannabis or any substance that would be self-impairing or interfere with one's religious duties. Just as wine was recommended in Hebrew scripture as part of the joy of life (Psalm 104:15), as well as recommended for health reasons in the Christian New Testament (I Timothy 5:23: "Drink no longer water, but use a little wine for thy stomach's sake and thine often infirmities"), and hashish was recommended by Al-Zakarshi also for medical reasons, then (insofar as the use of wine and hashish is analogous to cannabis) we conclude that cannabis use *per se* does not meet with a decisive objection from the religious ethics of Judaism, Christianity, or Islam. Consider, now, the initial four objections to cannabis use.

A Defense of Altered States

Reply to the problem of falsehood

A defense of cannabis use can take the same form as the defense of theatre in ancient Greek philosophy. Aristotle thought that the altered states that comprise the theatre are actually a vital forum for the development of one's moral identity. We can become better persons through entertaining possible states of affairs, and contemplate the dangers of hubris, our vulnerability to fortune or chance, and the value of integrity. Aristotle even prized poetry and theatre because it involved some escape or departure from history. History is concerned with actualities, but in poetic theatre we can think morally about instructive possible lives and fates. Aristotle's theory makes much of the cathartic impact of theatre, which many commentators think of as a kind of letting off steam (this is sometimes disparagingly called the *enema thesis*). But more recent commentators understand catharsis as a form of moral shaping or purifying. Insofar as cannabis use stimulates altered states (hallucinations, narratives), this can be, of course, a menacing tool, but it can also be a tool that assists us in enlarging our moral imagination.

Reply to the distortion of reason

Undoubtedly, excessive cannabis use can distort reason, but so can excessive consumption of wine. Pascal even held that without some wine, one's chances of success in seeking truth were on a par with abstaining from wine. In a clever (perhaps humorous) line, Pascal notes: "Too much and too little wine. Give him none, he cannot find truth; give him too much, the same."[7] The case of Medea does raise the deep worry in ancient

❦ CHARLES TALIAFERRO AND MICHEL LE GALL

Greek philosophy of the danger of mindless passion and revenge, and also warns us of the evil use of drugs (she uses evil potions to kill), but this may be seen as a warning against abuse, not against balanced use. (Medea was a master with herbs, but does that mean we should renounce herbs?)

William James raises a good point about the possible side-effects of some artificially induced moods – giving rise to the mere appearance of depth and brilliance – but artificially induced altered states may produce some good. A defense of inducing altered states might even be employed in the controlled use of cannabis. John Locke defended a view of freedom that employed the imagination. The problem with an alcoholic (from a Lockean point of view) is that at a certain point in the day, all he can think about and envisage is the tavern. A corrective of habitual, entrenched over-use could be an induced alternative state of mind.[8] Locke makes clear that the imagination alone is not sufficient to bring about change, but without the imagination (whether artificially assisted or not) the subject would not be able to act freely among open alternatives.

Consider, finally, the combined undermining of agency and the loss of freedom or the power of self-determination objections. We take essentially the same response to these objections that we have to the above objections. One can indeed have harmful impacts of excessive cannabis use, but one may also meet with the same outcome with excessive consumption of what we assume is licit: moderate consumption of wine and other alcoholic beverages (which are considered acceptable practices throughout ancient, medieval, renaissance, and modern philosophy). There have been some disagreements among philosophers about whether occasionally getting drunk is permissible,[9] but the vast majority who have addressed this issue (e.g., Cicero and Erasmus) counsel only moderation.

Cannabis in Particular

We have considered altered states in general, with a special focus on arguments over wine, hashish, and opium. We have defended the use of substances to bring about altered states, but if cannabis has a particularly damaging impact, worse than wine and such, then there will be additional arguments that come into play.

Some philosophers advocate a strong liberty principle that would prohibit third or second parties from interfering with voluntary self-harm.

This is where religious considerations also emerge. Witness Socrates' claim that we are not our own person, but are (as it were) property of the gods and "in this point of view it is not unreasonable to say that no one has a right to kill himself, until God has imposed upon him an absolute necessity of some kind."[10] Many (but not all) Jews, Christians, and Muslims have adopted negative views of self-harm largely on such grounds. Interestingly, however, there has been widespread tolerance of tobacco use in Jewish, Christian, and Islamic cultures, and so the precept against self-harm has in practice focused more on the prohibition against suicide than in smoking or otherwise consuming substances that may detract from, but not (necessarily) bring about death.[11]

For present purposes, we are content to have argued for the following: assuming that cannabis can produce altered states of consciousness and that it is no worse than alcohol, we think that the philosophical and religious reasons against it are not decisive.

NOTES

1 For more information, see Elbert Nevius Sebring Thompson's *The Controversy between the Puritans and the Stage* (New York: Henry Holt, 1903).

2 *Euripides' Medea*, trans. A. J. Podlecki (Newburyport: Focus Classical Library, 1998), p. 62.

3 William James, *The Varieties of Religious Experience* (New York: Collier Macmillan, 1961), p. 305.

4 *Discourses*, Book 1, Chapter 19.

5 Thomas De Quincy, *Confessions of an English Opium Eater*, ed. Alethea Hayter (London: Penguin, 1971), p. 30.

6 Franz Rosenthal, *The Herb: Hashish v. Islamic Society* (Leiden: Brill, 1971), p. 64.

7 Blaise Pascal, *The Pensees*, ed. and trans. Roger Ariew (Indianapolis: Hackett, 2004), p. 12.

8 John Locke, *An Essay Concerning Human Understanding*, Book II, Chapter 21.

9 See Plato's *Laws* 666b.

10 Plato, *Phaedo*, trans. E. M. Cope (Cambridge: Cambridge University Press, 1875), p. 11.

11 If we assume that tobacco use is not possible in moderation and will always lead to death, then matters change. Alan Donagan has claimed that religious and secular morality that is part of what he calls "common morality" does not rule out all addictions as being contrary to human goodness and welfare. "Nor, as the tolerance of tobacco by both Judaism and Christianity shows,

has addiction to a drug been traditionally considered unfitting to a human being. Inasmuch as the relief and enjoyment afforded by a drug compensate for any ill-effects it may have, then it is permissible to use it. But it is contrary to the precept forbidding the impairment of health to use drugs as to incapacitate oneself for the ordinary business of life." Alan Donagan, *The Theory of Morality* (Chicago: University of Chicago Press, 1977), p. 80.

BRIAN R. CLACK[1]

CHAPTER 6

CANNABIS AND THE HUMAN CONDITION

"Something of the Kind is Indispensable"

 Some of the pleasures human beings seek are clearly and immediately intelligible. There is little mystery as to why people enjoy holidays, sexual intercourse, or evenings in the company of friends. The use of intoxicants is somewhat harder to understand. Why should a substance such as alcohol – not infrequently the cause of embarrassing situations, bilious sensations, and dreadful hangovers – be so highly prized? Cannabis poses for us similar problems. Acrid fumes are taken into one's lungs, and these fumes, among other effects, make one feel drowsy, thickheaded, and dizzy. And one risks prosecution for doing this. Why would human beings engage in such a practice? One possible answer to this question is provided by Sigmund Freud, the founder of psychoanalysis.

In *Civilization and its Discontents*, Freud gives voice to a markedly pessimistic view of the human condition, one in which human beings are fated to lives of unhappiness. This inevitable discontent is in part due simply to the stresses and strains of existence: "Life, as we find it, is too hard for us; it brings us too many pains, disappointments and impossible tasks."[2] Freud proceeds to list the three inescapable sources of our suffering: our bodies, prone to illness and doomed to decay; the merciless natural forces of the external world; and our volatile relations with other people. The pains experienced as a result of these three are worsened and magnified by a basic feature of human beings: our pursuit of happiness as the goal of life. In Freud's own vocabulary, "what decides the purpose of life is simply the programme of the pleasure principle," that primary process of the mind which drives the person to seek pleasure and avoid pain.[3] The inherent problem of human life, accordingly, is this: we are programmed to pursue pleasure and happiness, and yet have found ourselves thrown into a world that is singularly incapable of delivering those desires. "There is no possibility at all of [the plan of the pleasure principle] being carried through; all the regulations of the universe run to counter to it. One feels inclined to say that the intention that man should be 'happy' is not included in the plan of 'Creation'."[4] Given the clash between human desires and the cold heartlessness of the universe, suffering is inevitable.

Freud's despairing view of the human condition has an important antecedent in the pessimistic philosophy of Arthur Schopenhauer, who likewise located suffering in the gap between the way the world is and way we would like it to be. No writer has ever documented the ills befalling humanity with such an unflinching eye and with such a complete absence of hope. For Schopenhauer, life just *is* suffering, a constant struggle in which physical pain and mental anguish are ever present, so much so indeed that one's judgment must be that it would be better if nothing had ever existed at all:

> If you try to imagine, as nearly as you can, what an amount of misery, pain and suffering of every kind the sun shines upon in its course, you will admit that it would be much better if on the earth as little as on the moon the sun were able to call forth the phenomena of life; and if, here as there, the surface were still in a crystalline state.[5]

As with Freud's analysis, Schopenhauer also stresses that suffering is due to the failure to attain the happiness-producing goals one desires; however, Schopenhauer also contends that whenever one *does* attain what is willed or desired, no abiding satisfaction is produced, but merely a sensation of *boredom* (a sensation concerning which Freud, tellingly as we shall see, says nothing). This inability to be satisfied leads Schopenhauer to declare that human existence is nothing other than an *error*:

> Human life must be some kind of mistake. The truth of this will be sufficiently obvious if we only remember that man is a compound of needs and

necessities hard to satisfy; and that even when they are satisfied all he obtains is a state of painlessness, where nothing remains to him but abandonment to boredom. This is direct proof that existence has no real value in itself; for what is boredom but the feeling of the emptiness of life?[6]

In Schopenhauerian perspective, therefore, life oscillates between want and boredom, between suffering and tedium, and his diagnosis of our condition is the same as Freud's: happiness presents itself to us as the goal and proper aim of our lives, and yet it is impossible to attain. No animal, consequently, is worse adapted to the conditions of its existence than the human.

One may wish to take issue with the unremitting bleakness of the Freudian-Schopenhauerian outlook – surely, we want to say, *some* degree of happiness, contentment, and fulfillment can be found in life. And yet it would undeniably be foolish to protest that the terrible features of life highlighted by these pessimistic writers are not present, conspicuous, and unavoidable. Do not all of us encounter heartache, loss, regret, bodily discomfort, illness, anxiety, boredom, frustration of purpose, and then – hovering inescapably in the background of all our endeavors – there is death, horrifying both because of its uncertain elements (when will it occur, how much pain will I need to endure before nothingness engulfs me?) and because of the threat it poses to any sense we may have of the meaning of life (what is the point of all my striving if death may rob me of my life at any moment?). It is hard to escape Schopenhauer's conclusion that we really are like lambs playing in a field while a butcher eyes and then selects first one and then another for slaughter.[7] Such indeed seems to be our shared condition: whether or not we have been successful in our lives, have escaped from poverty, have managed to find episodes of enjoyment, we all nonetheless await our moment in the slaughterhouse.

According to Freud, then, existence is a terrible burden, and "in order to bear it we cannot dispense with palliative measures."[8] This is an extraordinary thought. There is no cure for the human condition, but only palliative care: measures which can be employed to soften and ameliorate the worst of our suffering; analgesic cultural and psychological tools and techniques which might just soothe the pain of our dreadful and terminal situation. "Something of the kind," he writes, "is indispensable."[9] Freud discusses four specific palliatives. *Religion* constitutes one such palliative. It functions, Freud thinks, by denying some unpalatable element of reality and setting up in its stead a representation of things

❦ BRIAN R. CLACK

more in step with our wishes. Belief in a loving God and a blissful after-life are just two examples of wish-generated beliefs which can serve to soften the harsh realities of life. *Art* for Freud is a finer and more respect-able palliative, and, to those who value it, it is a source of great pleasure and consolation in life. Aesthetic enjoyment, however, is something accessible, he thinks, only to a few people and even then such pleasures are only mild, and do not "convulse our physical being."[10] *Love* is per-haps the most sought-after palliative and it provides both an enormous amount of comfort and the most intense sensations of pleasure available to us, the pleasures of sex. As a treatment for the human condition, how-ever, romantic love carries a degree of risk, since "we are never so defence-less against suffering as when we love, never so helplessly unhappy as when we have lost our loved object or its love."[11] For our purposes here, though, it is the fourth palliative Freud lists which is of principal interest. He calls this "the crudest, but also the most effective" method for amel-iorating sensations of suffering: *intoxication*.

The thoughts of the inventor of psychoanalysis will be worth listening to in any discussion about drugs and intoxicants, since Freud – occasionally enthusiastic about cocaine and catastrophically dependent upon tobacco – must have known their various effects well. It is worth quoting at length what he writes about these psychoactive substances in *Civilization and its Discontents*:

> I do not think that anyone completely understands its mechanism, but it is a fact that there are foreign substances which, when present in the blood or tissues, directly cause us pleasurable sensations, and they also so alter the conditions governing our sensibility that we become incapable of receiving unpleasurable impulses. The two effects not only occur simultaneously, but seem to be intimately bound up with each other. . . . The service rendered by intoxicating media in the struggle for happiness and in keeping misery at a distance is so highly prized as a benefit that individuals and peoples alike have given them an established place in the economics of their libido. We owe to such media not merely the immediate yield of pleasure, but also a greatly desired degree of independence from the external world. For one knows that, with the help of this "drowner of cares," one can at any time withdraw from the pressure of reality and find refuge in a world of one's own with better conditions of sensibility.[12]

In this passage, we find all the elements of the Freudian view of intoxi-cants-as-palliative: existence is difficult, at times *too* difficult for us; it leaves us with discomfort both mental and physical; intoxicating substances can be used to soothe these travails of life and to produce in the user sensations of pleasure otherwise unavailable; they thus provide a kind of "refuge" and can, at least for a while, free us from the world and its troubles. Freud quotes approvingly Wilhelm Busch: "The man who has cares has brandy too."

It may seem that Freud has a rather one-sided and unbalanced view of drug use here. His emphasis upon intoxication as a "refuge" from life's troubles may make it appear as though drugs were sought out merely for their sedative properties. But this is surely false. Not all drugs are barbiturates; and for every sedative there is a stimulant; for every person seeking anxiety reduction by means of a Valium or a Quaalude we can find another using psilocybin or LSD to achieve a hallucinogenic state, another in search of the stimulation and energy promised by coffee or amphetamines, and so on. Of course, Freud does allow for the possibility that drugs might do something other than sedate, might do something other than have a merely tranquilizing function: recall his observation that intoxicants are used for the removal of unpleasant sensations *and* for the production of pleasant ones. Nevertheless, the general thrust of Freud's psychological theorizing is to emphasize precisely the reduction of unwanted stimuli rather than the quest for new stimulation. According to his principle of *psychic inertia*, first advanced in the early "Project for a Scientific Psychology," the mind seeks, as far as possible, to eliminate all tension within it. By the time he came to write *Beyond the Pleasure Principle*, Freud was contending that the "dominating tendency of mental life, and perhaps of nervous life in general, is the effort to reduce, to keep constant or to remove internal tension due to stimuli."[13] He referred to this as the "Nirvana principle" and saw it as indicative of a *death instinct* within the human being, an instinct which aims "to conduct the restlessness of life into the stability of the inorganic state."[14] This undeniably leaves its mark on his account of the motivations for drug use, for from the principle of psychic inertia it is easy to move to the conviction that the great appeal of drugs is their promise to deliver a state of sensationless Nirvana.

Freud's emphasis on the desire to dispose of stimulation and excitement may be regarded as a weakness in his theory of the mind and its workings. At the very least it requires amending. His view, as we have seen, is that human beings seek mental tranquility and regard powerful emotions as undesirable intrusions which need quickly to be discharged, thus producing a state of quietude. "*Protection against* stimuli is an almost more important function for the living organism than *reception of* stimuli."[15]

In this scheme of things there is an emphasis on "stimulus overload" but little or no place for what psychiatrist Anthony Storr has called "stimulus hunger," the need human beings have to seek out stimuli when they find themselves in a tedious or monotonous environment, a reality which can be demonstrated by observation of (for example) prisoners who have spent considerable periods of time in solitary confinement. Stimulus hunger occurs in such a condition and the individual involved will engage in strenuous mental activities in order to excite her mind and avoid sinking into despair.[16] Freud, however, does not seem to recognize that tedium may result from a lack of excitation.

That boredom is a psychological problem so entirely ignored by Freud is strange, though not totally unexpected, given his account of the economics of the mental apparatus.[17] This need not undermine an account of drugs which stresses their palliative role. We need only supplement Freud's account of the problems of human existence with Schopenhauer's comparable contentions, noted earlier. The unsatisfactory nature of the human condition was not there regarded as solely due to pain and the overwhelming stresses of existence (stimulus overload), but also to the vacuity of the state of boredom (stimulus hunger). Human life swings back and forth between these two poles. Might not drugs function as distinct (perceived) remedies for one or other of these states, for pain and for boredom? The great and abundant variety of psychoactive substances suggests that this may be so. Some drugs (sedatives, for instance) may serve to ease our troubled and anxious minds. Others may be singularly unfitted to that particular tranquilizing task, and may instead *introduce* excitation into a mind uninspired by the common order of things. One might here recall Sherlock Holmes' explanation that his use of artificial stimulants was necessitated by "the dull routine of existence" which he so abhorred,[18] or may note Fernando Pessoa's complaint about "the contrast between the natural splendour of the inner life, with its natural Indias and its unexplored lands, and the squalor . . . of life's daily routine."[19] Even the nightmarish experiences sought by the PCP user may perhaps be illuminated by such an approach, since the hellish excitement of a trip on angel dust may contrast favorably with a life which is otherwise pedestrian and bland. Hence, drugs are often used both when the world has become too much for us *and* when it has become too little; both when there is too much going on *and*, conversely, when there is not enough. We can put this point another way by adapting a memorable image offered by Ronald Siegel.[20] Excitation in the brain may be regarded as a fire: sometimes the fire needs to be dampened, while at other times it requires stoking. Sedatives dampen the fire in the brain; hallucinogens and stimulants stoke it up.[21]

Cannabis is particularly interesting from this point of view, since its effects are highly varied, this variety depending upon the potency of the preparation.[22] The strongest psychoactive chemical within the cannabis plant – delta-9-tetrahydrocannabinol (THC) – is found in differing levels of concentration and it is this which determines the kind of experience the cannabis user will have. Low-grade marijuana, made from all the leaves of both sexes of the cannabis plant, may have less than 1 percent THC; high-grade marijuana (or sinsemilla), made from the flowering tops of the female plant kept in isolation from male plants, can have between 4–8 percent THC; while, at the highest end of the potency spectrum, hash oil may contain up to 70 percent THC. The concentration levels of THC are determined, moreover, by the stage of maturation at which the plant is harvested: THC is found in the plant's resin, which is most concentrated in the flowers. A plant harvested at its floral peak has a very high level of THC, and has relatively little sedative effect. If the plant is allowed to mature beyond this peak stage, however, marijuana with a heavier, more sedative effect will be produced. The different feelings associated with peak-harvested and late-harvested marijuana correspond to the differences between being "high" and being "stoned." Users report, indeed, an extraordinary range of feelings and experiences while under the influence of the drug, including drowsiness, dizziness, relaxation, hilarity, contemplativeness, and a heightened appreciation of conversation, music, visual images, and sense perceptions.

On our modified Freudian view of drugs-as-palliatives, then, cannabis can be seen to attend to some of the deficiencies of the human condition. In its analgesic capacity, it can sedate and relax; it can ameliorate anxiety;[23] and, of course, its capacity to lessen the suffering caused by such conditions as cancer, glaucoma, and multiple sclerosis is, by now, well known. As well as lessening the reception of painful sensations, cannabis use also directly causes pleasant sensations (thereby functioning in the dual manner described by Freud): the heightened appreciation of emotional, perceptual, and intellectual matters and the production of sometimes uncontrollable laughter[24] – such effects are understandably sought in a world which may often strike one as intolerably sad or just plain dull. Even the dizziness experienced as a result of smoking marijuana is something *different* from the everyday, and just as explicable as a child's self-produced sense of dizziness through spinning or the effects produced by some frenetic fairground ride: dizziness is *exciting*.[25] If the human condition is

❦ BRIAN R. CLACK

understood in the manner set out in *Civilization and its Discontents*, therefore, the term "medical marijuana" might be extended well beyond its reference to a treatment for agonizing physical ailments. There is, at the very least, an argument for contending that *all* cannabis use is medicinal, and for concurring with Siegel's view that all intoxicants (cannabis included) are "medicines, treatments for the human condition."[26]

A view which stresses the palliative function of cannabis and other intoxicants is not to be confused with the common and frequently heard complaint that drug use constitutes merely an "escape from reality," a view expressed by Massachusetts judge Joseph Tauro when upholding his state's marijuana law: "Many succumb to the drug as a handy means of withdrawing from the inevitable stresses and legitimate demands of society. The evasion of problems and escape from reality seem to be among the desired effects of the use of marijuana."[27] It is of course true that some people will on occasion take refuge in intoxication when reality threatens to overwhelm them.[28] But it does not follow from this that all intoxicant use, and all use of cannabis, is driven by a desire to escape from reality. Intoxicants are palliatives, but so are religious beliefs, love affairs, and the joys of art and music. Each of these runs the risk of falling into mere escapism – religion is frequently nothing other than a set of wish-driven delusions; romantic love is not uncommonly enmeshed in irrational overvaluations of the loved person; immersion in art is sometimes immersion in mere fantasy – but they are not uncommonly more, much more, than this. The joys of a love affair, the delights offered by art and music, the depth of understanding found within a mature religious faith – it is surely wrong to think of such things as constituting merely an escape from life and reality. Rather, they augment, embellish, and beautify it. Our lives would be poorer without one or other of these, maybe even intolerable. Is it not possible that the same could be said of intoxicants and of cannabis?

One might reasonably resist this rather upbeat conclusion. Legitimate concerns about the effect of cannabis on physical and mental health may make one reluctant to embrace or recommend it; while Freud's own rider concerning the "danger and injuriousness" of intoxicants itself deserves noting: "They are responsible, in certain circumstances, for the useless waste of a large quota of energy which might have been employed for the improvement of the human lot."[29] This is undeniably true. And yet when one comes to make a moral judgment about the use of cannabis, or when the vexed issue of its proper legal status is raised and considered, one might do worse than to reflect upon the difficulties of the human condition and the tools used to soften and beautify it. Our judgments on cannabis, both moral and legal, may then cease to be, as they typically are in our time, so very harsh. Existence might just require this sort of augmentation.

NOTES

1   I am grateful to Gary Jones, Christina Printz, and Patti White for their help-ful comments on a previous draft of this essay.
2   Sigmund Freud, *Civilization and its Discontents*, in *The Standard Edition of the Complete Psychological Works of Sigmund Freud* (hereafter *SE* followed by vol-ume number) (London: Hogarth Press, 1953–75), vol. 21, p. 75.
3   Ibid., p. 76.
4   Ibid. And again: "The programme of becoming happy, which the pleasure principle imposes on us, cannot be fulfilled" (ibid., p. 83).
5   Arthur Schopenhauer, *Studies in Pessimism* (London: Swann Sonnenschein, 1900), p. 7.
6   Ibid., p. 22.
7   Ibid., p. 6. See also Pascal's analysis: "Imagine a number of men in chains, all under sentence of death, some of whom are each day butchered in the sight of the others; those remaining see their own condition in that of their fellows, and looking at each other with grief and despair await their turn. This is an image of the human condition." Blaise Pascal, *Pensées* (London: Penguin, 1995), p. 137 [§434]).
8   Freud, *Civilization and its Discontents*, p. 75.
9   Ibid.
10 Ibid., p. 80.
11 Ibid., p. 82.
12 Ibid., p. 78.
13 Sigmund Freud, *Beyond the Pleasure Principle*, *SE 18*, pp. 55–6.
14 Sigmund Freud, "The Economic Problem of Masochism", *SE 19*, p. 160.
15 Freud, *Beyond the Pleasure Principle*, p. 27.
16 Anthony Storr, *Music and the Mind* (London: Harper Collins, 1997), p. 28.
17 In the standard edition of Freud's works there are only three references to boredom: *all* of these occur within Josef Breuer's solo contributions to the *Studies on Hysteria*.
18 Arthur Conan Doyle, *The Sign of Four* (Kelly Bray: Stratus, 2001), p. 2.
19 Fernando Pessoa, *The Book of Disquiet* (London: Penguin, 2002), p. 365.
20 Ronald K. Siegel, *Intoxication* (Rochester: Park Street Press, 2005), pp. 227–8.
21 None of this is to deny that what people actually seek from the use of intoxi-cants varies markedly, nor that the catalogue of motives is infinitely extendable,

but simply that those unsatisfactory elements of the human condition outlined by Schopenhauer and Freud may provide a useful context for understanding the reasons underlying a large amount of drug use.

22 See Cynthia Kuhn, Scott Swartzwelder, and Wilkie Wilson, *Buzzed* (New York: Norton, 2003), pp. 134–61. The information in this paragraph about the chemistry and harvesting of cannabis has been gleaned predominantly from this source.

23 Cannabidiol, a component of marijuana, has anti-anxiety effects, and in the *Artharvaveda* (an Indian scripture), cannabis is described as one of a number of herbs which "release us from anxiety." See Richard Rudgley, *The Encyclopaedia of Psychoactive Substances* (London: Little, Brown, 1998), p. 48.

24 For a remarkable first-hand description of the hilarity induced by hashish, see Théophile Gautier's "The Club of Assassins," in Charles Baudelaire and Théophile Gautier, *Hashish, Wine, Opium* (London: Calder and Boyars, 1972).

25 Cf. Siegel, *Intoxication*, pp. 210–13.

26 Ibid., p. xi.

27 G. Joseph Tauro, quoted in Jacob Sullum, *Saying Yes* (New York: Tarcher/Penguin, 2004), pp. 106–7.

28 And real life is, of course, not infrequently overwhelming. Recall T. S. Eliot's famous lines in the *Four Quartets*: "Go, go, go, said the bird: human kind/Cannot bear very much reality."

29 Freud, *Civilization and its Discontents*, p. 78.

PART III

CREATIVELY HIGH

You got to hold that muggles so that it barely touches your lips, see, then draw in air around it. Say "tfff, tfff," only breathe in when you say it. Then don't blow it out right away, you got to give the stuff a chance. . . . The first thing I noticed was that I began to hear my saxophone as though it were inside my head. . . . Then I began to feel the vibrations of the reed much more pronounced against my lip. . . . I found I was slurring much better and putting just the right feeling into my phrases. . . . All the notes came easing out of my horn, like they'd already been made up, greased and stuffed into the bell, so all I had to do was blow a little and send them on their way, one right after the other, never missing, never behind time, all without an ounce of effort. . . . I felt I could go on playing for years without running out of ideas and energy. There wasn't any struggle; it was all made to order and suddenly there wasn't a sour note or a discord in the world that could bother me. . . . I began to preach my millenniums on my horn, leading all the sinners to glory.

Milton Mezzrow and Bernard Wolfe,
Really the Blues, 1946; quoted in Martin Booth,
Cannabis: A History, 2003

CHAPTER 7

HALLUCINATORY TERROR

The World of the Hashish Eater

Cannabis is not a very exciting drug when it comes to literary texts about drug experiences. There are others that have been involved in creating more exceptional literature. Thomas De Quincey created the genre with his *Confessions of an English Opium Eater*, William Burroughs' *Junky* and *Naked Lunch* showed the effects of opiate abuse in its modern form, Aldous Huxley produced exciting texts about his experiments with mescaline (as did Henri Michaux), Terence McKenna documented his search for various shamanic plants and his love affair with the psilocybin mushroom, Hunter S. Thompson discussed most modern recreational drugs, and let us not forget Charles Bukowski's alcohol-fueled stories and poetry. The interesting philosophical questions that come up in most of the texts in the genre concern the nature of addiction and our perception of reality. In this respect, the problem with cannabis, if we may call it that, is that it is not that addictive and, furthermore, people do not usually take large enough quantities to create situations where the fundamental nature of reality seems to shatter. In the case of cannabis, one of the best descriptions that can compete for a place in the canon of autobiographical drug narratives is Fitz Hugh Ludlow's 1857 *The Hasheesh Eater: Being Passages from the Life of a Pythagorean*.

What enables Ludlow to vie for a place among the genre's other literary greats is the fact that he did not know that in terms of physical addiction, cannabis is not a very harmful drug. Having read De Quincey, he was very anxious about addiction even while he found the effects of the drug irresistible. He also used concentrated hashish oil which got him very, very high. Most importantly, however, he was a learned man with a good command of the classics, as well as an enthusiastic reader of the modern philosophy of his time. Without his education in philosophy, literature, and languages, nothing like the *Hasheesh Eater* would exist today.

A young American student at the time, Ludlow sets the scene by portraying himself as a Faustian character who has studied all possible drug worlds known to him and his chemist and supplier, Mr. Anderson. One day, engaged in his usual "pursuit for remarkable emotions,"[1] he finds a vial of hashish oil from the Cannabis Indica plant at his friend's Poughkeepsie apothecary and is intrigued. After hitting the books, he decides it is safe to go ahead and experiment with the hashish oil which at the time, we are told, was used as a remedy for lockjaw. He gets a feel for the correct dose after a few bungled attempts and is taken on an astonishing and frightening first trip.[2] His prose indicates that he stumbled on a very potent form of cannabis. As he hallucinates his days away, his experiences grow ever more frightening and finally he decides to wean himself off the drug, and it is during this period he wrote his account. The writing process acted as his therapy, recommended to him by a physician friend, and helped him get his mind off the craving for a state of mind and body where he found "all conceivable desires satisfied" (35).

In Ludlow's account, the mundane becomes epic page after glorious page. God himself is feared dead, years before Nietzsche's pronouncement,[3] and is found alive again. Time stretches into infinities; spaces which were a few steps away vanish into the distance. There is even what we today might call a UFO encounter. So violent are these experiences that Ludlow thinks two people, one intoxicated by hashish and the other not, can never meet at the same "plane of thought" (113) and communicate successfully. In fact, "a virtual change of worlds" (ibid.) takes place and language breaks down when the impossible stares at the hashish eater and demands description. Conversely, it is possible, says Ludlow, for someone clever enough to lead the hallucinating person through all sorts of visions by the mere power of suggestion. Words, it seems, can install visions into the mind of the hashish eater, but they cannot extract them from his mind intact.

Ludlow was a great admirer of De Quincey and was not apologetic of his emulation of the pioneer of the *Opium Eater*. Comparing the two authors, it is obvious that De Quincey is the stronger writer, but Ludlow does have his moments. What we find in his descriptions of the hashish experience is a man overjoyed and appalled by a succession of hallucinatory images produced by a strange drug whose effects were not yet well known, at least in Poughkeepsie. The hallucinations he experienced were something that could not be shared with his peers, because few had felt the peculiar effects of hashish and, consequently, there was little language in existence to describe them. Related to this problem is the fact that describing impossible objects using the slippery instruments of language is a task that has its own difficulties. Ludlow returns to the impossibility of the experience over and over again even as he does his best to convey the immense intensity of the visions. The ridiculous amount of hyperbole in the descriptions of his visions conveys the effect that language never does enough for Ludlow. He has excellent linguistic tools as he is a widely read man, the son of a minister, and a serious student of philosophy, but what is required to capture the experience would have to be a supernatural speech, a miraculous link from one mind to another. There is experience and there is description of experience, and never the two shall meet by mortal means.

"How can these things be?"

Ludlow is a strict dualist who sees himself and others as souls trapped in bodies whose porous composition is not fine enough to let the mind of one penetrate another's. At the height of one of his many deliriums, he even has an out of body experience and swears that it is his actual soul leaving his actual body and no dream or hallucination. In other words, he makes a categorical distinction between the hallucinatory and real experiences brought on by hashish: there are true experiences such as the sensation of thirst and there might also be visions which are completely false. Then, it seems, there are those experiences which do not fit neatly into the categories of truth and falsity because of their ambiguous state of being.

Many of Ludlow's hallucinations take this more subtle ontological form and he, of course, asks: "How can these things be?" (108) It is a strikingly practical question of metaphysics and one that must be asked by anyone who is in the peculiar position of seeing things that should not exist. Specifically, it is a question of ontology which asks what sorts of things there are in the world and of what things we can say that they are not in the world. The answer in this case is that hallucinations, however clearly visible or otherwise present to any of the other senses, in some sense are not. They are not reflections of some incoming perception distorted by the senses confused by hashish – this would be an illusion where the object does exist in some form in the outside world and is processed and mangled by the senses.[4]

There is something obviously strange about the ontological status of hallucinations even before we begin a metaphysical investigation. Metaphysicians are notorious for dreaming up ways of making everyday objects seem strange by examining them from odd perspectives. For instance, a table could be said to be composed mostly of empty air if we looked at it on the atomic level, where most of its body appears to us as the vast expanses of space between the nuclei and electrons of its atoms. Were we to zoom even closer we would arrive at the quantum level, where the solid matter that composes the table becomes the possibility of its particles being at a certain place at a certain time. For the moment, let us maintain a distinction between hallucinations as immediately ontologically ambiguous things and things like tables, which are solid material objects before metaphysicians gather around them and confuse them with atomic air and probabilities.

In other words, hallucinations are experiences of objects that are missing the one final ontological screw which would fasten them onto what we are pleased to call reality. Furthermore, this is their defining characteristic. However, we cannot merely say that hallucinations are and are not and think we have answered the question in any meaningful sense.[5] If, then, hallucinations are not in the world or exist in the same sense everyday objects exist, how can they be? Could they, for instance, exist as independent perceptions that do not have an external source like illusions have and, if so, how did these independent perceptions come to be? What we are faced with – if we deem them perceptions without an external object – is an object whose ontology we must somehow untangle in the senses.

Ludlow begins this untangling by looking back to his childhood. He tells a story of an incident involving two thinkers engaged in idle discussion who come to the conclusion that we never sense the essence of things, only the qualities they project onto our senses. The young Ludlow is impressed by this thought, as it contains no technical language and yet manages to present fascinating opportunities for philosophical discovery. He thinks it might be an empty sophism made for the sake of argument. After all, he knows that "metaphysicians love to argue" (223). In order to test the hypothesis he goes to a tree and experiments with his senses. He feels the tree, smells and tastes its bark, taps it and listens, looks at its colors. He finds that all he can detect are the qualities of the tree transmitted through his senses. These qualities, in turn, are a sign of the fact that the world as it is in itself is out of our direct reach, that before we can do anything else we have to explore the ways in which information about the world gets through to us. The story is also Ludlow's introduction to the philosophies he wishes to discuss in the latter part of his book: the skepticism of David Hume and what he calls the Transcendentalism of his own age.

Ludlow is a great defender of Hume even as he condemns his philosophy. The basic framework of Hume's thought came from the empiricist tradition and specifically John Locke's 1689 *Essay Concerning Human Understanding*, an essay so influential, says Ludlow, that Hume really had no choice in choosing the fundamental makeup of his own philosophical system. In short, Locke's position was that the understanding has to work on ideas which in turn come from either perceptions or reflection on things derived from perceptions.[6] This goes against any notion of innate ideas, the view that knowledge is somehow independent from particular experiences of things in the world – that we *just know* some things. The mind is furnished from experience alone.

As a religious man, Ludlow sees that this view can lead to heresy, but as a learned man he also knows there are always ways around heresies. He establishes that in his *Enquiry Concerning Human Understanding* and *Treatise of Human Nature* Hume treated Locke as a starting point to ponder the questions with which he himself wrestles; and, in fact, anyone who gives some thought to the subject has to face the same questions sooner or later. He presents Hume's view as a charming soliloquy:

> I find that my senses give me nothing but the phenomena of things – tell me merely how objects act upon me. My eye acquaints me with color and outline; my ear with vibrations of diverse intensities; and so on with all the rest of the organs. All give qualities of things, operations which things have a capability to perform on me, appearances of things, but never things themselves. How do I know that they do not? By reflection, certainly; reflection on the data afforded by sense. But why do we all believe, and act upon the belief, that we see, hear, feel, smell, and taste things? It must no doubt be sense that tells us so; that is the only conjoint source of knowledge with reflection. Then I have within me, and so has every one else, two exactly opposite verdicts. I do know things, and I do not know them. Now which is the lie? (227)

Crucially, as Ludlow also notes, Hume did not provide a simple answer to this problem. What Hume did do was to open up the possibility that all our sensations may in some sense be hallucinatory: mere sense perceptions without corresponding objects of sensation or reactions to sense perceptions with no certain origin. This has grave epistemological consequences since these perceptions are all we have to go on when it comes to the outside world. We simply cannot know if we know what is out there and what is not. We could pair the Lockean system with the conviction that God has equipped man with senses with which we can view his creation and base it on faith. After all, what would be the point of giving human beings senses that deceive him? The senses can get things wrong, sure, but in the grand ontological scheme of things, we would do all right if we followed a Locke reinforced with faith. However, Hume makes the world disappear from view by saying (with a wink and a nod, of course) that we cannot distinguish the view we have of the world from the world itself. We have found our object, our independent perception without an external object, but instead of getting closer to the answer of our question about hallucinations, we have lost sight of the world and suggested that the world might be merely a function of our senses. This will not do.

Reason's Transcendental Climb

It is the possibility of this radical doubt and not a rank disbelief that makes Hume's thought revolutionary. His is not a disbelief that says we cannot know the world or, as Ludlow seems to think, a dramatic Pyrrhonistic[7] renunciation of the possibility that we could even be in a position to doubt. It is an in-your-face attitude that suggests that all of us, philosophers as well, may just be making it all up as we go along. However, we do seem to take pleasure in our senses and want to discover the world around us through them by our very nature.[8] We play with our senses by making them distort (or indeed normalize) the everyday world through the use of various drugs. We also use tools like microscopes and telescopes to enhance the senses and help us discover things we cannot sense directly. A metaphysician might even argue that the equations physicists use to study very small and very large things can be seen as similar instruments and go on to claim that we transcended the limitations of our senses a long time ago.

What all this suggests is that if we are to get beyond the senses we must study the senses to see if we can get beyond them. Luckily, says Ludlow, there is a group of philosophers who can save us from all this skepticism and offer us an option beyond the crippled empiricist framework. He calls them Transcendentalists, but instead of the philosophical movement whose figurehead was Emerson he refers to Kant, Fichte, Hegel, and Schelling.[9] They are, says Ludlow, able to climb "over that ring-fence of knowledge brought in through mere physical passages, with which a tyrannous oligarchy of reasoners would circumscribe all our wanderings in search of facts and laws" (230). Unfortunately, he also says, these philosophers do use technical language and terminology that require study, but for good reasons. First, they wrote in German. Second, they really were making it up as they went along, because nothing quite like what they were trying to do had ever been done. Third, and most importantly, Immanuel Kant, the man who created the basic framework for this Transcendentalism, was in fact trying to make a science out of metaphysics.[10] Philosophical investigations which aspire to the rigorousness of scientific exactness need jargon just like a scientist needs his tools to keep everything in order. In any case, given time, the practitioners of such investigations do not find their terminology strange. Ludlow writes:

> When we complain of the sailor for speaking of his masts as spars, instead of calling them sticks, to meet the comprehension of some land-lubber . . . when, in fine, public opinion shall compel all men to talk of the delicacies of their arts in street slang or boudoir twaddle, then, and not till then, will it be time to deride the science, wherein, more than all others, rigorous exactitude of expression is required, for having a peculiar, even though it be not a universally intelligible language. (232)

The task was, and still is, hopelessly convoluted and this is reflected in its language because what is at stake is a description of the mind engaged in the description of its own workings. There is, however, a way into this mess and it begins with Kant's *Critique of Pure Reason* (1781) and his Copernican revolution, which turned the attention of metaphysicians from the world to the ways in which the world can be known.

Kant divides the world into the *phenomenal* and the *noumenal*. The phenomenal world is the one we experience through our senses, the noumenal world is the one of thing-in-itself (*Ding an sich*), which by definition is beyond empirical sensation. We are stuck with the phenomenal world, but even in our ignorance we can draw some conclusions. For one thing, we can derive the fact that the noumenal world exists from the way it is manifested in the phenomenal. And how does it manifest itself in the phenomenal world? It is colored by the senses and if we cannot say anything meaningful about a thing-in-itself other than that it exists, we can say certain things about the way the phenomenal world becomes experienced by us by creating certain kinds of propositions. That is, we can say something about things prior to experience, or *a priori*, and contrast these propositions with empirical, or *a posteriori*, propositions.

Now, we cannot simply assume that we can say all sorts of things independent from experience, as this would lead to all sorts of trouble, not to mention go against the scientific exactness that has to be the model of language in our pursuit of the hallucinatory with Kant's help. The way we say things can be either *analytic* or *synthetic*. The analytic proposition "A bachelor is an unmarried man," for instance, is obviously true, because bachelors, by definition, are unmarried and to say otherwise would be a contradiction and therefore false: there are no married bachelors. That is, we can look at the proposition and figure out that it is true without any external input: bachelors (*subject*) are unmarried (*predicate*) – the meaning of the predicate term (are unmarried) is contained in the subject term (bachelors). Furthermore, the proposition is necessarily true. Synthetic propositions, on the other hand, are like plain statements from experience such as "Nigel is an unmarried man," where we know this is true because we happen to know Nigel is a bachelor and not because Nigels, by definition, have to be unmarried. That is, we cannot figure out if the statement is true or false just by analyzing the statement: it would be much easier to call Nigel and ask him. Furthermore, if we call him and discover his marital status, we will have gained new information about the world through experience. This is another property of synthetic propositions.

The game gets interesting when we begin to combine the possibilities of the *a priori* and *a posteriori* with the analytic and synthetic kinds of propositions. We get four possibilities: (1) *analytic a priori*, (2) *analytic a posteriori*, (3) *synthetic a priori*, and (4) *synthetic a posteriori*. The last of these options (4) are common propositions from experience. The first one (1) are like the above analytic proposition about bachelors. We do not have to worry about (2) – analytic *a posteriori* propositions – since it is unnecessary to justify analytic propositions using experience as the basis for such justifications. The most important and interesting kind of proposition among the possibilities is (3), the synthetic *a priori*. What we need is a proposition that does not contain the meaning of the predicate term in its subject term. Furthermore, we need a proposition that gives us new information about the world, is prior to experience, and also necessarily true. Propositions in geometry are like this, says Kant, as are those of mathematics. That is, it is possible to find such propositions and Kant seems to think that this possibility is not caused by features of objects in the outside world, but by the way our sensory and conceptual apparatus orders the world for us.

Where Were We?

How does it do that? Well, we must look at the way we look at the world as existing in space and time. In fact, we have performed a kind of transcendental climbing-over in our reasoning by acknowledging the existence of the synthetic *a priori* and found things which are not given to us by the senses and yet apply universally. Space and time can be said to resemble such things, too. What Kant saw was that we view the world through space and time as *pure forms of intuition*. They are not objects in the world, but all objects in the world are necessarily conditioned by our view through space and time. Furthermore, according to Kant, it is useless to try to look for direct intuitive experience. There is no consciousness before we combine intuitions with *concepts*. Kant says: "Without sensibility no object would be given to us, without understanding no object would be thought. Thoughts without content are empty, intuitions without concepts are blind."[11]

We do not experience pure intuition or pure concept, but we can know that these things exist because we experience our world through them. Ludlow never went into all these details in his book, but he does tell of dramatic distortions of space and time. And it is here we can finally begin to trace the ontology of hallucinatory experiences. The Copernican revolution of Kant's philosophy is, in essence, the recognition that objects in the world must conform to certain intuitions and related categories we can discover through the use of reason. That is, through reason, we are able to discover that the objects we perceive must in some ways conform to the ways in which we perceive them. Strangely enough, it turns out we can know things about objects independently of experience and climb over the fences placed around knowledge by empiricists. This was a relatively new development in philosophy in Ludlow's time and he found it immensely liberating.[12]

Now we can come back to Ludlow's original question about the nature of hallucinations from a new angle. Instead of experience itself, we have had to look at language and what can be said about experience. We have also come to look at a question not of ontology *per se*, but a question of epistemology. In fact, we have come to look at the conditions of the possibility of experience. Unfortunately, Kant left many holes in his system and philosophers and metaphysicians have had their hands full trying to patch it up ever since. On the bright side, thanks to Kant, some of them are even today able to make a living trying to sort out the ensuing patchwork. Nevertheless, he made it clear that the senses are definitely not all we have to go on or else we could not conceive of things like pure intuitions or synthetic *a priori* statements. We have reason to help us figure out the metaphysical nature of the descriptions of hallucinations, if not hallucinations in themselves.

As a conclusion, we can suggest one final formulation of the answer to the question: "How can these things be?" Namely, we can say that Ludlow's reports of hallucinations are a response to the distortions produced by his drugged sensory apparatus. This much is abundantly clear. But hallucinations are not objects in the outside world or objects in his senses – we cannot really say that they exist or that they do not exist. They might not be objects at all, but the manifestations of the opportunities opened up by the perceiver in his hashish state. They could be called potentially existing objects. What this means is that when Ludlow tells the reader that a virtual change of worlds takes place in the intoxicated party in relation to his sober companion, he is not speaking metaphorically. The senses and thought have been affected in ways which Ludlow believes warrant the separation of another world for the hashish eater. The parties do not have a shared world or a shared life in which a shared language would make sense. That is why communication between them is doomed to failure. We can, however, get some sense of the hallucinatory world of another through a skillful writer like Ludlow and find out in the end that their language is not even supposed to make complete sense. That is one way hallucinations can be. A full description of the experience is always out of our reach and what remains outside of it can only be seen in the sputtering of language as it tries to describe the indescribable.

NOTES

1 Fitz Hugh Ludlow, *The Hasheesh Eater* (New Brunswick: Rutgers University Press, 2006). p. 207. From now on, I will include page numbers from *The Hasheesh Eater* in the body of the text.

TOMMI KAKKO

2   Terence McKenna produced an inspired reading of the first chapter of Ludlow's book which recounts his first cannabis experience. Copies of the recording can be found online.

3   As Donald P. Dulchinos notes, Friedrich Nietzsche was still a boy when *The Hasheesh Eater* was published. For the story of Ludlow's life as well as a useful bibliography, see Donald P. Dulchinos, *Pioneer of Inner Space: The Life of Fitz Hugh Ludlow, Hasheesh Eater* (New York: Autonomedia, 1998).

4   Another possibility one might want to consider in this context is a mirage, which is an image that has been distorted by the medium between the object and the person viewing the object.

5   Aristotle says in the *Metaphysics*: "To say of what is that it is and of what is not that it is not is true, whereas to say of what is that it is not and of what is not that it is is false." This sounds obvious, but sometimes in philosophy it pays to say obvious things. Aristotle, *Metaphysics, Books I–IX* (Cambridge, MA: Harvard University Press, 1933).

6   It is always foolish to summarize complicated philosophical treatises and arguments in a sentence or two, but often essayists get little choice in the matter. Those curious about the actual argument of Locke's groundbreaking work should of course look to Locke's original essay.

7   Pyrrho was an Ancient Greek skeptic who gave his name to an extreme form of skepticism. Many other kinds of skepticism can be found in Richard Popkin, *The History of Scepticism from Savonarola to Bayle* (Oxford: Oxford University Press, 2003).

8   This is the thought with which Aristotle begins his *Metaphysics*.

9   Dulchinos, *Pioneer of Inner Space*, p. 54, says that Ludlow's professor, Laurens Perseus Hickock, shares part of the blame for this German connection.

10 Kant famously said that he was awakened from his dogmatic slumbers by Hume. Almost equally famously, Bertrand Russell quipped in his *History of Western Philosophy* (London: Routledge, 2004) that soon after waking up Kant went back to sleep, lulled by his own philosophical musings.

11 Immanuel Kant, *Critique of Pure Reason* (London: Penguin, 2007), p. 86.

12 To get an idea where Ludlow's work can be placed in the history of philosophy in terms of experience, the reader may want to consult either Martin Jay, *Songs of Experience: Modern American and European Variations on a Universal Theme* (Berkeley: University of California Press, 2005) or, for a more literary approach, Marshall Berman, *All That Is Solid Melts Into Air: The Experience of Modernity* (New York: Simon and Schuster, 1982).

CHAPTER 8

MARIJUANA AND CREATIVITY

Marijuana is associated with many things, ranging from David Chapelle, the munchies, Robert Mitchum, and a way to treat glaucoma. For the senior author, it brings back memories of a classmate in high school who lost a shoe on the roof of a class. He managed to find a ladder and carried it across the quad during lunch, only to stop and eat lunch at one of the tables. An association that more people are likely to have is that marijuana use improves creative performance. Just as athletes (often unethically) use steroid cocktails to improve their performance on the field, so have many artists, musicians, and writers embraced it as a means to improve their creative feats. However, marijuana has also been embraced by people like our neighbors, whose greatest contribution has been lowering the neighborhood's property value with their garbage bag landscaping.

What exactly is the origin of this belief that marijuana use increases creativity? We will provide a historical overview of creativity research, North American drug laws, scientific results from research in the field, and comments on the socially accepted collective feelings about the topic. With this information, the reader will be more informed on the topic and will be able to sort through the controversy.

Early work on creativity often involved more mysticism than science. Divine inspiration reigned, and scholars talked about daemons and muses. The Greeks had quite a sophisticated system worked out with a specific muse for specific types of creativity. For example, if a poet needed to recite an epic poem such as the *Iliad*, he would call upon the assistance of the muse Calliope. However, the approach of the psychological study of creativity took a somewhat different route centering on the self. Early creativity research resulted mostly as a byproduct from work on heredity, intelligence, genius, and madness. Current work took off around the 1950s, when the President of the American Psychological Association, Joy P. Guilford, used the occasion of his presidential address to hype the need for creativity research.

In psychological research the first step is to figure out exactly what is being discussed. In this case, what exactly *is* creativity? How could you measure it? People use the word "creative" to refer to a genius, an outfit, a child, or a painting. Guilford approached this topic by organizing creativity into a larger framework of intelligence. He organized human cognition along three dimensions; of interest to this chapter is the one he called "operations." Operations can be thought of as the mental gymnastics required for any kind of task. A "free runner" practicing *parkour* and maneuvering through a business district, a four-year-old learning addition, and a rapper spontaneously delivering a freestyle spoken word poem, all use mental operations.

One type of mental operation is divergent thinking. This concept is the ability to come up with many novel answers for an open-ended question. For example, we could ask you to list as many different uses for a bottle as possible. Responses are then translated into a score based on four criteria. The first criterion, *fluency*, is just the number of responses produced. The second, *flexibility*, is how many types or categories of ideas are produced. If a list of responses includes "break the bottle" and "smash the bottle on someone's head," these two scores would fit in the same category and count as one. The third criterion, *originality*, is how unique the ideas are. Using a bottle to entertain party guests by suspending it in a corner is a much more novel idea than using a bottle as a weapon in a bar fight. Finally, *elaboration* is a measure of how developed the ideas are. Using a bottle as a musical instrument for a folk band in the post-zombie apocalypse is a much more developed idea than "hit it to make music." Although most psychologists consider creativity to be much more complicated than merely divergent thinking, the ability to generate many novel ideas is nonetheless integral to creativity.

The psychological study of creativity commonly uses the working definition that creativity involves being both original and appropriate to the task at hand. If we were to ask you to solve the math problem $40 + 2 = x$

and you blurt out "*x* equals pistachio," that would not be creative. While pistachio would certainly be an original response, it would not be appropriate to the task at hand. However, if you were to blurt out "the answer to life, the universe, everything," we would give you a thumbs up for being familiar with *Hitchhiker's Guide to the Galaxy* by Douglas Adams.

The scientific research on marijuana comes with a history of restrictions, due to many countries banning it as an illegal substance (including the US). The history of marijuana's control in the US begins in the 1930s when Harry J. Anslinger became the Commissioner of Narcotics in the Bureau of Narcotics. He personally led a campaign portraying marijuana as a substance capable of destroying the motivation of American youth, thereby creating the era of "Reefer Madness." Decades later, during the "War on Drugs," the Controlled Substances Act (CSA) was codified into law by Congress. The CSA is the Federal drug policy of the US which uses a scientific panel to regulate the manufacture, distribution, and possession of controlled substances. The list of controlled substances is divided into different classes. Marijuana belongs to the Schedule I group which includes drugs like LSD, heroin, PCP, and ecstasy. For a drug to belong to the Schedule I group it must have high potential for abuse, no currently accepted medical use, and a lack of accepted safety for use under medical supervision.

Research on Schedule I drugs requires a great deal of registration and communication with the DEA, along with other groups, and is often very restricted. Given this history of restricted access, it may be unsurprising that there is a particularly small amount of actual research on creativity; highbrow types tend to focus on topics that seem more important. The current research on creativity and marijuana often comes from other countries, such as Holland and Canada, whose laws regarding the research and testing of marijuana are less restrictive.

What exactly does the research say about marijuana's effects? Aside from making people hungry, the amount of research on cognitive effects makes the answer a bit controversial. The existing collection of research typically demonstrates that marijuana reduces the ability to learn.[1] A study on heavy marijuana users among college students demonstrated an inability to focus and sustain attention for as long as 24 hours after their last use of the drug.[2] Another study examined former users of at least five years who had been abstinent for at least two years. These people still showed moderate cognitive impairments. These results have led to the controversial hypothesis that long-term heavy use could result in progressive cognitive deficits.[3] Although an exact relationship between

♦ RYAN E. HOLT AND JAMES C. KAUFMAN

long-term use and the length of the lingering deficits has not been concluded, users should be aware that it takes long periods of abstinence to return to normal levels of cognition due to the slow rate of THC (the active psychedelic substance) elimination in the body.

In being creative, it certainly helps to be able to focus and have basic human cognitive abilities. However, what does the research on creativity and marijuana have to say?

The effects of marijuana use on creativity through a divergent thinking task were examined under two experimental conditions: "with marijuana" or "with a placebo."[4] The two groups were given biscuits with or without active THC (we wonder how they arrived at that method of administration, which is at least preferable to a suppository). The results of the study led the researchers to conclude that the use of marijuana did not have any effect on creativity (positive or negative). Whereas the scores between THC-loaded biscuit eaters and the placebo group were not comparably different, the placebo group had slightly higher scores. In other words, the group tripping out on oregano biscuits actually did a tiny bit better on the divergent thinking task, but not enough for the numbers to be statistically different.

Another study piggybacks off of the previous experiment with the same two previous conditions (THC biscuit and non-THC biscuit), along with a third that did not receive any biscuits whatsoever. The researchers also used two groups of participants (novice marijuana users and regular users). The results for the novice group (who at least claimed they never used marijuana before) showed that none of the three conditions had any effect on divergent thinking. For the group of regular users, the people in the placebo condition showed increased fluency, whereas those that ingested THC showed *reduced* fluency and flexibility.[5] In other words, the placebo condition group (the ones that thought they were high) came up with more ideas. The marijuana condition group probably discussed other times that they had been high and forgot what they were supposed to be doing. This study shows a strong expected effect of marijuana – if you think you're high, you're more creative. If you actually are high, you are less creative.

A further interesting finding was that the regular users had lower scores on elaboration than did novices – across *all* conditions. We cannot help but be reminded of the song "Tribute" by Tenacious D, which describes playing the best song in the world without specifically explaining what it is.

It would seem that as a society we accept the cost of creativity to include mental disorders, depression, alcoholism, and drug use. If the rewards of creativity are so great (successful harnessing of AC/DC current,

Impressionist paintings, the first transatlantic plane flight by a woman), then certainly it should cost something (eventual bankruptcy, a lost ear, mysterious disappearance). Some researchers argue that we want this relationship of costs and rewards to exist.[6] Creativity becomes more mysterious, and therefore the burden some people may feel to be creative is removed. In addition, they note that the creativity-drug connection may provide a convenient excuse for adolescents to experiment. Indeed, other researchers studied adolescent explanations for using illicit drugs, and one of the five reasons was to enhance creativity (the other four reasons were belonging, coping, pleasure, and aggression).[7] However, other research has found no correlation among college students between creative personality traits and alcohol, tobacco, and marijuana beliefs and use.[8]

However, there are many examples of music groups that function and thrive with drug use, despite the possible negative effects, and still produce creative products. Gronnerod investigated the use of alcohol and cannabis among amateur rock bands in Finland.[9] While this was not a purely "scientific" study with controlled conditions, it examines the attitudes and beliefs of drug use among amateur rock band members. The interviews conducted seem to shine light on the reasons for drug use while being mediated by a complex mutual understanding. Most bands use marijuana or alcohol together to aid the cohesion of the group by chemically setting everyone in a shared mood. Because most amateurs perform outside of their locale, the move, set up, and performance all require cohesion among the group to pull off a successful show. Experience with this pattern of set up, band member influence, and stage conditions can all modulate the appropriate time for drug use to occur. Whereas drug use certainly influences the behavior of the band (perhaps impeding success, given the risk of addiction and/or overdose), the remaining successful bands are able to make it work. It appears that the main reasons for drug use include mood alteration, group cohesion, and a belief that drugs can boost creativity. Regardless of the consistent research finding that marijuana use does not help (and may hinder) creativity, this association persists in the public eye.

Why does the drug-creativity connection persist? Could the reason for drug use be rooted in social expectancy? Researchers interested in this question gave participants either tonic water or tonic water mixed with vodka, and then (randomly) told them that the drinks were either non-alcoholic or alcoholic. They found no pharmacological effects of alcohol on creativity – but they found a strong placebo effect, indicating that the social expectation of alcohol's effect on creativity is more important than the alcohol itself.[10] Other researchers, in a seven-year study of LSD and

✿ RYAN E. HOLT AND JAMES C. KAUFMAN

artistic creativity, found that artists believed that LSD had improved their perceptions and made a difference in their art – but little aesthetic difference was found in the artwork itself.[11] In addition, it is not uncommon for people who use drugs to use more than one type of drug. This behavior can create unpredictable pharmacological effects. It is hard to conclusively see any relation between a specific drug and creativity outside of a controlled environment.

Even though the existing research mostly points to no effects, the belief of a connection between cannabis and creativity seems to endure. One reason for this association is the idea of the spurious correlation. This idea is that two things may seem to be unrelated, but in fact a third factor causes both things. For example, you may notice that you rarely see attractive people walking around in skimpy clothing during your annual Christmas vacation in Boston. It is possible for you to make the assumption that people do not like being half-naked because Santa may be watching. Much more likely, however, is that people are wearing more clothing because it is freezing cold outside (because it is December, when Christmas occurs). A similar spurious correlation may happen with marijuana and creativity. If you think of people like Cheech and Chong, Jack Black, and Seth Rogan, you may make a connection between marijuana users and people who are creative (and funny). However, a third factor (such as being extroverted, or enjoying partying) may be the underlying cause of both marijuana use and creativity.

In addition, we notice unusual or impressive occurrences. We remember and note well-known pot users Bob Marley and Willie Nelson. They are famous and in the news, and we are more likely to read about them. We are much less likely to hear about Ralph, who takes marijuana every day and keeps writing the same terrible songs. There are no movies celebrating the dancing penguin that wants to dance better and smokes pot – and then dances in the exact same half-assed way. Granted, there are few movies about pot-smoking penguins, period.

Another factor shown by many of the research studies is that people assume drugs such as marijuana will increase their creativity. We would not expect people outside of psychology to diligently read psychological journals each night before going to bed (*we* don't even do that); therefore, most people will not be aware of the actual scientific research. It is unsurprising that this connection persists in most people's minds despite the evidence to the contrary.

Toxicomania is a field that focuses on prevention and intervention by modifying the motivation and beliefs of illicit substance users.

One motivation for using marijuana is the wish to increase creativity. However, it seems reasonable to conclude from the scientific research that any connection between drug use and creativity is largely manufactured in the drug user's mind. The actual creative work is likely not impacted. The spurious correlations and placebo effect will likely continue to support belief in this connection. Our guess is that people will continue assuming that marijuana increases creativity regardless of what the data say – and perhaps it will be this belief (and this belief alone) that may aid their creativity.

NOTES

1 R. I. Block and M. M. Ghoneim, "Effects of Chronic Marijuana Use on Human Cognition," *Psychopharmacology* 110 (1993): 219–28.
2 H. G. Pope, Jr. and D. Yurgelun-Todd, "The Residual Cognitive Effects of Heavy Marijuana Use in College Students," *Journal of the American Medical Association* 275, 7 (1996): 521–7.
3 N. Solowij, *Cannabis and Cognitive Functioning* (Cambridge: Cambridge University Press, 1998).
4 J. R. Tinklenberg, C. F. Darley, W. T. Roth, A. Pferbhaum, and B. S. Koppel, "Marijuana Effects on Associations to Novel Stimuli," *Journal of Nervous and Mental Disease* 166 (1978): 362–4.
5 M. Bourassa and P. Vaugeois, "Effects of Marijuana Use on Divergent Thinking," *Creativity Research Journal* 13, 2 (2001): 411–16.
6 J. A. Plucker and R. Q. Dana, "Alcohol, Tobacco, and Marijuana Use: Relationships to Undergraduate Students' Creative Achievement," *Journal of College Student Development* 39 (1998): 483.
7 J. Novacek, R. Raskin, and R. Hogan, "Why Do Adolescents Use Drugs? Age, Sex, and User Differences," *Journal of Youth and Adolescence* 20 (1991): 475–92.
8 J. Plucker, A. McNeely, and C. Morgan, "Controlled Substance-Related Beliefs and Use: Relationships to Undergraduates' Creativity Personality Traits," *Journal of Creative Behavior* 43 (2009): 94–101.
9 J. S. Gronnerod, "The Use of Alcohol and Cannabis in Non-Professional Rock Bands in Finland," *Journal of Contemporary Drug Problems* 29 (1990): 417–43.
10 W. M. Lapp, R. L. Collins, and C. V. Izzo, "On the Enhancement of Creativity by Alcohol: Pharmacology or Expectation?" *American Journal of Psychology* 107 (1994): 173–206.
11 O. Janiger and M. D. de Rios, "LSD and Creativity," *Journal of Psychoactive Drugs* 21 (1989): 129–34.

CHAPTER 9

NAVIGATING CREATIVE INNER SPACE ON THE INNOCENT PLEASURES OF HASHISH

There was once, my lord, crown of my head, a man in a certain city who was a fisherman by trade and a hashish eater by occupation. Whenever he earned a daily wage, he would spend a bit on food and the rest on a sufficient quantity of that hilarious herb whose extract is hashish. He took the hashish three times a day: once in the morning on an empty stomach, once at noontime, and once at sunset. Thus he never missed being extravagantly happy. Yet he worked quite hard at fishing, though sometimes in a very unusual way.

Tale of the Two Hashish Eaters,
Arabian Nights

Creative Inner Space

A philosopher stoned is not the Philosopher's Stone. I doubt very much that there are distinctive philosophical insights to be gained by smoking pot. If I thought there were, then, as a philosopher, I suppose I might want to get high all the time.

What one derives from cannabis at its best is a sense of experiencing something familiar as though for the first time, occasionally with a strange pulsating halo of significance. This sometimes intensely vivid impression of the newness of something already known leads thought even when it is back down on the ground to consider previously unexplored ways of thinking about old concepts, problems, and propositions in ways suggested by the experience of a good cannabis buzz. New associations may seem to present themselves to consciousness also as though for the first time, or with more apparently profound meanings than otherwise observed. The ideas must naturally be coming from the same mind, so it is as though the straight mind had previously denied these innovations admission to the privileged court of consciousness, until cannabis opens the door. It is easy when you are high to get carried away with the streaming train of ideas, to project one's imagination into many creative endeavors that one might never actually develop the talents to pursue. This is not to say that cannabis cannot be an invaluable ally in expanding and focusing whatever native creativity a person naturally possesses.

I call the feeling of creative potential, real or illusory, anecdotally reported by persons high on marijuana, *creative inner space*. The reason cannabis users speak of getting *high* is that the drug typically delivers the sensation of being partly weightless in space. When you are high, or, as it is also significantly called, spaced, it can sometimes feel as though you are able to mentally explore a previously unsuspected dimension of possible connections and associations between things that for the cannabis user seem entirely new to thought. As unexpected ways of understanding are presented to the imagination, and their peculiar combinations suggest ideas to be exploited in creative work, a cannabis user seeking inspiration can sometimes make productive use of different ways of looking at things that a soaring cannabis high affords. Some persons who like to get high on cannabis do so specifically for the sake of experiencing the impression that the drug frees them from the inhibitions that can straitjacket ordinary creativity.

There need not be scientific support for the existence of creative inner space. The whole idea after all is that creative inner space is no more than a projection of the imagination by persons high on cannabis. It should be enough if a number of cannabis users report a similar kind of experience, or if testimony about the alleged creativity-enhancing effects of cannabis can most plausibly be accounted for by making reference to what cannabis users have reported as their attention being directed inward to creativity-challenging problems in which new possibilities can be explored with more focused concentration. The result at some stage of the creative process of allowing one's thoughts to maneuver within a cannabis-induced creative inner space of unscripted associations might then be judged to satisfy ordinary expectations of the concept of creativity enhancement. The test is not necessarily whether a subject does something brilliantly creative when high on the good stuff, but at any point in the ongoing creative process that can plausibly be credited to cannabis as one of a number of background causes. If cannabis plays any role at all in helping to produce more creativity than would otherwise exist, even if it does not always work its enchantment immediately when a subject is high, then it can be properly described as a creativity enhancer, which is all that advocates of its creative virtues have ever proposed.

O True Apothecary! A Votary to Fond Desire

William Shakespeare might have smoked cannabis for precisely such purposes. If we are to believe the recent investigations of South African scientists Frances Thackery and Nick van der Werfe, reported by the BBC on November 5, 2000, then Shakespeare's house back in the seventeenth century was probably the scene of some joyful clandestine puffing.

Thackery and van der Werfe requested police laboratories to check two dozen clay pipe fragments found in the garden by Shakespeare's still-standing house in Stratford-upon-Avon, and discovered by means of gas chromatography that eight of the pipe fragments showed evidence of cannabis residue. Another three revealed detectable amounts of cocaine, which must have been rare at the time, fresh from unprecedented botanical discoveries in the New World. That there were pipes in Shakespeare's garden laden with cannabis residue clearly does not imply that Shakespeare himself used them, nor that anyone did so with the intention of getting high. Shakespeare in his day, however, cannabis or no, besides being a successful business entrepeneur and devoted family man, was a hip guy who moved in some interesting Bohemian circles. So it's not improbable that he might have had the opportunity of learning about cannabis and enjoyed getting high, and that he might have even believed its use to be creativity-enhancing in his own writing.

The work of literature, especially of Shakespeare's caliber, remains a matter of natural talent, determination, and hard effort that no psychoactive substance can magically replace. The composition of a play or sonnet, novel, short story, or the like, as with any written document, is the result of a complex process of back and forth reading, writing, criticizing, improving, and finalizing, not all of which stages can be profitably managed by an author persistently high on cannabis. A writer like Shakespeare with his gifts might nevertheless learn how to exploit the virtues and avoid the vices of cannabis to the greater profit of certain aspects of his personal creative process. As with other distinguished dopers, the experts for the most part do not want to imagine Shakespeare writing any of his theatrical inventions high. The evidence in support of the claim in any case is somewhat sketchy and circumstantial. Moreover, it doesn't change a thing about how Shakespeare's work is interpreted, performed, or appreciated to think that he might have smoked cannabis during some part of his creative activity. Chris Bennet, in *Cannabis Culture: Marijuana Magazine*, nevertheless exposes the squeamishness of Shakespeare scholars to acknowledge that the Bard might have smoked up for any but quasi-respectable medicinal purposes. "As could be expected," Bennet states,

> this information was not easily accepted in Shakespearian academic circles. Georgianna Ziegler, head of reference for the Folger Shakespeare Library in Washington, said scholars had no proof Shakespeare actually enjoyed toking up. "I'm not saying that Shakespeare would never have drunk, or eaten, or smoked marijuana, because it was used as a medical remedy at the time. But we have no evidence that he ever used it for pleasure."[1]

The thing is, no one denies that smoking marijuana is often pleasurable, so apparently we are to imagine that Shakespeare in all his solemn virtue smoked cannabis despite or with sublime indifference to its psychoactive effects. CNN was more forthright in its report of March 1, 2001, provocatively if less knowledgeably titled, "Drugs Clue to Shakespeare's Genius."[2] There may even be collaborative textual evidence that Shakespeare smoked cannabis for shits and giggles, and possibly even for literary inspiration, given his cryptic description in Sonnet 76 of finding "invention in a noted weed."[3]

Despite the lack of a literally smoking gun indicating that Shakespeare liked getting high as part of his creative work, the stigma that seems to attach to the use of cannabis and the embarrassment that many of Shakespeare's serious admirers have for any suggested association of the poet with marijuana is itself a topic deserving of philosophical reflection. It is as though if Shakespeare smoked pot then something is somehow taken away from his enormous contributions to world literature. Who would say this kind of thing if the Stratford Bard had preferred to limber up the creative juices like Ernest Hemingway with a vodka and tonic or rum and Coke? There would be no controversy surrounding the fact if broken liquor bottles had been found on the Shakespeare estate, except as testimony to how the poet may have spent some of his leisure time.

With cannabis the attitude is markedly different. If you are high and you write, then the writing must not come from you but from the dope. Could anything outside of anti-drug law enforcement bureaucracy be more naïve? The anti-marijuana forces don't want people to believe it, because logically it implies that marijuana has the potential for good things, such as the collected masterpieces of William Shakespeare. Nor, fie upon them, would Shakespeare be alone among revered artists using cannabis in their private moments and in a variety of ways when practicing their trade. Scores of writers and artists have done so, and while some, like Shakespeare, as has been conjectured, were virtually silent about their use, possibly for fear of being associated in the seventeenth century with witchcraft, others in later times, including François Rabelais, Alexander Dumas, Gerard de Nerval, Victor Hugo, Honoré de Balzac, Ferdinand Boissard, Charles Baudelaire, Edgar Allan Poe, Eugene Delacroix, William Butler Yeats, Arthur Rimbaud, Allen Ginsberg, Jack Kerouac, and Paul Bowles, among numerous others, enthusiastically used cannabis and openly proclaimed its virtues for their own pursuit of literary fine art. It doesn't take anything away from Shakespeare to consider that he might have sometimes worked high, just as it doesn't take anything away from the accomplishments of Jack London or Charles Bukowski to consider the role of alcohol in their lives and writings. If Shakespeare smoked up now and then, he merely joins a distinguished club of cannabis connoisseurs of artistic and philosophical disposition who have found the drug beneficial in their life and work. Would it be so surprising, then, for later readers such as ourselves to take pleasure in works that were created at least in part under the influence of this beguiling natural-substance-induced cerebral holiday?

Philosophers Gaining Altitude

It is hard but not impossible to imagine philosophers getting high much of the time. Given the statistics for worldwide soft drug use, it is not far-fetched to suppose that some philosophers get high, and even that some do so at one point or another during the complex process of identifying and reflecting on philosophical problems, as an aid in their work.

Philosophy needs to be interested in cannabis for other, more important, reasons, because of interesting but generally neglected problems of metaphysics, phenomenology, theory of knowledge, ethics and aesthetics, philosophy of law, and philosophical social activism, each of which is related in its own way to understanding the neurochemical and cognitive psychology of cannabis and the ethics of cannabis use under legislative prohibition.

The partnership between cannabis and philosophy is complex. It is not as though by smoking a little reefer a philosopher will suddenly have deep philosophical concepts revealed that can afterward be successfully applied in sober philosophical problem-solving. I seriously doubt that smoking marijuana offers a unique mind-opening road to important philosophical truths that cannot otherwise or at least as easily be discovered thinking straight. At least I have not credibly heard anecdotally about such incidents; although, again, it is only wise to remain open-minded. The deepest explicitly dope-related philosophical insight that I've ever encountered is owing to Freewheelin' Frank of the Fabulous Furry Freak Brothers in Gilbert Shelton's classic underground comics, when Frank sagely remarks: "Dope will get you through times of no money better than money will get you through times of no dope." I think, on the contrary, that regular cannabis use must eventually obscure the truth even as it wastes time for more serious study, at least where the effort to clarify and resolve technical problems in philosophy is concerned. If a philosopher gets high it is not to enter an otherwise locked vault of valuable philosophical treasures that will stand the essential test of criticism once they are reconsidered in the light of day. It is at most to snatch a little respite for overworked synapses, in the course of which, just as during an afternoon at the beach or an evening at the philharmonic, philosophical ideas might arise through the release of more uninhibited patterns of association, letting go of one's ordinary conscious constraints and opening the imagination to ideas that might otherwise be blocked by a censorious narrow-minded intellectual super-ego.

That said, there are many other ways to waste time, and we usually manage to trash about the same amount all told in different ways. Some people get high, others watch sports or surf endlessly on the Internet from topic to random topic. Some people get high *and* watch sports *and* surf endlessly on the Internet. Responsible cannabis use implies among other things that one ingests the substance only when there is approximately the same proportionate span of time as would equally be available to while away with alcohol or sports TV or the Internet. Can a responsible

DALE JACQUETTE

adult get high and do anything more interesting than watch TV or surf the Internet? Many creative persons enjoy marijuana and may report that they see, understand, and appreciate things differently when they are high that they can also use later in pursuing their normal straight activities and professional work. To some it might feel that cannabis is itself a releasing source of creative new ideas or at least an aid to creativity, as the drug sometimes intensifies and sometimes dulls other experiences, both cerebral and sensual. I have it on good authority in any case that time spent high is not subtracted from the sum total of one's life. Getting chalked now and then allows the user to be reflective in a way that feels different from straight thinking and seems to result in different conclusions because it permits thought to entertain many more combinations of ideas that straight thinking typically inhibits. Some of these are made vividly hilarious, and some of them vividly frightening, from whence results the stereotypical comic-tragic extremes of laughing at nothing and languishing in occasional waves of acute cannabis-induced paranoia.

What knowledgeable person disputes that occasional and in other ways socially responsible cannabis use is relatively harmless fun? It is clear then that either the user breaking the law or the law itself must be morally wrong. You watch a movie or listen to music, you have a passionate if not always legible conversation, you pursue your amateur hobbies with a special zest, and in any case you don't hurt anybody. Some users find that getting high is better appreciated when you return to it briefly again after significant periods of abstinence, others shine a bowl more regularly whenever they possibly can. Artists and truth-seekers of many kinds are obviously among those who use cannabis for recreational purposes, and they have sometimes expressed what might be described as a creative debt to the drug. The reports of users from the field frequently remark an experience in which obstacles to normal aesthetic appreciation, inspiration, spiritual exploration, and other cognitive experiences are lifted above the ordinary.

You have to experience that rush for yourself with cannabis singing in your veins in order to understand what is meant by being high. Once you have gotten lit, you can at least begin to formulate an educated opinion about whether or not cannabis could be a chemical ally in the philosopher's search for truth. Where is such an admission likely to lead? How, exactly, might cannabis contribute to advancing any of the established purposes of philosophy? When you are high it might feel vibrantly that the content and direction of philosophical reflection, and the occurrence of "new ideas" of which poetic and artistic users frequently speak, are the result of distinctively cannabis-induced or cannabis-altered patterns of thought. Those bright if short-lived bursts of enthusiasm do not ultimately sustain their stoned promised value, say, when the thinker of the cannabis-derived new idea comes down later and looks more critically at the results. The happy toker's opinion of cannabis-influenced ideation and later afterthought are often diametrically opposed, and when they are not, it is hard to know whether or not it is simply accidental. It is a cliché to feel chagrined after writing down one's "brilliant" ideas during the peak of a cannabis high, surrounded with a kind of glow of discovery and penetration into hidden truths, that what cannabis has delivered to introspection is generally devoid of genuine interest or even intelligibility in the sobering aftermath. The truth is that you think a lot of crap when you're high, just as you often do when you're straight, no matter how revelatory the flood of ideas may seem at the time. Can there be exceptions to the false impression of stoned insight? As a logical matter, yes, of course. And there are other ways in which cannabis can potentially assist creative persons in achieving works of art and intellect.

The difficulty epistemically is in trying to separate the multiple psychological effects of cannabis from those that might be said to contribute something special and distinctive to creative processes that could not equally be set free by a drug-free walk in the woods or soak in the tub. There is a lot more hard work to making worthwhile progress in philosophy than blowing dope and entering a cannabis-altered state of consciousness hoping for interesting ideas to present themselves. Aside from the joy and relaxation of getting a little high, there is no royal road to philosophical insight, and drugs can make things more difficult rather than lubricating the journey.

Insight and Delusion

This is not to say that a good synaptic retreat cannot contribute to creativity. Cannabis might even work such an effect quite frequently and reliably for certain persons. The evidence, however, is equivocal and unscientific at best. It does not allow us very easily to sort out the generally pleasurable cannabis high experienced by a creative person from whatever contribution cannabis might hypothetically be making to the creative mind's production of new worthwhile ideas.

As Allen Ginsberg famously remarks in his 1966 *Atlantic Monthly* essay, "The Great Marijuana Hoax: The First Manifesto to End the Bringdown":

> Marijuana is a useful catalyst for specific optical and aural aesthetic perceptions. I apprehended the structure of certain pieces of jazz and classical music in a new manner under the influence of marijuana, and these apprehensions have remained valid in years of normal consciousness.[4]

No doubt Ginsberg experienced something special listening to music high. The enhancing of and concentrated attention on a proportionately intensified pleasure, sensual or mathematical, has long been recognized as one of the drug's most attractive virtues. Perhaps marijuana allowed Ginsberg to appreciate aspects of musical structure that had otherwise remained concealed. It is interesting to see that Ginsberg in this connection makes a special point of emphasizing that experiencing music high offered insights that he continued to consider valid long after the effects of cannabis had passed. There is a recognition in this fact that so often what appears to the cannabis user as a worthwhile truth must later be dismissed as illusory. What is important for Ginsberg is his belief that cannabis enabled him to get hold of something whose value persisted even when he had come back down.

Regrettably, Ginsberg does not help us to better understand exactly what he thought he had learned. He does not, in the first place, explain whatever he means, straight or high, by *apprehending the structure* of jazz and classical compositions and arrangements, or what it is he apprehended that he thinks he otherwise would not have understood. If, a philosophical dilemma goes, Ginsberg just means what he would normally intend by apprehending a musical structure in the same sense that is meant when doing so straight, but in a new way, then there is nothing necessarily special, nothing distinctively cannabis-related, about apprehending musical structure while under the influence of marijuana. It just so happens that he caught sight of something interesting about music when he was high that he later thought retained its parcel of truth. Perhaps Ginsberg assumes that he would not have been as likely to happen upon such an apprehension of musical structure had he not been high merely because the insights happened to occur to him when he was flying. What we need to know in order to place more confidence in his conclusions, and Ginsberg as poet has no obligation to provide such assistance, is whether he repeated the experiment with different pieces of music. If he did, and found new intuitions into musical structure each time he made the experiment, then it would be interesting further to know if Ginsberg also apprehended the structure of the same music in the same way, new relative only to his straight conscious grasp of the structure. Or, if his experience was entirely new, whether his ideas were different relative even to his other previous high musical experiences. If, on the other hand, Ginsberg means something other than what is ordinarily meant by apprehending musical structure among persons who are not high on cannabis, then we will be rather at a loss to understand what he experienced and what is trying to say about it, even if we all get gloriously frosted ourselves listening to the same music as Ginsberg and compare notes afterward.

The problem for phenomenology as descriptive philosophical psychology is how to distinguish the enthusiasm users express for the effects of cannabis on their creative artistic and spiritual quests, the glow that metaphorically haloes high thinking, and the convictions that they would not have attained such creative and appreciative insights were it not for the effects of cannabis. How are we to know that such thoughts might not have occurred to the same thinker without the benefit of cannabis, lacking only the all-too-often misplaced cannabis-induced excitement, the false optimism and fanfare over trivial or in other ways simply dumb and absurdly overestimated and over-stated ideas that pass as profound insights only as long as the buzz lasts? It can be eye-opening to see how different high impressions of explanatory and aesthetic value can be not only from the standpoint of straight consciousness, but also from high consciousness about the same ideas on different occasions. An experienced cannabis user understands all this and develops a fondness for the excesses that come with being high, trying to avoid confusing the two.

I think it is only fair, then, that I should offer something concrete by way of my personal more recent experiences with cannabis. I performed the following experiment trying in cannabis-tolerant social surroundings to see and record whatever of creative interest might occur to me under the influence of hashish. Here is the result, which I present unedited for the sake of providing specific anecdotal data for reflection. The result, I am sure the reader will agree, is not too impressive, reinforcing my general point about the inefficacy of cannabis for creative work in philosophy. Note first that none of my own work is in Eastern philosophy, although I know something about its art, which I greatly admire, especially in classical Buddhist and Hindu traditions. I should mention also at the outset that there is a small reclining figure of Ganesha-sri on my coffee table,

❦   DALE JACQUETTE

holding a tiny television remote control in one hand. What I wrote in my notebook on the occasion I now reproduce here, the only thing of interest I jotted down on the occasion, that may have been indirectly inspired by this household idol:

> Ganesha is a great starter god; the Ronald McDonald of Hinduism. Yet he also has a dark and almost lascivious sensuous side. Well, why not? He's half-man, half-elephant (perhaps the percentages are more like forty-sixty or even thirty-seventy), or at least a man turned into an elephant. What would that be like? He reads books and plays the flute. He eats sweets from a bowl. He meditates and dances with unexpected grace, while his consort the wily rat dashes about trying to avoid those monstrous padded feet. Unlike Brahma, Shiva and Vishnu, Ganesha enjoys a good-natured laugh; yet he is also a serious scholar and an iconic patron deity of scholars. He is sometimes carved or cast in bronze writing out the epics of the Mahabharata with a piece of his own broken tusk. As such, he makes a brilliant introduction to the Hindu pantheon. A joyful but moody, literate and indulgent down-to-earth god, a lot more like the best of ordinary people – if you overlook the fact that most ordinary people are not half-pachydermal divinities. Ganesha makes you wonder what it would be like to create a godlike person out of the best of ordinary people's best parts, and hence to wonder what parts to choose and who seems to have them, seeking a trailhead also for oneself among the crisscrossing paths to perfection.

Life, Liberty, and the Pursuit of Cannabis

It's fun indeed to blow a joint when you have nothing more important to do. Watching *The Mighty Boosh*, or listening to Tabla Beat Science or Nusrat Fateh Ali Khan, absorbing each note as though hearing it for the first time with especially sharp attention, or reading and rereading a particularly enigmatic passage in Djuna Barnes, or, say, Plato's dialogues.

For the sake of such relatively innocent pleasures alone, one would think that the basic human right of pursuing happiness promised in the Declaration of Independence would include smoking cannabis. In the US, this would only be in keeping with the ideals of the eighteenth century Enlightenment founders of the American republic, cultivating weed on their own plantations as at least both George Washington and Thomas Jefferson are believed to have done for medicinal, recreational, or some other, spiritual or philosophical, purposes. Nor is it likely that Benjamin Franklin was unaware of cannabis and just said no to the evil weed, since it is known that he started America's first hemp paper mill, on which, ironically, original copies of the Declaration of Independence proclaiming the political ideals of a natural right to life, liberty, and the pursuit of happiness, were transcribed. Would the endlessly curious, pipe-smoking Franklin who mastered electricity for the new world not also have wondered about the interesting cones of flowers topping off the next standing crop of hemp newsprint basking in the sunshine? Should Franklin Washington, Jefferson, and who knows how many others in the early days of the American adventure have gone to jail?

No, a critic of the patriotic cannabis argument will always say. All that is necessary for logical consistency is to deny the argument's key assumption. For back then there was no law against marijuana, and now there is. Would those great leaders have broken the law? Of course not. True, they broke many laws against the British in waging the revolution. They wanted intelligent, sensible, locally answerable government, and they were prepared to take action against whatever existent rule they deemed unjust. These were the mature, educated, and accomplished gentlemen who founded the United States of America. Why would Washington and the others have gone against the laws instituted by a representative democratic government for the sake of getting high? We should suppose instead that if there had been a law against cannabis cultivation, sale, or use, which there was not in the United States until 1937, the founding fathers would have strictly observed the law's letter and intent, and, out of respect for the law, not illegally grown pot for any purpose – which, finally, as far as the historical record proves, was not necessarily recreational even in part.

The objection has a certain force, but manages entirely to miss the point of cannabis patriotism. The argument is not that whatever the founding fathers did in their time and circumstances is something we should also do, although as a nation Americans could probably take a few pointers. The claim is rather that it is a violation of the principle encoded in the Declaration of Independence, and presumably appreciated more globally, that people should be allowed to live their lives in pursuit of whatever they conceive to be their individual happiness without governmental interference, provided that in doing so they are not harming others. The same rationale that tolerates and in many instances even promotes alcohol consumption, that subsidizes tobacco growing from the public purse, should also tolerate cannabis, on pain

DALE JACQUETTE

of legal and social hypocrisy. If smoking a little dope contributes to your happiness, and if you're not hurting anybody including yourself in doing so, no more than you would by any other legal but private pursuits of a free person, if you behave responsibly when you are enjoying a high, as you have to do anyway, and which is less of a problem for persons high on cannabis than under the influence of alcohol and many other drugs, then the law should have no objection and there should be no enforcement of cannabis prohibition in a progressive free society.

That might be how things should be, but certainly not how they are. Or, is it rather that most of the most powerful industrialized democracies who most actively enforce anti-marijuana legislation, the United States, France, and Sweden, are not actually all that progressive or free? When you cut through the hype that most societies emerging as nations in the nineteenth century still like to project about themselves as promoting freedom and the just rule of law, how many have actually exercised wise judicial discretion by refraining from legally harassing their own otherwise law-abiding domestic marijuana users? People's lives are ruined because, despite aggressive law enforcement, they choose the desirable effects of these naturally occurring resinous flowering buds over the risk that they will actually suffer under the law. In doing so, they experience only a relatively harmless indulgence for responsible adults. In an obvious sense this is their risk and their fault, assuming they should have known the law. Reflecting on the plain facts of cannabis prohibition, it does not seem much like the policy of an enlightened and compassionate, or even frugal and prudent society with a developed sense of its own rational self-interest.

The reality of the situation remains that anyone who smokes a joint outside of the Netherlands and a few other high tolerance zones very seriously risks arrest, conviction, a criminal record, and incarceration. It is the kind of thing, for example, that could seriously screw up a promising professional career, not to mention a marriage and family life, and everything else of value available to a person who is not rotting in jail. Encouraging legalized cultivation at least by individuals at home for recreational, ritual, and medicinal purposes should also further open the door to the unlimited commercial and market potential for hemp products, much of which is currently grown from materially inferior non-psychoactive stock. The extensive farming of hemp, what Martin Booth, in his invaluable 2003 study, *Cannabis: A History*, calls "the fragrant cane," would be an economic boon to many societies in multiple ways, and countries that otherwise grow coca and opium might well be persuaded to trade in their hard drug agriculture for cannabis.[5] I'm sure at the same time that cannabis can be used to make excellent chocolate. To produce green-power liquid fuels for the airline industry, affordable lightweight bulletproof plastics, and a kind of shampoo that's gentler on your hair and better for the environment. Conceivably, I could think of even more marvelous applications if I weren't already stoned out of my tits. Chocolate, for example, might be improved by cannabis in at least two ways – by mixing it in with the other dull ingredients for added flavor and texture, or by smoking it before you eat the otherwise untouched chocolate just as it comes from the box. A truly versatile bit of botany for the future of humankind, and one that we should be embracing as though it were a gift from the gods rather than allowing the DEA to set fire to piles of it in the middle of the emerald fields they decimate.

The scientific evidence, which governments keep paying for only to ignore, is that cannabis is not a gateway drug, that it is not addictive, that it offers considerable health benefits and only minimal health risks, and that its users are not prone to acts of violence or other misbehavior. Here are some of the facts about the social impact of the battle against the bong compiled by an extra-governmental fact-finder. According to a recent 2007 study by Jon Gettman, marijuana reform activist and leader of the Coalition for Rescheduling Cannabis, the United States alone spends $42 billion per year in the effort to control cannabis. This breaks down to $10.7 billion on law enforcement and $31.1 billion in lost tax revenues. In recent times in the US, there have been as many as 829,627 yearly marijuana arrests, which means in effect that one American is arrested on a marijuana bust every 38 seconds.[6]

It all adds up to a lot of unnecessary misery. When one thinks about other worthwhile social expenditures, including education, healthcare, telecommunications infrastructure, public transportation, national security, and the legitimate battle against terrorism, the loss is truly appalling. When you visit the Netherlands you find some people peacefully choosing to enjoy marijuana or hashish without causing disturbances or committing the kinds of outrages associated with alcohol or hard drug intake, and you also find a society with excellent education, public healthcare, transportation services, and numerous other social amenities, a considerable part of which is paid for these days by taxing the cannabis industry. Cannabis, like prostitution, is tolerated under Dutch tax law as an "immoral" business, which, according to the Dutch Finance Ministry, generated about $600 million in tax revenue in 2008, as reported by the

Netherlands Information Service. In the meantime, the Netherlands enjoys one of the lowest percentages of violent crime and problem drug abuse in all of Europe.

And it's quite good shit. You know what you're buying there, choosing from a menu, and it's all up front. No sleazy dealers to negotiate with, no sliding a folded banknote across a park bench and looking over your shoulder as you scarf up a plastic bag of God knows what kind, freshness, or purity level of dope, and then try to restrain an anxiety attack creeping up as you exit the crime scene. Since there are estimated to be about 100 million regular cannabis users in the United States, and since with few exceptions they cannot obtain the substance legally, there has flourished a criminal supply chain that is believed to involve more than $113 billion annually in unregulated, untaxed, illegal marijuana trade, allowing violent organized crime to gain further footholds in the economy and in the social fabric more generally, precisely as it did during the roaring 1920s under the disastrous years of alcohol prohibition. If one didn't know better, one would almost think that it was the smug lawmakers who were high as a kite, although I suspect they would all be capable of better, more responsible judgment if they toked up a little now and then, instead of downing their bourbon and branch water, sharing a more relaxed perspective with what statistics show are approximately one out of three of their constituents.

If one day cannabis is finally legalized, there will presumably be next to nothing more to talk about on the subject than cannabis gourmandise, quality, availability, and price. And that is precisely how it should be. Cannabis need be no different in this respect than fine wine, cheese, chocolate, or caviar – a hedonistic indulgence like any other, extravagance or necessity, depending on one's point of view, for responsible discerning free adults who can afford the luxury of experimenting with consciousness by bending their cognitive states a little out of their ordinary all-too-familiar shape, and learning to appreciate the difference.

NOTES

1   Chris Bennet, in *Cannabis Culture: Marijuana Magazine* (June 13, 2001); available online at www.cannabisculture.com/articles/1943.html.
2   Available online at www.europe.cnn.com/2001/WORLD/europe/UK/03/01/shakespeare.cannabis.
3   William Shakespeare, *Shakespeare's Sonnets and A Lover's Complaint*, ed. Stanley Wells (Oxford: Oxford University Press, 1985), Sonnet 76, p. 90:

"Why is my verse so barren of new pride, / So far from variation or quick change? / Why, with the time, do I not glance aside / To new-found methods and to compounds strange? / Why write I still all one, ever the same, / And keep invention in a noted weed . . ."

4 Allen Ginsberg, "The Great Marijuana Hoax: First Manifesto to End the Bringdown," *Atlantic Monthly* 218, 5 (1966); reprinted in David Solomon (ed.) *Marijuana Papers* (New York: Bobbs-Merrill, 1969), p. 196.
5 Martin Booth, *Cannabis: A History* (New York: Bantam, 2004), pp. 15–34.
6 Jon Gettman, "Lost Taxes and Other Costs of Marijuana Laws," *Bulletin of Cannabis Reform* (2007): 1–37.

PART IV

PSYCHO-SOCIOLOGICAL DIMENSIONS OF CANNABIS CULTURE

The term "getting stoned" is confusing; it implies losing consciousness, rather than a higher awareness. But getting dulled has nothing to do with the psychedelic experience; using marijuana is more like what happens when a person with fuzzy vision puts on glasses. Listening to a familiar piece of music, such as a Bach orchestral suite, the mind is newly conscious of the bass line; listening to a conversation, the mind is more aware of the nuances of each voice. Music assumes shapes and comes out into the room, it is so vivid and so tangible. Grass is a subtle and delicate experience, an educated experience (one that has to be learned), and it is not too different from the heightened awareness that an unusually sensitive or artistic person has. . . . Used continually and to excess, drugs become a factor that dulls consciousness. They diminish awareness, cut off reality, and separate people from human contacts. Perhaps their greatest affirmative significance is to provide an initial breakthrough, a shattering of the euphoria and mythology of the Corporate State, a beginning of a new way of thinking. In the long run, they are not enough to support a new consciousness, and they may eventually become yet another bar to reality.

Charles A. Reich, *The Greening of America*, 1970

CHAPTER 10

CANNABIS AND THE CULTURE OF ALIENATION

Domain of Consciousness

The joy of smoking, eating, drinking, or otherwise ingesting cannabis consists in getting high. Yet what exactly does this mean – that is, to get *high*? Millions around the world who partake in the ganja (as it is known in India), either leisurely or in the face of the law, are intimately acquainted with the euphoric affects of cannabis and understand, at least experientially, what it means to get high; while other readers, having neither the opportunity nor the will, are more likely to be familiar with a number of caricatures for the experience. No matter how familiar you might be with the phenomenon of getting high, I would like to suggest that there is something rather mysterious about the culture of getting high – something that neither the experience itself nor a parallel caricature of the experience can capture.

Philosophically, by thinking about cannabis use in the Western world, notably in Western Europe and North America, we can imitate a discussion about the merits of our culture in general. When one thinks about the experience of "getting high" one is likely to think about the light-headedness cannabis induces, its euphoric daze, the laughter it incites, or the forgetfulness that affects some of its users. In order to fully grasp the meaning that stands behind the experience and situate its philosophical importance, we need to juxtapose it with our ordinary experience.

Philosophers are fond of saying that we have no concept of hot without the corollary concept of cold, that an awareness of the color black requires a familiarity with whiteness, and so on, such that in order to understand a phenomenon one needs to think about the binary opposites that help in defining a particular experience. In like fashion, if we want to understand what "getting high" means, we need to consider the opposite experience: what it means *not* to be high. In many ways, we shall see that "getting high" is a particular form of cultural and even philosophical resistance to ways of thinking that are indicative of the mainstream status quo. Furthermore, by investigating and distinguishing the relationship between a high experience of the world with one that is not, we shall discover that our everyday sobriety is not so innocuous as we might be led to believe.

First of all, consider what the phrase "getting high" literally means: to rise up, to stand above, to elevate, and so on; such that the very "lingo" of cannabis culture implies the possibility of an experience that is in some remote fashion transcendental. Whenever you see the word "transcendental" in a philosophy paper you should raise an eyebrow – for to speak of the transcendental is to enter into metaphysical terrain. Metaphysics, for those unfamiliar with the subject, can be summed up as essentially the study of what must necessarily be the case such that the physical world we see and live in is constituted as it is. Interestingly, the poet Allen Ginsberg calls cannabis the metaphysical herb.[1] As you can see, we have already begun to enter into a conversation that sounds obscurely philosophical. The task of philosophy, however, is not to offer up obscure and opaque ideas for understanding the world, but rather to bring what is obscure and opaque into the fresh light of inquiry. So, what gets transcended in the experience? My father, himself having been a hippie from the 1960s, once told me that in some sense the world seemed more real when smoking cannabis and that truth could more readily be perceived than it was ordinarily. Yet how queer is that? What could possibly account for this sort of intuition? Indeed, I think you shall see that there are many aspects of modern culture that invisibly recede into a background of normalcy, but that when reflected upon reveal startling features that ought to engender our resistance. Cannabis is a critical expedient for articulating a cultural diagnosis that, among other things, helps us to see our own society anew.

Of course, "getting high" is as old as the hills and people have been smoking ganja, as it were, for millennia. Historians tell us that cannabis has been used for spiritual, medicinal, and recreational purposes for generations, perhaps even dating back to the Neolithic epoch. The Ancient

Greek historian Herodotus records in his *Histories* that cannabis smoke was used for burial purposes by the Scythian people, for getting drunk,[2] and even bathing. In the second century AD cannabis was used for medicinal purposes in China[3] as well as in the ancient rituals of the Assyrians, Babylonians, and Palestinian peoples. Cannabis has been known by a slew of different names: charas, dagga, hasish, ganja, pot, weed, kanebosm, marijuana, kancga, kif, zamal, and others. Whatever the designation, the historical evidence is clear that cannabis is neither new nor has it always been viewed with such cultural suspicion and disputation.

Intriguingly, given that cannabis has figured in so many spiritual practices throughout history, we can begin to formulate a sense of the transcendental dimension to which "getting high" must refer. That is, "getting high" must in some sense refer to the ability to step outside or beyond one's normal state of consciousness and familiarity with the world. Such shifts in "consciousness" need not be linked with marijuana alone. For thousands of years, Buddhists and even Hindus have been training successive generations in meditative techniques which alter the normal flow of consciousness. Zen Master Thich Nhat Hanh is famous for teaching breathing meditations that aim to elevate one's consciousness from out of the ordinary drudgery of modern life. Perhaps one could think of marijuana as a chemical expedient for manifesting such shifts in spiritual and meditative consciousness. In his classic essay, "The Great Marijuana Hoax," Allen Ginsberg tells us that:

> the marijuana consciousness is one that, ever so gently, shifts the center of attention *from* habitual shallow, purely verbal guidelines and repetitive secondhand ideological interpretations of experience to *more direct, slower, absorbing, occasionally microscopically minute engagement with sensing phenomena.*[4]

Ginsberg suggests that cannabis consciousness can be distinguished from ordinary consciousness insofar as it enables one to rise above shallow, ideological, and routinely habitual forms of thinking. Cannabis ruptures the ordinary; it pulls one into the immediacy of experience where the world becomes a thing that is present to consciousness. While we may not be apt to admit it, the lives of most people on most days are rather routine, organized, and unreflective. When I wake up for work in the morning, everything is where I expect it to be, and I discover no need to rethink my life or radically reevaluate my choices. What cannabis ruptures, albeit temporarily, is the ordinary unreflective attitude in which I uncritically accept the world and my assumptions about that world as they are, as given. An interesting way for thinking about this sort of rupture in consciousness is to consider the novice art student. For some years I taught basic painting and drawing and invariably I was faced with the same task again and again: when a new student sits down for the first time to draw a scene or model in an art class, the first drawings are almost always horrible because beginning students tend to draw what they *think* they see rather than what they actually do see. Instead of drawing the shapes of dark and light which envelop and reveal the model's body, for example, my students would draw what they thought the model *should* look like. The task, however, was never to draw the figure of the model, but to draw what is actually seen, allowing the figure of the model to reveal herself. Another example would be to consider the color of a wall. As you sit reading this, look up and ask yourself what the colour of the wall is. Surely, you will be inclined at first to say that it is such and such color, red for instance. But if you take the time to actually inspect the colors that are before your eyes, you will see that the walls around you are actually a variety of colors and shades. Under the lamp, the red wall is actually orange; at the corner where the ceiling meets the wall, what I at first perceived as red is actually a dark maroon color; and where the sun reflects off the wall I actually see white, and so on. A good painter is attentive to both *what is seen* as well as *the idea of the seen*. Simply by attending to your experience in detail you will discover this distinction. The trick is to see that in many ways our ordinary experience is one which presumes the world and does not see it in all of its immediacy, presence, and richness. Ganja, by contrast, pulls one toward a radical reevaluation of the sensible world in which things that are always present are suddenly discovered as overflowing with meaning. To some degree, it is this sudden abundance of meaningfulness that I think corresponds to the feeling of getting high. Provisionally speaking, then, we can say that what cannabis allows us to transcend is an ordinary type of consciousness that inattentively prefigures and presumes the world as a totality according to a matrix of familiarity. But what sort of matrix is this that structures our experience of the world? Is it legitimate? Should it be resisted? What we have raised here is the preeminent question of cultural philosophy; that is, this is the question of *consciousness*.

Philosophers have debated and theorized about consciousness for centuries. Right up to this day, philosophers are mulling over about what it means to be conscious of anything and what sort of mental equipment must be in place so as to account for such an ordinary and yet fantastically complicated fact of waking life. They have distinguished a multiplicity

❋ MARK THORSBY

of types of conscious experience: from transitive consciousness, to creature consciousness, state consciousness, reflective consciousness, self-consciousness, or even political consciousness. In order to articulate what we mean here by consciousness, let us consider the etymology or history of the word itself.

"Consciousness," coming from "conscious," is derived from the Latin *conscius*, which means knowing or awareness. Morphologically, the word is a conjunction of the Latin *con-* which means to put together and the Latin *sci-* (as in *scire*) which means to know. From these same roots we get such words as *sci*ence, dis*ci*pline, *con*templation, *con*catenation, etc. So etymologically, we could rewrite the word "consciousness" as *together-knowing*, where the basic idea is that consciousness is the fact of being together with what is known. When we are conscious of something we are momentarily together with the thing we are conscious of. When you look at the color of your walls, your mind is in some sense together with the walls – and this is what it means to be conscious of something. When you forgot where you placed your mobile phone, your keys, or the ganja pipe, we say that you are *not* conscious of their place because their location is not presently combined with your awareness. Philosophers call this aspect of awareness the *intentionality* of consciousness, such that in every waking state one's attention is always directed, and henceforth together with whatever it is one is conscious of (whether that be an idea or a perception).

Roughly speaking, the question of consciousness is the concern over what and how the world is combined with our knowledge and awareness of it. Thus, in stating that cannabis somehow alters our consciousness, we can begin to see that what gets altered is the manner of our togetherness with the world such that an experience under the colorful euphoria of hashish, for instance, is a modification in both how the world comes together for us in experience – but also how we come together with the world. Additionally, we would be wise to take the counsel of philosophers who, since the days of old, have warned against the mistake of assuming that our ordinary consciousness of the world – sober consciousness, as it were – is wholly passive, objective, and indicative of the truth. Two such philosophers are Plato and Karl Marx. The first warns that our ordinary consciousness, so to speak, is riddled with changing illusions; and the latter, Marx, tries to get a grip on what sort of illusion(s) the modern world and ourselves have been seized by. To Plato first.

Plato, who lived more than 23 centuries ago (429–347 BCE) and came from the ancient city of Athens on the southern tip of the Greek peninsula, had a remarkably stunning and rich view of the world. He saw the physical world as illusory and the realm of ideas as truly and unchangeably real. His questions, dialogues, and meditations tower over the history of philosophy, having guided many thinkers to a life of examination and critical contemplation. Plato taught that in order to be conscious of truth it was essential that the philosopher elevate herself beyond the mere appearances and opinions we have of the world into a terrain of actual knowledge. He thought that philosophy, through its incessant interrogation of the world, was the means towards gaining true knowledge, and hence of achieving the best form of consciousness and life. In Book VII of the *Republic*, his most celebrated text, he likens the transition from a false consciousness of mere opinion to a consciousness of truth to the escape of a prisoner who previously having been forced to stare at a series of shadows on the wall of a cave, frees himself, working his way up and out of the darkness into the blanket of the outside light. Never having seen the light before, the prisoner would discover that what he had previously taken as real entities in the world, the shadows on the cave wall, are nothing but illusions, and that the real world has stood outside of his consciousness. The prisoner would be both terrified and liberated.

Plato asks:

> What do you suppose he'd say if someone were to tell him that before he saw silly nothings, while now, because he is somewhat nearer to what *is* and more turned toward beings, he sees more correctly. . . . Don't you suppose he'd be at a loss and believe that what was seen before is truer than what is now shown?
>
> And later, after becoming accustomed to the light . . .
>
> What then? When he recalled his first home and the wisdom there, and his fellow prisoners in that time, don't you suppose he would consider himself happy for the change and pity the others?[5]

If the prisoner, who having been freed from the chains of illusion, returned to free his companions and tell them that what they believed to be the truth of the world was merely a series of shadows and fictions, the other prisoners would likely commit violence against their liberator and kill him so as to protect their already defined opinions about the world. The lesson here is that ordinary consciousness can be ignorant of truth and violently rebel against truth. This last point is striking when you consider how many great liberators, from Jesus Christ to Mahatma Ghandi, or Martin Luther King, Jr., have been slain simply for seeking, speaking, and raising the question of truth into society's consciousness.

❧   MARK THORSBY

Plato's allegory of the cave reminds us of two things. First, we are reminded of the possibility that our ordinary consciousness may be in radical error. In living our lives, we presume a host of beliefs and assumptions that may in fact be false. Consider the fact that people used to believe that the world was flat and burn their neighbors as witches for odd behavior. How many false beliefs have been overturned throughout history? How much more is the possibility that we too suffer from forms of false consciousness? Simply because we are conscious of a world does not mean that we are conscious about what is true of that world. Second, Plato reminds us of the tremendous resistance most of us have to anyone or anything that might challenge our beliefs about the world. Philosophy interrogates our ordinary assumptions that prereflectively categorize our experience, casts them into the light of day, and asks us to evaluate their legitimacy. We need not become disciples of Plato to recognize the truth of his teaching: namely, that the consciousness of our ordinary experience ought not be taken as the truth. Within the greater context of our discussion, perhaps we can say that cannabis ruptures ordinary consciousness as a humbly enjoyable reminder of the fragility and arbitrariness of consciousness.

In parallel fashion, but in an utterly different way from Plato, Karl Marx challenges the legitimacy of our ordinary, average, everyday form of consciousness. He argues that our modern cultural consciousness has been disfigured and skewed by our society's form of economy – that is, by the capitalist system of production. At the heart of the matter, Marx argues that modern consciousness has become *alienated*. What exactly does this mean? Well, in order to grasp at least his central idea we need to remind ourselves of some of the basic elements of capitalism. In a capitalist society, there are essentially two types of persons within the economic order: there are *laborers* who produce products for a set amount of pay, and there are the *employers* who own the products of that labor which are sold for profit. If a company flourishes and sells a lot of products, then the employer gains greater and greater wealth *because* she need not share her profit with the employees under her care. The reason capitalism is the most productive form of economy the world has yet known is precisely because of the relationship between the laborers and the employers, or capitalists. Because workers do not own the products of their own labor, a system is created in which the increase in wealth can pool in the hands of a few. The organization of this system is one of alienation or estrangement because workers are alienated from the fruits of their own labor. For example, in nature, if a beaver builds a dam, we say that the dam is the beaver's. If we see a bird build a nest, we say that the nest is the bird's. Or if we discover a teepee built by aboriginal peoples, we say that the teepee is theirs. What this means is that naturally we say that the work of a being is a part of or owned by that being. But in modern society, if a carpenter builds a set of cabinets for his employer, they are not said to be his, but rather the owner's. What Marx wants us to see is that the laboring classes have become divorced from their work, and so are to some degree in a state of alienation. He writes:

> The alienation of the worker in his object is expressed according to the laws of political economy as follows; the more the worker produces, the less he has to consume; the more values he creates the more worthless and unworthy he becomes; the better shaped his product the more misshapen is he.[6]

In other words, modern society is structured in such a way that we have become alien to ourselves.

The alienation of consciousness can be summarized as the inability to recognize this feature of modern life; that is, the inability to consciously see oneself as alienated from oneself – that the value of your life and work is not your own. In a much later text, *Das Kapital*, Marx speaks about a fetishism of commodities, which simply refers to the mysterious fact that in the activity of daily economic life, we tend to see the value of products as inherent within the products themselves, divorced from the laborers who produce them. We do not see that in fact the source of material value is another person. When most of us go into a restaurant, order a meal, and the food arrives, we generally do not think of the cooks who in the kitchen will have touched, prepared, and dressed our meal; no, we generally think that the meal has value because of what it is and not because of how it came about. In so doing, we adopt a form of consciousness that falsifies and alienates us from ourselves, from nature, apart from our fellow human beings, and even from the species as a whole. We need not become political Marxists in the sense of socialist activists to see that there is some truth to this critique of modern society and that we should fearlessly ask whether or not our ordinary assumptions about life are illusory, as Plato warned.

The question we need to ask is whether or not the sort of transcendence that cannabis propels consciousness towards can be understood as a kind of resistance to the alienation of modern life. Currently, the World Health Organization (WHO) estimates that over 147 million people worldwide consume cannabis regularly, with the largest growth sectors located in the developed world: the United States, Western Europe, and

Australia. But why would the largest growth sectors be in the developed world where capitalism is most productive? If cannabis use were simply a matter of escaping and coping with life's difficult conditions as I think many people assume, then shouldn't we expect to see the highest growth of cannabis consumption in the third world, where it can be grown quite easily under the harshest of social conditions? Or conversely, could there be a link between the flourishing and growing use of cannabis among Westerners and the type of consciousness that those societies adopt?

In his extraordinarily insightful and provocative work, *To Have or To Be?*, psychologist Erich Fromm postulates that there are two essential psychological modes of living in the world. There is the mode of *having* in which the value, direction, and choices of one's life are defined and determined according to what one has rather than who one is. The mode of *being*, by contrast, is a paradigm of consciousness in which the value of life is guided by what type of person one wishes and chooses to *become*. A person's identity and subsequent consciousness is either determined by what they *have* in the first case or who they *are* in the second. Fromm convincingly argues that the modern commodification of Western culture into a society of consumers has resulted in the dominance of having, a veneer of happiness, and a loss of what it means to *become* a good person. Provocatively, he writes: "Consuming has ambiguous qualities: It relieves anxiety, because what one has cannot be taken away; but it also requires one to consume ever more, because previous consumption soon loses its satisfactory character."[7] If Fromm is right about the mode of having and if it is endemic to Western culture, then we can say that our consciousness is continually alienating, never satisfying, and like a treadmill keeps our consciousness stationary despite consuming more and more. The shift of consciousness that cannabis incurs is notable for its temporary alleviation of this condition. We live in a culture of alienation where *having things* guides our actions. The answer to our initial question, I think, is that when we talk about "getting high" we are in part talking about rising above the ordinary routes of consciousness which have enslaved, belittled, and defined us. Cannabis offers a momentary escape from the desert of alienation we find ourselves stranded upon, despite the colorful trappings of materialism. Ultimately, cannabis cannot rectify the alienating affects of modern culture, but it can lead us into a critique over the legitimacy of our world and our consciousness of that world. What cannabis can help us to see philosophically is that we ought to resist certain forms of consciousness, otherwise we may find ourselves condemned to live in Plato's cave, chained to a series of illusions.

NOTES

1 Allen Ginsberg, "The Great Marijuana Hoax: First Manifesto to End the Bringdown," *Atlantic Monthly* 218, 5 (1966): 104.

2 Herodotus, *The Histories*, 4.73 and 1.202.

3 See Hui-Lin Li, "The Origin and Use of Cannabis in Eastern Asia: Their Linguistic-Cultural Implications," in Vera Rubin (ed.) *Cannabis and Culture* (Paris: Mouton, 1975).

4 Ginsberg, "The Great Marijuana Hoax," p. 104.

5 Plato, *The Republic*, 2nd edn., trans. Allan Bloom (New York: Basic Books, 1991), 514a–517b.

6 Karl Marx, "Economic and Philosophic Manuscripts," in *Early Philosophical Writings*, ed. Lawrence Simon (Cambridge, MA: Hackett, 1994), p. 61.

7 Erich Fromm, *To Have or To Be?* (New York: Continuum), p. 23.

MARK THORSBY

TUOMAS E. TAHKO

CHAPTER 11

REEFER MADNESS

Cannabis, the Individual, and Public Policy

Introduction

Why is cannabis not our drug of choice? On the face of it, cannabis seems so much better than legal drugs: it does not cause aggression, it gives the user no hangover, makes everything seem funny, and appears to be a lot healthier. Of course, at the dark end of the spectrum, cannabis is thought by some to act as a gateway drug, gets the user involved with criminals, causes social isolation and depression, and can lead to psychosis or even schizophrenia. Regardless of the supposed pros and cons of cannabis use, it certainly *is* the drug of choice for many. For instance, 22.7 percent of English and Welsh 16 to 29-year-olds had used cannabis in the previous 12 months in 2001/2002.[1] The popularity of cannabis raises concerns that the use of less popular drugs perhaps does not; namely, how does the use of cannabis affect the quality of life and what sort of socioeconomic impact does it have? Given the widespread use of cannabis, the implications that it may have should be taken under careful consideration. In what follows, I will examine both the adverse effects as well as potential benefits that cannabis use is likely to have in the light of recent research. The inquiry will be divided into two sections: the implications of cannabis use from the point of view of the individual on one hand, and from the point of view of society on the other.

Cannabis and the Individual

The use of any drug starts with the same thing: acquiring it. In the case of illegal drugs this part becomes considerably more complicated. Indeed, the legal status of cannabis is perhaps the most problematic aspect of cannabis use from the individual's point of view. The problem is not so much that cannabis is difficult to acquire. In fact, it appears that for most users the legal status of cannabis causes little or no hindrance in this regard: for instance, more than half of cannabis users in San Francisco are able to get hold of the drug within half a day.[2] What seems to be more problematic from the individual's point of view are the risks that the criminalization of cannabis brings with it, specifically, the risk of getting caught and facing legal action. In San Francisco, two-thirds of cannabis users have reported being afraid of these implications at least sometimes,[3] even if the actual risk of getting caught is rather small, with only 8 percent of the same sample group ever having faced legal action.

Another concern for the cannabis user is that one may have to deal with criminals to acquire the drug, although this is unlikely to be a major concern. At least in San Francisco, the vast majority of cannabis users deal with their friends and the link to a dealer is established through trusted channels.[4] Accordingly, most cannabis users will never have any contact with the organized crime network which undoubtedly is behind a substantial portion of cannabis trafficking. In fact, by acquiring cannabis, or distributing the drug to one's friends, the individual becomes a criminal as well. Since the vast majority of cannabis users are likely to be normal, law-abiding citizens in other regards, the situation may seem rather disconcerting for many users. There are at least two factors to consider here. Firstly, due to the extremely widespread use of cannabis, its criminalization turns a substantial part of the population into *de facto* criminals. It is at least noteworthy that a substantial part of all criminals, perhaps even *most* criminals, are criminals strictly because they are cannabis users. This is not to mention the problems that this causes for law enforcement: due to the vast number of cannabis users, the police can do very little to maintain a credible threat for the cannabis user. In reality, small offenses are often simply ignored. Secondly, while most cannabis users might never face any legal consequences, it is very possible that the credibility of the legal system diminishes in their eyes if it considers such a widely accepted activity as criminal. If the use of the drug is condoned by one's social circle, then its legal status may seem unjustified.

❧ TUOMAS E. TAHKO

Yet another issue regarding the source of cannabis is that at least some cannabis that originates from less reputable sources is likely to be of inferior quality. As an extreme example, in recent years in the UK, there have been concerns that cannabis may have been contaminated with small glass particles.[5] The motive for adding glass particles to cannabis is unclear, but it is likely to have something to do with increasing the weight of the product. This and other cases of contaminated cannabis are of course a direct consequence of the legal status of cannabis and the fact that some distributors of the drug will do anything to increase their profits. This obviously increases the risk of adverse health effects for the end user.

Effects on health are certainly one of the major concerns for cannabis users, and also for society more generally, due to public health implications, so some discussion about these issues is necessary. Folk knowledge among cannabis users suggests that it is, in general, considerably healthier than either alcohol or tobacco, but rigorous studies especially into the long-term effects of cannabis are still scarce. The acute health effects of cannabis, however, are fairly well documented. Because of the low toxicity of cannabis, the major risks are either derivative, i.e., increased accident-proneness, or psychological. A survey of the first is not necessary in this connection. I take it that any responsible drug user will be aware that, for instance, driving under the influence is not advisable. There have been a number of studies about the effects of cannabis on driving performance and it is not surprising that it will increase the risk of accidents, although considerably less than alcohol does.[6] In any case, this is not something that will be a major concern from the point of view of the individual, since it is easily avoided. As acute effects go, the only other notable adverse effects are perhaps occasional anxiety, panic attacks, and paranoia.[7]

The effects of chronic cannabis use on health are much more difficult to assess. This is partly because the medical histories often include the use of other drugs, and partly because heavy cannabis users often come from socioeconomic groups that are at higher risk to begin with, so the effects of cannabis are difficult to isolate.[8] In any case, it appears that adverse psychological effects are the ones that users should be concerned about. Other adverse health effects that chronic cannabis use may have include a number of illnesses associated with the respiratory system. These illnesses are of course due to smoking cannabis, which is by far the most common method of using it, which could be avoided entirely by using a different method. It is clear that smoking cannabis increases the risk of certain illnesses of the respiratory system, such as chronic bronchitis, but in many cases the results have been mixed.[9] The same is true of the connection between cannabis and certain types of cancer; it seems at least that smoking tobacco carries greater risks.[10] While chronic cannabis smoking certainly has some adverse effects for the respiratory system, a health-conscious individual could avoid the majority of these by using alternative methods, such as oral administration.

Given the relatively mild adverse effects that cannabis appears to have on one's physical health, the greatest risks are perhaps psychological. I would include cannabis dependence in this section as well, for it is well known that cannabis does not cause significant physical dependence. In fact, before the modern understanding of dependence emerged in the 1970s, cannabis was simply considered not to cause dependence at all.[11] However, cannabis dependence is now recognized as the most common form of drug dependence after alcohol and tobacco in the USA and Australia, and it is cannabis dependence that is likely to be responsible for the amotivational effects that are often associated with cannabis, although there is very little evidence that suggests that even chronic cannabis use would cause any type of unique amotivational syndrome.[12]

One of the best-known adverse effects of cannabis is that it impairs cognitive functions such as short-term memory, so that there may be a risk that chronic use will cause permanent damage to cognitive faculties. Indeed, there is some proof that this is the case, but once again the adverse effects of cannabis would seem to pale when compared to those of alcohol:

> Cannabis use does not produce *gross* cognitive impairment like that seen in heavy consumers of alcohol. There is growing evidence, however, that long-term daily cannabis use produces more subtle impairments in memory and attention. Expert opinion is divided on the significance of these differences in cognitive performance. Some sceptics still argue that we cannot exclude the possibility that these differences indicate pre-existing differences in cognitive ability, differences in other drug use, or a failure to ensure abstinence from cannabis. Increasingly more commentators believe that there are real, if small, differences in cognitive functioning between long-term cannabis users and controls. They argue that recent better-controlled studies make the sceptics' explanation implausible.[13]

It appears that at least heavy cannabis use is likely to cause *some* cognitive impairment, although it is less clear whether the reduced performance in certain laboratory tests will translate into any effects whatsoever in everyday life. This nevertheless seems to be a very widely accepted conclusion.[14]

TUOMAS E. TAHKO

However, cannabis use, correctly or incorrectly, is also commonly associated with psychotic disorders and even schizophrenia. If there is any truth to the claims that cannabis can cause severe psychological problems such as these, then this is surely something that cannabis users should take into consideration. That cannabis could cause such disorders is not difficult to see, as it is after all a potent psychoactive substance. The key question is: How strong is the causal link between cannabis and psychotic disorders? At least in the case of schizophrenia, there appears to be a clear statistical link between cannabis use and the illness,[15] but the interpretation of this statistical link is controversial.[16] Isolating the effects of cannabis is one of the problems, but it is also possible that there is some type of a deviant causal link in effect. For instance, people who are at risk to develop schizophrenia may be more likely to become regular cannabis users. A recent systematic review of the link between cannabis use and psychotic disorders suggests that the odds ratio for those who have ever used cannabis to develop a psychotic disorder is 1.4 (95 percent confidence interval: 1.20, 1.65).[17] However, another study of alcohol, cannabis, and tobacco use among Australians suggests that cannabis is not associated with anxiety or affective disorders, whereas alcohol dependence and tobacco use are associated with both of these disorders.[18] Finally, a recent study conducted in Norway concludes rather paradoxically that there is no link between cannabis use and depression, but that it may increase suicidal ideation and suicide attempts in later life.[19] In light of these results, it is probably safe to conclude that using cannabis increases the risk of psychological problems at least slightly, but probably not significantly more than the use of alcohol and tobacco.

The conclusion that we may draw at this point is that although there are various health risks associated with the use of cannabis, these seem to pale in comparison with the adverse health effects of alcohol and tobacco. While cannabis is by no means harmless, people with no previous health problems are relatively unlikely to suffer major adverse effects, at least if cannabis is used only occasionally. Perhaps the biggest risk is the possibility of some type of psychological addiction: cannabis is the third most common drug "addiction" after alcohol and tobacco. Whether this is reason enough to abstain from cannabis use altogether is another question; a question which requires discussion concerning the potential *benefits* that the use of cannabis may have.

There are a number of medicinal uses for cannabis that have received a fair amount of attention. These include the use of cannabis to treat glaucoma, as an appetite stimulant, to relieve chronic pain in AIDS and cancer patients, to alleviate seizure disorders, and so on.[20] However, these medicinal uses are hardly a reason to use cannabis for the majority of the population. The question is whether the use of cannabis can be beneficial for a healthy individual. Unfortunately, this is where the availability of systematic academic studies ends. Any discussion of the topic that one is likely to encounter will be based on anecdotal evidence and will thus be of little value for any kind of rigorous investigation of the matter. One of the few attempts at a survey of the benefits of cannabis, at least that I am aware of, is by Bello,[21] which certainly lacks the rigor that one would hope to see in such a study and appears mainly to consist of statements of the following type: "Regardless of the model used, marijuana resolves conflict by de-emphasizing extreme aggressiveness and stroking the receptive sides of human nature. This unification or balance, however, may be responsible for changes in goals and values. It is the healthy balancing nature of marijuana that is most beneficial to the individual and most threatening to modern society."[22]

But is there nothing that we can say about the potential benefits of cannabis that would not seem like the rambling of a devoted pothead? The manner in which I would like to engage with this question would be with the help of systematic interviews with cannabis users, but that is obviously not possible in this context. However, I believe that at least a few speculative remarks are in order. At the very least it can be said that for those who use drugs anyway, cannabis may be the least harmful choice – there is certainly good evidence to this effect. Given that very few individuals abstain from drug use entirely, this fact on its own constitutes a strong argument in favor of cannabis. Whether this is really a *benefit* of cannabis use is another question. If cannabis does have any actual benefits for a healthy individual, they are most likely to be of a psychological nature. There has been some research into the motives for using cannabis, although the questionnaires used in these studies may not be as accurate as we would like.[23] The results, as one might expect, suggest that cannabis use is primarily motivated either by hedonistic motives such as relaxation or entertainment, or by coping motives such as to reduce social anxiety or depression. What is more interesting is that these studies strongly suggest that the adverse psychological effects of cannabis are associated with coping motives. For instance, a study of young Swiss adults discovered that only cannabis users with coping motives manifested the typical adverse psychological effects associated with cannabis, whereas users with social motives did not differ from non-users in terms of psychological disorders.[24] This suggests that many of

✿ TUOMAS E. TAHKO

the adverse effects of cannabis may be due to previous psychological problems. It is not surprising that the use of drugs would only emphasize such previous problems. It would be interesting to examine how the sub-group of cannabis users whose motives are social or hedonistic differs from non-users, if at all. There is certainly at least a possibility that these individuals have *better* mental health than non-users. The problem is that any effect of this type would be masked by problem-users in studies that do not moderate for the motives of cannabis use – something that is lacking in nearly all studies.

So, could it be that cannabis use may be beneficial for one's mental health? Anecdotal evidence may suggest such benefits, but before we see a rigorous study about this that adjusts for the motives of use as well as other background conditions such as previous mental health problems, it is difficult to answer this question. I suspect that some mental health benefits are indeed likely, but probably in a preventive capacity rather than as a cure for acute problems. Why would this be the case? Two things come to mind: firstly, cannabis makes you laugh, and laughing is certainly good for you; secondly, cannabis has an introspective element. Where alcohol numbs your mind, cannabis makes you aware of yourself, and this is surely the first step towards a healthy mind. Be that as it may, I shall conclude simply by recommending further research into the potential benefits of cannabis use – strong anecdotal evidence in favor of such benefits surely warrants the research.

Cannabis and Society

From the point of view of society, it is difficult to see how the use of any drug could be beneficial. Even if there are individuals who use drugs in a manner beneficial to them, it is likely that any possible benefits will be very small compared to the harmful effects of drugs. Hence, the question becomes: What is the most effective way to reduce the harmful effects of drugs?

Quite clearly, a total ban of all drugs will not be the solution. Humans have always used drugs and they will always find a way to do that, no matter what measures society takes. Perhaps the biggest problems concerning drugs from society's standpoint are adverse health effects and the cost of treatment. Crime is another major problem, whether in acquiring drugs or as a result of their effects. We have already discussed the health effects of cannabis in the previous section, so in this section we will mainly focus on ancillary effects, such as crime and social isolation. The obvious question is: Which policy is the most effective in countering the adverse effects of cannabis?

With cannabis having recently been reclassified from class C to class B in the UK, meaning that the law once again allows up to five years imprisonment for possession of the drug, it seems that society there is fixed on the idea that a tough anti-marijuana policy is the answer. However, the message to the public is mixed to say the least, since the reasons for moving cannabis from class B to class C are still as valid as they were in 2004 when the downgrading was done. In their report preceding the reclassification of cannabis to class B in January 2009, the Advisory Council on the Misuse of Drugs (ACMD) recommended that cannabis should remain in class C:

> After a most careful scrutiny of the totality of the available evidence, the majority of the Council's members consider – based on its harmfulness to individuals and society – that cannabis should remain a Class C substance. It is judged that the harmfulness of cannabis more closely equates with other Class C substances than with those currently classified as Class B [such as amphetamines].[25]

The ACMD issued 21 recommendations to the government concerning cannabis. The government accepted all but one of these recommendations, the remaining recommendation was that cannabis should remain in class C. While this is quite baffling, it is perhaps not surprising if the policy towards cannabis will never be quite as liberal in countries such as the UK as it is in countries like the Netherlands. For one thing, the increased measures being taken against tobacco smoking make it difficult to build a case for cannabis smoking, and no one can claim that cannabis would not cause *any* harm, so the case for legalizing cannabis would need to be based on reduced harms.[26] Is there any research that would suggest reduced harms if cannabis were to be legalized, or at least decriminalized?

One major question concerns the connection between the use of cannabis and other illegal drugs, i.e., the notorious "gateway" hypothesis, suggesting that cannabis use leads to the use of more harmful drugs in later life. This hypothesis has received plenty of attention and the consensus seems to be that although there may be some truth to it, the usual story is vastly exaggerated.[27] Most notably, Cleveland and Wiebe[28] conclude that

TUOMAS E. TAHKO

patterns of drug use appear to have more to do with genetically influenced developmental trajectories, rather than there being any real gateway effect at hand. Similarly, Choo et al.[29] discovered that students in Tennessee who are likely to move from cannabis to other drugs tend to be the ones who manifest certain previous risk factors as well as being subject to environmental factors which contribute to problematic behavior. What little plausibility remains for the hypothesis is likely to be explained by the availability of other drugs: often, the source of cannabis is also a source for other illicit drugs. What makes this interesting is that if cannabis were to be legalized, at least part of this effect might disappear due to natural market separation. In San Francisco the source of cannabis is over three times more likely to have other drugs available than the source of cannabis in Amsterdam, where cannabis is usually acquired from coffee shops.[30]

Another factor to consider, which has not received quite so much attention, is social isolation. It is obvious that the legal status of cannabis encourages users to secrecy and forces them to abstain from using the drug in public. Some cannabis users may also have to hide their use from their friends and family due to the social unacceptability of cannabis. Furthermore, because cannabis users may have to hide their habit, it can be difficult to seek assistance for any potential problems that a user might encounter, such as addiction. All this contributes to social isolation, the consequences of which can be severe, especially for those who may require help. Some aspects of this social isolation are beginning to take ludicrous forms: in May 2009 the *Guardian* reported that in these tough economic times, UK employers are starting to use drug tests to get rid of staff without having to pay redundancy fees.[31] Most often these drug tests will reveal cannabis use, as it can remain detectable even after several weeks. However, whether this has any effect on the efficiency of the employee is questionable at the very least. One move that could alleviate these problems is the Dutch coffee shop model, where cannabis may be used in an environment where it is condoned.[32] Accordingly, from the point of view of harm reduction, decriminalization might very well be a sensible policy.

Indeed, the consensus among public health experts is that the tough policy towards cannabis which was set in the 1961 Drug Convention is utterly obsolete. For instance, one conclusion of the convention was that cannabis has no medical value, and this has certainly been disputed.[33] Reflecting these opinions, the Beckley Foundation's 2008 Global Cannabis Commission Report put forward the following recommendation:

The principal aim of a cannabis control system should be to minimize any harms from cannabis use. In our view this means grudgingly allowing use and attempting to channel such use into less harmful patterns (e.g., by delaying onset of use until early adulthood, encouraging all users to avoid substantial daily use, driving a car after using, and smoking cannabis mixed with tobacco).[34]

The same report speculates about potential methods to proceed accordingly. There are apparent problems that any government wishing to minimize the harms of cannabis use will face, perhaps the most obvious being that there are international agreements concerning drug prohibition, such as the 1961 Drug Convention. Any country that hopes to change the legal status of cannabis would somehow have to get around this. However, these problems can certainly be overcome, and they are, at any rate, merely political problems. A common reply is that changing the legal status of cannabis would "send the wrong message," but what is so wrong about minimizing harms? Clearly, the current drug policy is not doing its job: in 1998 the UN General Assembly special session declared its ten-year plan to eliminate the use and production of illicit drugs.[35] However, as the 2008 World Drug Report clearly indicates, the production and use of illicit drugs, far from having been eliminated, has in fact increased significantly.[36] In the case of cannabis, the number of users has increased steadily since 1998 and was at an all-time high of 166 million people in 2006/07, and has probably increased since. Despite the utter failure of the previous policy, the UN Commission on Narcotic Drugs that took place in March 2009[37] committed itself to essentially the same policy that it did a decade ago, with hardly any attention being given to cannabis and its 166 million users. In light of these facts, the whole idea of international agreements on drugs seems completely absurd: no good can come from repeating the same mistakes over and over again.

Unsurprisingly, I wish to conclude by revoicing the opinion of public health experts and recommending an altogether novel approach to cannabis. With the use of cannabis being more widespread than ever, we must face the fact that it will probably never be eliminated and any policy that aims at eliminating its use will surely fail miserably. The only viable option is to adopt a harm reduction policy. It cannot be disputed that using cannabis is potentially harmful, but given the moderately tame adverse health effects that cannabis appears to have, we should perhaps be more concerned about what kind of social implications the legal status

❧ TUOMAS E. TAHKO

of the drug has. As I have demonstrated above, factors such as social isolation and the risk of facing legal action or plain persecution may be far more harmful than any potential adverse health effects. However, these problems are strictly a consequence of a failed drug policy that with a little political will could certainly be overcome.

NOTES

1   Home Office, *British Crime Survey*; available online at www.homeoffice.gov. uk/rds/bcs1.html.
2   C. Reinarman, "Lineaments of Cannabis Culture: Rules Regulating Cannabis Use in Amsterdam and San Francisco," *Contemporary Justice Review* 10 (2007): 393–410.
3   Ibid., p. 34.
4   Ibid.
5   Public Health Link, "Update on Seizures of Cannabis Contaminated with Glass Particles" (2007); available online at www.nelm.nhs.uk/en/NeLM-Area/News/490687/490847/490854/.
6   M. N. Bates and T. A. Blakely, "Role of Cannabis in Motor Vehicle Crashes," *Epidemiologic Reviews* 21 (1999): 222–32; M. Asbridge, C. Poulin, and A. Donato, "Motor Vehicle Collision Risk and Driving under the Influence of Cannabis: Evidence from Adolescents in Atlantic Canada," *Accident Analysis and Prevention* 37 (2005): 1025–34; A. Smiley, "Marijuana: On Road and Driving Simulator Studies," in H. Kalant et al. (ed.) *The Health Effects of Cannabis* (Toronto: Centre for Addiction and Mental Health, 1999), pp. 173–91; W. Hall, "The Adverse Health Effects of Cannabis Use: What Are They, and What Are Their Implications for Policy?" *International Journal of Drug Policy* 20 (2009): 458–66.
7   W. D. Hall and R. L. Pacula, *Cannabis Use and Dependence: Public health and Public Policy* (Cambridge: Cambridge University Press, 2003), p. 38.
8   J. Macleod, et al., "Psychological and Social Sequelae of Cannabis and Other Illicit Drug Use by Young People: A Systematic Review of Longitudinal, General Population Studies," *The Lancet* 363 (2004): 1579–88.
9   Hall, "The Adverse Health Effects of Cannabis Use."
10 Ibid.
11 Hall and Pacula, *Cannabis Use and Dependence*, p. 71.
12 Ibid.
13 Ibid., p. 85.
14 See also N. Solowij, *Cannabis and Cognitive Functioning (International Research Monographs in the Addictions)* (Cambridge: Cambridge University Press, 1998).

15 S. Andreasson et al., "Cannabis and Schizophrenia: A Longitudinal Study of Swedish Conscripts," *The Lancet* 2 (1987): 1483–6.

16 Hall and Pacula, *Cannabis Use and Dependence*, pp. 92–3.

17 T. H. Moore et al., "Cannabis Use and Risk of Psychotic or Affective Mental Health Outcomes: A Systematic Review," *The Lancet* 370 (2007): 319–28.

18 L. Degenhardt, W. Hall, and M. Lynskey, "Alcohol, Cannabis and Tobacco Use Among Australians: A Comparison of Their Associations with Other Drug Use and Use Disorders, Affective and Anxiety Disorders, and Psychosis," *Addiction* 96 (2001): 1603–14.

19 W. Pedersen, "Does Cannabis Use Lead to Depression and Suicidal Behaviours? A Population-Based Longitudinal Study," *Acta Psychiatrica Scandinavica* 118 (2008): 395–403.

20 M. L. Mathre (ed.) *Cannabis in Medical Practice: A Legal, Historical and Pharmacological Overview of the Therapeutic Use of Marijuana* (Jefferson: McFarland, 1997).

21 J. Bello, *The Benefits of Marijuana: Physical, Psychological and Spiritual*, 2nd edn. (Susquehanna: Lifeservices Press, 2000).

22 Ibid., p. 51.

23 For example, J. D. Buckner et al., "Marijuana Use Motives and Social Anxiety Among Marijuana-Using Young Adults," *Addictive Behaviours* 32 (2007): 2238–52; J. Brodbeck et al., "Motives for Cannabis Use as a Moderator Variable of Distress Among Young Adults," *Addictive Behaviours* 32 (2007): 1537–45; C. Lee et al., "Development and Preliminary Validation of a Comprehensive Marijuana Motives Questionnaire," *Journal of Studies on Alcohol and Drugs* 70 (2009): 279–87.

24 Brodbeck et al., "Motives for Cannabis Use."

25 Advisory Council on the Misuse of Drugs, "Cannabis: Classification and Public Health" (2008); available online at www.drugs.homeoffice.gov.uk/ publication-search/acmd/acmd-cannabis-report-2008.

26 See Hall, "The Adverse Health Effects of Cannabis Use."

27 A. L. Bretteville-Jensen, H. O. Melberg, and A. M. Jones, "Sequential Patterns of Drug Use Initiation – Can We Believe in the Gateway Theory?" *Journal of Economic Analysis and Policy* 8 (2008); T. Choo, S. Roh, and M. Robinson, "Assessing the 'Gateway Hypothesis' Among Middle and High School Students in Tennessee," *Journal of Drug Issues* 38 (2008): 467–92; H. H. Cleveland and R. P. Wiebe, "Understanding the Association between Adolescent Marijuana Use and Later Serious Drug Use: Gateway Effect or Developmental Trajectory?" *Development and Psychopathology* 20 (2008): 615–32.

28 Ibid.

29 Choo, Roh, and Robinson, "Assessing the 'Gateway Hypothesis'."

30 C. Reinarman, "Lineaments of Cannabis Culture: Rules Regulating Cannabis Use in Amsterdam and San Francisco," *Contemporary Justice Review* 10 (2007): 393–410.

31 D. Taylor, "Rise in Use of Drug Tests to Sack Staff Without Redundancy Pay," *Guardian* (May 18, 2009); available online at www.guardian.co.uk/society/2009/may/18/drugs-testing-workplace-redundancy.

32 See A. J. Suissa, "Cannabis, Social Control and Exclusion: The Importance of Social Ties," *International Journal of Drug Policy* 12 (2001): 385–96.

33 See, for example, Mathre, *Cannabis in Medical Practice.*

34 Beckley Foundation, "2008 Global Cannabis Commission Report," p. 183; available online at www.beckleyfoundation.org/policy/cannabis_commission.html.

35 UN General Assembly, "Twentieth Special Session: World Drug Problem," available online at www.un.org/ga/20special/.

36 UNODC, "World Drug Report 2008," available online at www.unodc.org/unodc/en/data-and-analysis/WDR-2008.html.

37 UNODC, "2009 Commission on Narcotic Drugs," available online at www.unodc.org/unodc/en/commissions/CND/session/52-draftresolutions.html.

CHAPTER 12

SOFT VS. HARD

Why Drugs are Not Like Eggs

 When I go to a restaurant and order poached eggs, the waitperson often asks whether I'd like them soft or hard. I understand that question perfectly. "Soft" means "runny" or something along those lines and "hard" indicates much more cooked and firm – no runny yolk. It's true that, like many distinctions, there's a large gray area – eggs that are somewhere between soft and hard. But I understand that, too. There's a smooth spectrum along a single line, one end of which is soft and the other end of which is hard.

People often distinguish between soft and hard drugs as well. There are a variety of ways the distinction is drawn. Sometimes "hard" means "addictive," "soft" means "non-addictive," and like eggs, there is then something like a spectrum of "hardness" and "softness" along a single vector. Other accounts leave out the hallucinogens – LSD, psilocybin mushrooms, sometimes MDMA and/or Extasy. These are then seen as a kind of "middle ground."[1] But the way the distinction is most frequently drawn is this: "soft drug" typically refers to cannabis products – marijuana, hashish, hash oil, etc. "Hard drug" refers to all the other illegal and recreational drugs – the aforementioned hallucinogens, plus cocaine, crack, methamphetamine, heroin, morphine, and so forth. When I was growing up and learning about drugs, this was clearly how the distinction was drawn. The so-called "gateway" theory of cannabis use presupposes this as well. According to proponents of this theory, we can concede for the sake of argument that cannabis – a *soft* drug – is not so risky or dangerous or addictive. But the problem with it is that it "leads to" the use of *hard* drugs – any or all of the others. This account of the distinction also underwrites the much-discussed drug-use policy of the Netherlands. Small amounts of cannabis are tolerated, but not "hard" drugs.[2] So when people use the soft drug/hard drug distinction, it's typically a distinction between cannabis and all other illegal or recreational drugs. I'll refer to this as the "traditional distinction."

But while that's the way the traditional distinction is made and used, we need to ask whether there is some feature of reality to which it refers. With eggs there is. Some eggs really *are* runny. Other eggs really *are* firm and not runny at all. Still other eggs *are* somewhere in between. But is there some reality to which the traditional distinction refers? Is there some sense in which soft drugs really *are* soft and hard drugs hard? The more I think about it, the less plausible this seems to me. Indeed, far from being a helpful characterization of reality, the distinction is a fairly gross distortion of it. Or so I wish to argue in what follows here.

In denying the merits of the traditional distinction, I do not mean to follow those who deny a distinction because they think *all* drugs are hard. Rather, I want to suggest that there is no single spectrum of different drugs, one end of which is soft and the other end of which is hard. Different drugs have different properties, to be sure. But not, I'll argue, in any meaningful respect that would warrant distinguishing between hard ones and soft ones. And because the way people think about drugs is heavily shaped by perceptions like a distinction between hard and soft drugs, and because the way people think shapes public policies on the use of such drugs, it's worth cleaning up this conceptual mess a bit.

I propose briefly to consider three candidates for "hardness," three features such that drugs with the feature in question merit being called "hard" and those without "soft." One might be called "phenomenological." By this I simply mean the sort of experiential state experienced by the user. Perhaps the hard drugs are much more disorienting, confusing, disabling, or whatever. A second candidate is addictiveness. Perhaps the difference between cannabis and the "hard" drugs is that the latter are addictive and the former not, or the latter such that addiction is much more likely to occur than with cannabis. The third candidate is slightly more generic. It might be said that cannabis is a lot less "dangerous" than the hard drugs. One is running a much higher risk of death or disabling injury or disease with a hard drug than with cannabis.

While properly addressing these candidates involves empirical questions the thorough answering of which will be beyond the scope of this essay, I want at least to cast serious doubt of a speculative kind on each of these candidates. These don't exhaust the possibilities for the basis of the distinction, of course. But as I see terms like "soft drugs" and "hard drugs" bandied about in public discourse, I think one or other of these three are usually what the user of the terms has (vaguely) in mind. Casting doubt on each of these three possibilities will take us some way towards exposing the spurious nature of the traditional soft drug/hard drug distinction.

Before proceeding further, however, one important preliminary point needs to be made. It's far from clear why the distinction should apply only to *illegal* drugs. The picture of reality painted by common usage is that there are legal drugs and illegal drugs, and the latter break down into soft and hard. But this can be immediately seen to be preposterous. If we're worried about phenomenological properties, addictive properties, or dangerousness, whether a drug is legal or not is completely irrelevant. Imagine someone confronted with the obvious truth that alcohol has addictive potential, and much more so than, say, LSD. And suppose that someone says, "Yeah, but alcohol is legal." We'd be well within our rights to regard this as an abrupt change of the subject. Part of the reason, I think, that the traditional distinction seems precritically to have some merit is that some of the "hard" drugs – alcohol and nicotine, for example – have already been ruled out of consideration by an irrelevant implicit appeal to their legality. Consequently, any meaningful discussion of the distinction should include legal drugs as well as illegal ones, and I'll avail myself of that in the discussion to follow.[3]

Phenomenological Considerations

When people use the phrase "hard drugs" they sometimes seem to mean drugs which, from the standpoint of the user, make one "higher," more "out of it," more "blasted," or some such thing. What is intended here is that the effects of the drug in question are somehow more extreme, less manageable, more frightening, "weirder" or more "far out," or in some such way greater or more pronounced than the experiential state one is in when one has smoked cannabis. So, while you can certainly get "high" on cannabis, it's only a soft drug. Hard drugs, by contrast, have more extreme first-person effects than cannabis does.

It's difficult to evaluate this claim as such. Indeed, it's not obvious that it's even fully intelligible. Consider first the obvious point that how high one gets from consuming a drug depends hugely on how much of it one consumes. To even begin to evaluate the phenomenological claim one would need to find some way of managing this. Someone smoking several joints would surely get higher than he or she would from, say, a single line of cocaine. (If not, the quality of the cannabis would need to be seriously investigated.) So to say that drug $D1$ makes one higher than drug $D2$, one would need to elaborate by saying something like taking n amount of $D1$ is comparable to taking m amount of $D2$. And then one might be able to show that n amount of $D1$ makes one higher (or less high) than m amount of $D2$. But while I'm no researcher and may thus be insufficiently resourceful or imaginative, I can see no way of establishing "comparable" amounts. In which case, there seems to be no way of showing or refuting any claim to the effect that one drug makes one higher than another.

Even putting that to one side, though, how might the investigation go exactly? How does one tell which, of two people high on drugs, is the "higher" *from their perspective*? Maybe we could administer some cannabis to a number of people and a "comparable" amount of hard drug to a number of people and ask them to evaluate how "high" they were on a scale of 1–10. But while I can imagine such an exercise to be entertaining, I battle to see how it could be enlightening. First, we'd need to ask *which* hard drug? Cocaine? Heroin? LSD? Or what? Presumably one would need to compare cannabis with the hard drug on a hard-drug by hard-drug basis. The claim would then be that people generally claimed to be less high on cannabis than on each hard drug (assuming one could control the amount ingested in each comparison). And thus the distinction.

I take it, though, that one person's 5/10 is another person's 7/10 is another person's 3/10. It seems hopelessly implausible to me that any meaningful information could be revealed, even if we put the "comparable amounts" problem to one side. Perhaps with a large enough sample these differences could be ironed out. Or perhaps, instead of giving different people different drugs, we'd give different drugs successively to the same people. They could then compare how high they were on cannabis last week to how high they are on Extasy now and look forward to seeing how high they'll be next week on LSD? Putting to one side the obvious worry that it would be a feeble ethics committee which would give such research the green light, I find it almost impossible to imagine that, lo and behold, people consistently reported being less high on cannabis than on each of the hard drugs. When one reflects, then, on the comparability problem as well as the dubiousness of interpersonal (or intrapersonal) comparisons of "highness," it seems virtually impossible to provide any meaningful evidence for the claim that hard drugs make one "higher" than cannabis.

What *is* evident, both anecdotally and from any thorough drug-information literature based on phenomenological reports of users, is that there are quite different *kinds* of high provided by distinct drugs.[4] Thus, while there is some individual variability, the sort of high provided by cannabis differs qualitatively from the sort of high provided by Extasy, or amphetamine, or LSD, or heroin, etc. This fact, though, is of little use to the person who would distinguish soft and hard drugs on the basis of their phenomenological properties. Are we to say that cannabis provides a "soft" high, while each of the other drugs, despite the vast differences between them in their qualitative effects, produces a "hard" high? I can't see how this suggestion bears serious consideration. And, indeed, it compounds the problem mentioned above of weighing and comparing different degrees of "highness." (Is this cannabis-type high more or less high than this amphetamine-type high or LSD-type high, or what have you?) At best, the phenomenological criterion seems impossible to establish (or refute), and on reflection seems highly doubtful as a basis for a distinction between soft and hard drugs.

What one might have in mind is that, based on tests of coordination, cognition, memory, or some other variable, the person high on one drug fares worse than the other. While not strictly phenomenological, this would have the virtue of being empirically ascertainable. What counts as "higher" is the relative inability to perform observable functions or tasks in comparison with the "less high." The one faring worse would, when this is a pattern observed from a scientifically suitable class of observations, be on the hard drug, the other on the (relatively) soft drug. Then the claim would be that people high on cannabis tend to fare better on such tests, or be able to function better (in general, say) than those on any of the hard drugs.

This is clearly an empirical matter, and if we grant for the moment that a solution to the comparability problem can be found, it would be in principle possible to show that, for instance, the cannabis users fared better on some set of tests or other (or in, say, their ability to drive a car, clean the house, or, I suppose, cook eggs) than did the users of any hard drug. I strongly suspect that such research has been undertaken. And since I'm not familiar with it, honesty compels me to admit that we must allow that it might in fact be the case that cannabis makes one less "high" in this observable and testable sense. It's conceivable that the hard drugs are more *incapacitating* than the soft drug cannabis. But while I suspect this is no doubt true of some hard drugs, I doubt that the person high on cannabis would do better at cleaning the house, driving a car, or cooking eggs than the person "comparably" high on cocaine or amphetamine (never mind *remembering* that they had cleaned the house, driven a car, or cooked eggs). While we clearly need to be open to contrary evidence, then, I think we're right to be very doubtful that what distinguishes soft drugs from hard drugs is their phenomenological properties.[5]

Addictiveness

Perhaps, then, what is meant when a distinction is drawn between cannabis and the hard drugs is that the latter are much more *addictive* than cannabis. Cannabis users can use it in some genuinely "recreational" way; while perhaps some users use it too much, or find themselves craving it more than they are comfortable with (which is clearly true), they can still stop if they want to. Unlike heroin or crack cocaine, the cannabis user is still in charge of the direction of his or her life and able to manage, at least usually, the relationship she or he has to the drug. And thus cannabis is "soft" and the other drugs "hard."

As I mentioned earlier, this is the sort of thing that some people have in mind by the traditional hard drug/soft drug distinction. On that version of the distinction, it would be true by definition that hard drugs are hard in virtue of their addictiveness while soft ones are soft in virtue of their lack thereof. It's for this reason that those who draw the distinction this way treat LSD and the other hallucinogens as soft drugs. Whatever else may be true of them, they're more or less universally recognized as non-addictive.

For this very reason, addictiveness can't be the basis for the traditional version of the distinction with which we're dealing here. Putting to one side disputes about the potential for "dependency development" of cannabis, a whole range of hard drugs as thus cast by the distinction are not addictive. Thus, it's simply false to assert that addictiveness is the criterion of "hardness" of a drug. On the traditional distinction LSD and other hallucinogens are hard drugs. They're not addictive. So this can't be the basis for the standard hard drug/soft drug distinction, and we need not discuss it further.[6]

Dangerousness

We come, then, to the third of our three possible underpinnings for the traditional distinction. Hard drugs, it is sometimes said, are hard because they're much more *dangerous* than cannabis, *qua* soft drug. "Danger," of course, is a very generic category. Something can be dangerous because it can be deadly, lead to serious mental or physical injury or impairment, cause violent behavior, be addictive, or any of a number of other possibilities. I want to suggest momentarily that this insight gives us reason to recast drug classifications in a more sensible way than does the traditional distinction. But for the moment, note that by appealing to "dangerousness" as the criterion, a certain level of plausibility is achieved. Maybe the idea is that the hard drugs are more dangerous than cannabis *in some way or other*. Thus, while not addictive, LSD might be more dangerous than cannabis in some other respect – leading to mental illness, say, or putting one at risk of harming oneself while "tripping." And ditto for other hard drugs. After all, if something is dangerous, and is more dangerous than something else, it would be irrational to insist that it be dangerous in some particular *way*. So maybe the fact that hard drugs pose a significantly higher risk of some harm or other than does cannabis is the reason we should regard cannabis as soft and the others hard.

This, I think, is the most plausible candidate for supporting the distinction, and I also suspect that it comes closest to what users of the distinction have in mind, however unconsciously. And since it's clearly an empirical matter, a proper assessment would require a foray into the empirical literature that would not be appropriate here. In casting doubt on the plausibility of this as a defensible division of drugs into soft and hard, I fully admit, as I did above, that we will have to reevaluate things should the evidence require it.

Still, as I say, I do want to cast some doubt on even this as a basis for a meaningful hard drug/soft drug distinction. I want to do so via three claims. First, on the empirical evidence, it's far from obvious that it's true. Second, insofar as it is supported by empirical evidence, the aforementioned cordoning off of legal drugs from the scope of the distinction does a good deal of the work here. And third, even if there is a defensible sense in which cannabis is less dangerous than the hard drugs, a division into "soft" and "hard" is far from the most accurate representation of what's less dangerous about cannabis.

First, its truth. As noted, a proper investigation of this would take us into a substantial empirical literature. But without such an inquiry, it's worth noting that there *is* credible evidence that it isn't true. Not decisive, obviously. But enough to suggest that, as noted above, it's far from obvious that it's true.

One particularly widely discussed study – widely discussed because it was published by reputable researchers in a reputable professional journal and cast grave doubts on the rationality of the UK's drug classification system – was published in 2007 in *The Lancet* by David Nutt and colleagues.[7] To make a long story short, Nutt's group considered a combination of risk of physical harm to the user, addictiveness, and social destructiveness, called that "harm," and assessed the dangers of various drugs, legal and illegal, in light of that combination. The results took many people by surprise. While less dangerous than many drugs – including heroin, cocaine, alcohol, and nicotine – it was also rated as *more* dangerous than several "hard" drugs, including LSD and Extasy. More recently, in early 2009, Nutt published an editorial in the *Journal of Psychopharmacology* in which he says, roughly, that Extasy is no more dangerous than horse-riding.[8] (From which, I take it, it follows that cannabis use is *more* dangerous than horse-riding.)

Now this is only one research group and one study, so one can't (and I don't) claim to have refuted the theory that hard drugs are more dangerous than cannabis. But since this is hardly the only study which casts traditional drug classifications into doubt, supporters of this basis for the traditional distinction should be careful about helping themselves to the thesis that cannabis is "soft" because it's less dangerous or harmful than the "hard" drugs. It's not at all clear that it is, at least in comparison with some "hard" drugs. And as such, we have at least some reason to be skeptical that the distinction is viable on the basis of differential dangerousness.

Secondly, though, the traditional distinction trades, as I've said, on the exclusion of legal drugs. No one disputes that alcohol is more dangerous, more addictive, and more responsible for social harm than most of the "hard" drugs, not to mention cannabis.[9] When this is pointed to by supporters of decriminalization of some or all currently illegal drugs, the response is not usually to deny the relative dangers of alcohol and the illegal drugs, but to point to the dangerousness of alcohol as a reason not to "make things worse" by legalizing other drugs as well. We can, of course, designate alcohol, nicotine, and other legal drugs as "hard" on these grounds. But this is not how they're designated by the traditional distinction. They're not treated as illegal in the Netherlands, which tolerates cannabis but not hard drugs. No one worries that cannabis will be a "gateway drug" to alcohol and nicotine. While one *can* include alcohol and nicotine under the heading of "hard drugs," the simple fact is that the traditional distinction doesn't. And the best explanation for why it doesn't is because they're legal, a fact which I argued earlier is irrelevant to a classification of drugs into hard and soft (or anything else, other than "legal" and "illegal"). Whatever we say about the relative dangers of cannabis and hard drugs, their respective dangers can't easily be thought to underlie the traditional distinction.

Finally, while I conceded that dangerousness *in some way or other* could, if true and sufficiently inclusive of the range of drugs, underwrite the traditional distinction, the fact that the dangers and risks of harm come in several varieties suggests a more accurate way of classifying drugs. So, for instance, while addictiveness and potential for dependency development are concepts themselves needing some unpacking, it makes sense to think of a spectrum of drugs ranked along a line of addictiveness. Some drugs are really addictive, others hardly at all, and others in between. Similarly, think of risk of death or physical harm. This, too, is problematic in that this surely depends on how the drugs are used. As one writer nicely puts it in the course of suggesting that the traditional distinction is "rather artificial," "there is a hard use of soft drugs and a soft use of hard drugs."[10] But that aside, I can envisage a spectrum of drugs which, when used as they're normally used, are more or less dangerous in this respect. Some drugs pose a great risk of death or physical injury, others very little, and others in between. I can envisage the same for risk of mental or emotional injury or impairment. Each of these is a distinct thread or line, reflecting quite distinct continua of drugs and their properties. In each case the various drugs will come out in a different place in the spectrum relative to the others. With each individual sort of danger, there is something like a line joining more dangerous in respect r, and less dangerous in respect r'.

This suggestion is nevertheless hopelessly obscured by the traditional classification of drugs into "hard" and "soft." That image suggests that, as with eggs, we have a single thread containing a spectrum of softer and harder drugs. If what I've said above is true, this is not the case. There are drugs with distinct properties, which possess those properties to greater or lesser extents depending on the properties in question. But there is no single spectrum of hard and soft. And in this important respect, the traditional distinction is simply false. Drugs are not, in this respect, like eggs.

NOTES

1 See, for instance, the *All Experts Encyclopedia* website entry on hard and soft drugs at www.en.allexperts.com/e/h/ha/hard_and_soft_drugs.htm (accessed August 14, 2009). Cf. *Wikipedia*'s account which counts the hallucinogens as "soft" drugs, at www.en.wikipedia.org/wiki/Hard_drugs (accessed August 14, 2009).

2 This isn't, or hasn't been, *quite* true. One online travel guide, *World 66*, suggests that the tolerated "soft drugs" include psilocybin mushrooms. See www.world66.com/europe/netherlands/amsterdam/drugs (accessed August 14, 2009). It seems, however, that that only applies to fresh mushrooms. The dried ones that are normally the ones used by people were considered "hard" on the Dutch distinction. According to the *DutchAmsterdam* online travel guide, however, even those have been removed from the soft/tolerated category. See "Sale of Hallucinogenic 'Magic' Mushrooms Banned Starting December 1, 2008," at www.dutchamsterdam.nl/542-hallucinogenic-magic-mushrooms-netherlands-amsterdam (accessed August 14, 2009). So now the Dutch distinction is that mentioned in the text.

A helpful brief characterization of the Dutch system can be found in "In 2010, Will There Be No More Coffeeshops in the Netherlands?" at www.dutcham sterdam.nl/545-coffeeshops-netherlands (accessed August 14, 2009).

3 In fairness, some discussions of soft and hard drugs do include such drugs as alcohol and nicotine, and the latter two are usually classified as "hard" in such discussions. But this is not the case with the traditional distinction, as discussed in the text. And, in any case, my argument in the section on dangerousness below will undermine the distinction even with alcohol and nicotine classified as hard.

4 See, for example, Cynthia Kuhn, Scott Swartzwelder, and Wilkie Wilson, *Buzzed: The Straight Facts About the Most Used and Abused Drugs from Alcohol to Ecstasy*, 2nd edn. (New York: Norton, 2003). This book discusses a wide variety of drugs, divided into sections of similar kinds of drugs. Each drug discussion includes a section called "The Buzz" in which the phenomenological effects generally associated with each drug are described.

5 A few years ago the BBC reported that journalists took 46 swabs from toilets in the European Parliament and that 41 of them tested positive for cocaine. We don't know, of course, that it was parliamentarians themselves or their staff members who had been snorting the cocaine. But suppose it was (which would not be highly surprising, pardon the pun). Would we be relieved to hear that reports of their cocaine use was mistaken, and that all they'd really been doing was smoking dope? I certainly wouldn't, and I doubt that no one not already in the grips of the view that cocaine is phenomenologically "harder" than cannabis would either. See "Cocaine Traces at EU Parliament", *BBC News*, July 15, 2005, at www.news.bbc.co.uk/2/hi/europe/4685693.stm (accessed July 23, 2005).

6   I leave out of the discussion the additional truth that alcohol and, even more, nicotine are highly addictive. A number of sensible discussions of drugs are up-front about this and class them as hard drugs. I said earlier, though, that the traditional distinction is frequently only invoked once we've (illicitly) set aside legal drugs. As such, the addictiveness of alcohol and nicotine further undermines the addictiveness criterion for the distinction as usually portrayed.

7   David Nutt et al., "Development of a Rational Scale to Assess the Harm of Drugs of Potential Misuse," *The Lancet* 369 (March 24, 2007): 1047–53. Nutt was at the time the chairman of the Advisory Council on the Misuse of Drugs in the UK.

8   See "Ecstasy 'Not Worse Than Riding'," *BBC News* (February 7, 2009) at www.news.bbc.co.uk/2/hi/uk_news/7876425.stm (accessed August 28, 2009). Those wishing to read the editorial itself can see David Nutt, "Equasy: An Overlooked Addiction with Implications for the Current Debate on Drug Harms," *Journal of Psychopharmacology* 23, 1 (2009): 3–5. "Equasy," for the benefit of the curious, is Nutt's coined term for, "Equine Addiction Syndrome, a condition characterized by gaining pleasure from horses and being prepared to countenance the consequences, especially the harms, from falling off/under the horse" (p. 4, col. i).

9   Nutt et al. rank it fifth, well ahead of among other things ketamine, amphetamine, tobacco, and cannabis.

10 See Félix Guattari, "Socially Significant Drugs," trans. Mark S. Roberts, in Anna Alexander and Mark S. Roberts (eds.) *High Culture: Reflections on Addiction and Modernity* (Albany: State University of New York Press, 2003), pp. 199–208.

PART V

CANNABIS ETHICS AND POLITICS

Penalties against possession of a drug should not be more damaging to an individual than the use of the drug itself; and where they are, they should be changed. Nowhere is this more clear than in the laws against possession of marihuana in private for personal use. . . . Therefore, I support legislation amending Federal law to eliminate all Federal criminal penalties for the possession of up to one ounce of marihuana.

US President Jimmy Carter, Message to Congress, 1977

JACK GREEN MUSSELMAN, RUSS FROHARDT,
AND D. G. LYNCH

CHAPTER 13

"SMOKING POT DOESN'T HURT ANYONE BUT ME!"

Why Adults Should be Allowed to Consume Cannabis

Moral Argument

In the fall of 2008, Michael Phelps, the American swimmer who won a record eight Olympic gold medals, was photographed at a party in South Carolina while inhaling marijuana smoke from a large pipe. When that photo hit the Internet the public outcry was predictable. Phelps apologized for behavior that was "regrettable and demonstrated bad judgment," adding he acted in a "youthful and inappropriate way." He and his family said in television interviews this was a one-time lapse of judgment and that Phelps did not regularly use drugs. The USA Swimming organization suspended him from competition for three months and the local sheriff in South Carolina threatened arrest if he could determine that Phelps was really smoking marijuana.[1] Finally, to finish the tragicomic tale, representatives of Kellogg Foods, which had placed Phelps's face on their cereal boxes, decided not to renew his endorsement contract and tried to dissociate the company from this alleged drug user by donating myriad boxes of Frosted Flakes and Corn Flakes to a San Francisco food bank – only to find some of those very boxes for sale on eBay soon thereafter.[2]

This high-profile case is a tragicomic tale because it puts one of the central moral and political problems with making the moderate use of marijuana by rational and competent adults illegal in high relief: viz., such drug use need not clearly and distinctly harm second parties and may only harm the competent adult user. And cases like Phelps's draw away social attention and resources from preventing or regulating far greater second-party harms caused by legal drugs like tobacco and alcohol. In short, in cases like Phelps's the public could better spend its time, energy, and money preventing the more severe physical and social harms shown to be caused by alcohol and tobacco.

Of course, Phelps is not your average adult, pot smoking American, since the Olympic champion's bong picture may well lead untold American teens into a life of drug use and abuse. Moreover, Phelps probably freely and willfully signed a clear and explicit contract with Kellogg to plaster his face on cereal boxes in exchange for hefty licensing fees, and that contract likely had a so-called morals clause that would forfeit those fees in the event he did something, like smoke pot, that Kellogg found bad for business. Thus, to present this essay's central claim that moderate use of cannabis by competent and rational adults does not harm anyone but the user (especially when contrasted with the way alcohol and tobacco are used), and to defend our claim that social regulatory efforts would be better spent on alcohol and cigarettes, it would be quite helpful to have a more representative user than Phelps to make our case.

For the sake of argument, we will build our case on our hypothetical friend Patrick the pot smoker. Our Patrick is a white male in his thirties, a college-educated, middle-class professional who has a steady job, spouse named Penelope, and a four-year-old son, Paul.[3] To avoid the problem that his purchase of illegal drugs might subsidize the violence of drug kingpins, we will assume Patrick grows cannabis in his basement, does not sell his stash, and has an understanding with his wife to smoke marijuana on Friday nights with friends on the back porch (so his son will not inhale the smoke and so Patrick will not be driving his car home later), the same way adults might get together for drinks at a friend's house.

What, then, can be morally said in Patrick's defense? On John Stuart Mill's classic formulation of the Harm Principle, we are generally only warranted to use law or physical force to compel Patrick to stop smoking pot, and thereby restrict his freedom to choose his own path in life, if we are engaging in "self-protection" from some unjust harm he causes us. That is, Patrick's autonomy, or self-governance to freely choose, as a

❧ J. G. MUSSELMAN, R. FROHARDT, AND D. G. LYNCH

competent and rational adult, his own way of life, leaves decisions about his self-regarding harm up to him.

We might, of course, argue with Patrick that smoking pot is bad for his lungs or beg him to stop because risks to his health might diminish the time he has on Earth to spend with his family. But for Mill, arguing or begging a rational and competent adult is one thing; coercing him by legal or physical force to stop harming himself is something else altogether. For the latter violates Patrick's "sovereign" form of "independence" over his "own body and mind."[4] As Mill adds, if Patrick is of "full age," so that he can maturely and competently make his own decisions, and has the "ordinary amount of understanding," so that he knows the consequences of his actions, then he should have "perfect freedom, legal and social, to do the action and stand the consequences"[5] even if those outcomes from smoking pot might include harm to his body and spirit.

Of course, if Patrick has friends who disapprove of his pot smoking, they need not join him Friday nights. They might judge him an idiot for polluting his lungs or decide not to "seek his society" any longer because they think he is foolishly trying to re-live his carefree days from college.[6] That is, Patrick's "perfect freedom" to engage in self-regarding harm does not, and should not, prevent his friends from criticizing his choice to fill his lungs with pot smoke or keep them from avoiding his company. Only Patrick, the "person most interested in his own wellbeing,"[7] can and should decide if these friends are worth keeping if he has to give up smoking pot to do so.

His wife and son, on the other hand, might make a different claim by insisting that smoking pot does not, for Patrick, merely cause self-regarding harm. After all, Penelope might argue she agreed Patrick would damage his lungs with pot smoke only because it helped Patrick to relax after a long week at work. Just the same, Penelope can add that, like Patrick's friends who do not come over Friday night, she worries Patrick is trying to foolishly recapture his college days as he smokes pot and discusses philosophy with his "stoner" friends. Worse than that, she might add, he should not harm himself so much that he might then get ill and die, thus depriving her and Paul of a husband and father for the rest of their lives.

This argument attempts to move Patrick's self-regarding harm into the realm of the other-regarding injuries, and Penelope may have a point. That is, when does one's apparently self-regarding harm entail illicit harm to second parties? Of course, anything Patrick might do at home (i.e., make a sandwich for lunch) could be considered harmful to members of his family (e.g., depriving them of specific food they might have eaten). Thus, unless we are prepared to give up all self-regarding activities (harmful or not) because those very same activities might in some sense harm others, we need to come up with a way to distinguish the self-regarding harms that rational and competent adults may choose from those that they may not especially choose when one's family is involved.

Fortunately, Mill suggests how to draw this line and thereby protect an adult's individual autonomy. For Mill, when those, like Patrick's wife and son who are "nearly connected" to him, are, "through their sympathies and their interests," harmed in such a way that Patrick violates his "distinct and assignable obligations" to them, then when he smokes pot he not only harms himself but illicitly harms them, too. Mill's examples about such obligations to others include a man who cannot pay his financial debts or support or educate his family because of "intemperance or extravagance,"[8] and a police officer who is punished not for "simply for being drunk" but for being drunk on duty.[9]

It appears Mill is arguing that when adults have or take a clear (or distinct) vow (or promise) to care for (or protect) certain others, such adults thereby freely have assigned to themselves extra duties not to hurt these others by engaging in harmful self-regarding behaviors. Thus, it may be that Patrick has clear or distinct duties, assigned to himself by virtue of his promise to be (or his role as) husband and father, to not smoke pot if this has a negative effect on his special, personal, and unique relationship to his family.

Of course, Patrick could very well respond that not all his self-regarding behaviors have the same kind of (perhaps illicit) negative effect on his family. By smoking pot on Friday nights, Patrick might claim he does little or nothing to violate the clear and distinct role-responsibilities inherent to being (or promising to be) husband and father. That is, Patrick might recognize he has a duty to support and provide for – and even coexist for a long time with – Penelope and Paul, but smoking pot on Friday night does not necessarily restrict his ability to work during the week, or be a loving father and husband all week long or for years thereafter. In fact, Patrick might argue that similar to the perfectly legal Marlboro cigarette and glass of Jack Daniel's whiskey he might have with friends Friday night, the otherwise illegal pot smoking helps clear his mind and relax his body so that he is a more loving husband and father. And as for the harm it may do to his body, smoking pot on Friday night may be no worse than the many kinds of things he did not clearly promise to assign to himself as duties to his family by choice or role, such as

❦

avoiding chocolate ice cream for dessert because he might gain weight in such a way that he would not otherwise live as long with his family.

Ultimately, Patrick can argue that the way he smokes pot does not entail an illicit form of harm to any second parties (including his family), and so he should have the freedom to smoke pot to pursue this own good way of life in his own way. As Mill argues in the third chapter of *On Liberty*, such freedom allows rational and competent adults to pursue their own vision of the good life and thus develop more fully as human beings by their own lights. As Mill suggests in this very chapter, such freedom, when unconstrained unless it unjustly harms second parties, allows individuals to pursue creative projects that interest them and benefit society.

To put this another way, by drawing on Mill's other famous work, *Utilitarianism*, if the experience of pleasure – especially the higher, intrinsically better, intellectual pleasures and not just the physical ones[10] – is the only moral good in itself, unjust paternalistic limits on pot smoking do not enable a competent and rational adult like Patrick to autonomously pursue his own vision of the pleasures of the good life. That is, if Patrick gives his friends a rain-check on Friday night while Penelope takes Paul to visit her family, suppose he decides to smoke pot to enhance the full range of divine aesthetic beauty and perfection offered by a majestic view of the Grand Canyon, or something similar offered by sitting in the preternatural blue glow of the stained glass windows of Marc Chagall's chapel in Nice, France. Unrestrained by the paternalistic restriction of law and policy, he might well be inspired to write a computer program or poetic verse that brings much pleasure to Internet users or readers of poetry. And if that is true, the net social gain of respecting Patrick's liberty to smoke pot would seem prima facie justified on utilitarian grounds, too – even before examining the net social benefits of spending our regulatory time and energy not on enforcing marijuana laws against people like Patrick, but instead restricting more empirically grounded physically and socially harmful legal drugs like tobacco and alcohol.

Science and Health Argument

Now let us consider the validity of the empirical claim that Patrick is really only harming himself. First let us consider Patrick's pot smoking behavior and how it might impact his role as a loving husband, father, and provider for his family. Given the pattern of his use (Friday nights), there is no evidence to suggest that the active components of marijuana would remain in his system beyond Friday night (1.4 and 1.5 hour elimination half-life in serum and oral fluid, respectively, for low and high doses).[11] Therefore, he would be lucid and engaging with Penelope and Paul over waffles and orange juice on Saturday morning, and he would certainly be unaffected on Monday morning when he reports to work.

Furthermore, Patrick's hypothetical argument proposed above, that his pot smoking behavior is no worse than legal cigarettes, is relatively understated. While there is substantial evidence that tobacco has dramatic negative consequences on the health of those who smoke it,[12] specifically lung cancer and other pulmonary diseases, the equivalent risk for lung cancer is not associated with marijuana use.[13] In fact, some compounds found in cannabis have been shown to kill numerous types of cancer, including lung cancer.[14]

Once more, should Patrick live into his golden years and be sitting on his porch looking back on his accomplishments and the memories that he shared with his family and friends, there is evidence that his Friday evening sessions may prove beneficial for preserving those memories, as some studies have shown cannabinoids to be neuroprotective, particularly against some of the pathology brought on by Alzheimer's disease.[15] This evidence suggests that Patrick's promise to his family to be a caregiver and companion is not endangered by his Friday evening marijuana imbibing; rather, he may be protecting himself against the comparative risks of ubiquitous legal drugs such as tobacco and alcohol.

What if Patrick were to break out of his innocuous routine and smoke in the house while Penelope and Paul are present? Similarly, what if one of Patrick's friends, Pete, came over on Friday night but did not actively smoke? Would the secondhand (passive) cannabis smoke be deleterious to their health? Would Pete fail his random drug test at his job working as a clinical psychologist for the Veterans Affairs (VA) hospital the next day? Evidence suggests that this passive exposure would not be a risk, or a minimal risk at worst.

While tetrahydrocannabinol (THC), the main psychoactive component of cannabis, is present in exhaled (or mainstream) smoke and smoke burning from the tip of the cigarette (or sidestream smoke), the amount of THC present in the latter has been estimated to be roughly 40 percent of the original THC content in cannabis[16] – and passive exposure to high levels of passive smoke (i.e., four active smokers with one non-smoker in a closed van) has been shown in some tests to be below detectable levels for the non-smoker.[17] Of course, any form or amount of smoke can be an

☘ J. G. MUSSELMAN, R. FROHARDT, AND D. G. LYNCH

irritant, increasing coughing, and exacerbating the effects of existing respiratory problems (e.g., asthma); however, the exposure to the active ingredients of marijuana smoke appears to be minimal, even in relatively extreme conditions. So at the very least, Patrick's family is not getting high if they come out to the back patio to ask him to unscrew the lid on the pickle jar and Pete would not (due to drug tests alone) lose his job at the VA's office.

These data do suggest a lack of harm to those other than Patrick and even relatively minimal harm to him, but that is not to say that a pot smoker does not take on personal risk by regularly consuming marijuana. Smoke from tobacco and cannabis contain many of the same carcinogens and tumor promoters,[18] hot gasses, and irritating particulate matter; however, the THC present in cannabis smoke has been shown to be protective against pro-carcinogens,[19] while nicotine has been shown to activate the carcinogenic effects of tobacco smoke.[20] These results lead many to argue that cannabis and tobacco smoke are not equally carcinogenic,[21] but not that smoking cannabis is harmless. Not to mention, if Patrick or his friends decide to drive while under the effects of cannabis, there is a notable and dose-dependent impairment on the pot smoker's ability to drive, although not as deleterious or consistent as the debilitating effects of alcohol on driving.[22]

Moreover, removing the smoking part of consuming pot (via vaporizing or eating) eliminates nearly all of the health risks associated with ingesting the active ingredients of the marijuana plant.[23] The arguments of the sections above lead many, then, to ask why policies regarding the use of marijuana in this country have not changed given our increased understanding of the risks and benefits associated with it, especially relative to tobacco and alcohol.

Social Policy Argument

From the realm of social policy, what can be said in defense of our protagonist's cannabis use? To answer this question, let us first review the stated reasons why cannabis is illegal, at least in the United States. The government publishes many overlapping policy positions on cannabis (e.g., Department of Justice, White House's Office of National Drug Control Policy, Federal Register, National Institute of Health, Food and Drug Administration, etc.), but its official stance is perhaps best summed up by the title of a chapter from the Drug Enforcement Agency's cannabis position paper: "Marijuana is Dangerous to the User and Others."[24]

In addition, according to the government, not only is cannabis bad, it is *really* bad. So harmful, in fact, that it is labeled as a "Schedule I" drug.[25] Other Schedule I substances deemed as injurious as cannabis are LSD, heroin, and PCP. To earn this designation, a given substance must have "a high potential for abuse," "no currently accepted medical use in treatment in the United States," and "a lack of accepted safety for use of the drug or other substance under medical supervision." Schedule I drugs cannot be cultivated, sold, bought, possessed, consumed, or traded anywhere in the country.

Legally speaking, therefore, Patrick should not consume cannabis in the US because it is prohibited in order to protect him and society from its damaging effects. This, of course, begs the question why reasonable, rational adults can enjoy several grain alcohol cocktails, or deeply inhale numerous filterless cigarettes, yet not consume cannabis legally. It is well documented that these legal substances can harm the user, as well as directly and indirectly endanger members of society, particularly when abused.

Numerous studies supporting this fact – from the dangers of firsthand and secondhand cigarette smoke, to drunken driving and alcoholism – do not need to be listed here. Still, perhaps one fact is illustrative: in the US, cigarette smoking causes one in five deaths.[26] Curious, then, that the number one preventable cause of death in the US, tobacco (alcohol is number three),[27] is in turn supported by the very same government's financial incentives for farmers who grow tobacco. In fact, given cigarette smoking's documented high rate of abuse (and addiction), as well as alcohol's nearly perfect inability to function as "currently accepted medical use in treatment," one wonders aloud: "Why are not tobacco and alcohol labeled as Schedule I substances as well?"

The reasonable adult cannabis user, while potentially causing some lung damage when smoking, is not harming herself or himself very much at all, particularly when compared to sanctioned use of alcohol and tobacco. In fact, given cannabis's medicinal properties, as well as its potential to fight lung cancer, Patrick's moderate cannabis use may offer some benefit to his health.

Cannabis is also illegal because it supposedly endangers others. As detailed above, Patrick's moderate cannabis use is not necessarily harmful, directly or indirectly, to his family. Likewise, his abstaining friends will not necessarily be injured by Patrick's illegal habit if they seek his company. And if Patrick continues his current pattern of moderate use at home in the evenings after work, he will not endanger others by driving a car or heavy machinery, his recreational activities will not affect his job performance, and his enmellowment will not effect his family and friends by either making him infirm and/or unsafe (although they may want to hide the snacks).

Still, there is one way that cannabis is harmful to others, although not for the typically stated reasons. Unlike Patrick, the majority of users in the US purchase cannabis from illegal markets. And this black market is substantial. According to economist and public policy expert Dr. John Gettman, the estimated retail value of the marijuana underground is $113 billion, more than wheat and corn combined, thus making cannabis America's most lucrative crop. Additionally, this illegal market for cannabis costs taxpayers about $42 billion in law enforcement and unrealized tax revenues.[28]

A byproduct of prohibition, this shadow economy has grave and often deadly consequences. Outlawing cannabis helps create competition for illegal profits among dealers, which in turn leads to turf wars, drive-by shootings, execution-style murders, etc. These problems are largely caused by cannabis's illegality, not by crazed cannabis smokers. And penalizing moderate users, in turn, diverts police resources from violent crime, some of which, paradoxically, is caused by prohibition itself.

Knowledge of this fact is not new. One main reason Patrick can legally quaff a rye on the rocks is expressly because we learned, with alcohol in the US, that prohibiting moderate substance use causes more problems than it aims to prevent. There is likely one simple reason why the Eighteenth Amendment to the United States Constitution is the only amendment that has ever been repealed: it did not work and made things worse.

The National Commission on Law Observance and Enforcement, commonly known as the Wickersham Commission, was a group christened by President Herbert Hoover in 1929 to determine the causes of increased crime. In its report the Commission found out that, as a result of prohibition, both alcohol intake and law breaking escalated, while social policy and the legal system were damaged.[29]

By analogy, prohibiting the use of cannabis sends typically non-violent, otherwise infraction-free individuals into the court system. Using FBI and Census Bureau data, it is estimated that nearly half of nationwide drug arrests involve cannabis possession.[30] This not only restricts the freedom and abilities of productive members of society, it creates additional harm by diverting increasingly limited government resources from treatment options and violent offenders. And what does it say in the archives of human history that the US – supposedly the richest, most liberty-loving country in the world – has the highest incarceration rate and largest number of criminals behind bars on the big blue marble? America is home to 5 percent of the global population, yet houses 25 percent of its inmates (not including secret prisons and black sites).[31]

Of course, not all prohibition is bad. There are good reasons why Patrick's son Paul cannot fix himself a highball. As a four-year-old, he is not sufficiently emotionally or cognitively developed to weigh the pros and cons of consumption, and he is not experienced enough to predict the consequences of his actions on himself and others. Hence, as with other legal substances, laws should outline the legal age of cannabis con-sumption – not a wholesale prohibition by otherwise functioning, rea-sonable, and productive adult citizens. Do not prohibit Patrick's benign use of cannabis. Instead, charge his neighbor Packard with a crime after he gets grossly overserved on cannabis and proceeds to publicly embrace his otherwise-latent nudist tendencies while jogging at night. As we learned with the inevitable consumption of alcohol, when it comes to substances: focus on the abuse, not the use.

In any discussion of drug laws, the Netherlands and its drug policies will inevitably be raised. Clearly, Dutch and American citizens differ cul-turally, historically, and socially. Still, overall, the Dutch experiment has been successful. And one statistic is telling. In spite of the prediction that Holland's relaxed drug laws would lead to rampant substance abuse, it remains true that drug use rates in the US – in every category as cited in relevant government studies – are higher than those in the Kingdom of the Netherlands.[32]

The success of coffee shops in Holland that sell personal amounts of cannabis is not the only data that support changing cannabis legislation. In 2001, Portugal eliminated criminal penalties for personal drug posses-sion, thus essentially decriminalizing all drug use. Empirical data informed these policy decisions instead of historical inertia or fear mon-gering. The results of this policy sea change were both powerful and com-pelling. First, none of the doomsday predictions made by decriminalization critics – drug use would skyrocket, particularly among the young; Portugal would become a tourist destination for drug users, etc. – became reality. Second, drug usage rates in Portugal are currently among the lowest in the European Union, and drug-related pathologies (e.g., deaths caused by drug use) have decreased markedly since decriminalization.[33] Not surprisingly, then, these laws have widespread public support. There is no substantial discussion in Portugal about whether drugs, including cannabis, should be re-criminalized.

To quote a recent *Time* magazine article about Portugal's cannabis decriminalization: "Compared to the European Union and the US, Portugal's drug use numbers are impressive. Following decriminalization, Portugal had the lowest rate of lifetime marijuana use in people over 15 in the EU: 10 percent. The most comparable figure in America is in people over 12: 39.8 percent. Proportionally, more Americans have used cocaine than Portuguese have used marijuana."[34]

Since Patrick could conceivably be arrested for safely consuming a substance potentially no more harmful than a mug of beer, another one of the government's stated reasons why cannabis should remain illegal is that it has no viable medical application. Given this assertion, it is ironic, to say the least, that the US government grows and distributes cannabis as a medication to selected needy individuals. And it has been doing so for over three decades, under the *Compassionate Investigational New Drug* (IND) initiative, a program run by the National Institute on Drug Abuse.

Under advice of his doctor, one of the patients in this program, Florida stockbroker Irvin Rosenfeld, has smoked a dozen joints a day for a quarter of a century to cope with a rare and painful form of bone disease. Not only has cannabis successfully helped Rosenfeld manage his disease, but comprehensive physical examinations of him and others in the IND program showed no ill-effects of smoking cannabis.[35] One hand of government literally gives cannabis as medicine to sick folks, yet strangely the other one lobbies for cannabis to remain, for the rest of us, highly illegal.

In addition to refuting the three stated reasons why cannabis should be outlawed – bad for you, bad for others, no medical use – there are also pragmatic reasons to change current cannabis laws. Given the current global economic recession, one of the main advantages to permitting cannabis use is potential government revenue from taxation. Cannabis use should be treated like alcohol and tobacco, that is, with restrictions upon when, where, and at what age it can be purchased, compliance with quality standards and truth in advertising regulations, taxation, and the like.

Of course, since it grows more readily, this titular weed would not be as easy to tax as tobacco, but there is no question that people would be happy to purchase a pack of Pall Mall Verde due to convenience alone, even though doing so may be more expensive than self-harvesting. Revenue would go into state and federal coffers, whereas now money goes out for cannabis-related law enforcement. According to a 2005 study conducted by Jeffrey Miron, a Harvard University economist, legalization of marijuana *à la* tobacco and alcohol in the US could potentially generate over $6 billion in revenue, while simultaneously saving at least $7.7 billion in law enforcement costs.[36] California alone was forecast to raise about $1.3 billion in revenue, not including savings from the penal system.[37] This tokin' economy, if you will, is a fiscal no-brainer.

Since the government's laws against cannabis spread like a blunderbuss, even hemp, the non-THC-concentrated version of the plant, is outlawed. This, in spite of the fact that smoking hemp cannot get you high. Additionally, hemp contains many beneficial properties. Along with being a hardy and easy-to-grow plant (it is one of the planet's fastest growing biomasses), commercial hemp can be used for food, textiles, fiber, biodegradable plastics, paper, clothing material, fuel, construction, and more.[38]

So, in the end, is it harmful to use cannabis? The short answer: if so, probably not much. It can be harmful to the user, particularly if abused, or if it is smoked by someone with respiratory problems. Then again, if you are one of the patients in the federal IND program, you depend on cannabis as essential medicine. Does cannabis use harm society? Certainly not any more than the equivalent use of alcohol and tobacco, and likely a lot less, while even sometimes being good for one's health. What does damage society, however, is prohibition. It imposes unnecessary punitive controls, creates incentives for crime, while at the same time diverting enforcement resources away from more crucial matters.

Additionally, reasonable cannabis use raises important questions about personal liberty and social morality. Here are the immutable social facts. Drugs are not going away. Thus, people will consume them. Prohibition does not work, so making adult substance use illegal causes more problems than it supposedly prevents. Therefore, if use of a given substance like cannabis is inevitable, it seems prudent to permit reasonable, adult use, reduce the harm, tax the process, and treat the abusers in the public health realm, not the penal system.

Revisiting Mill's Harm Principle, we should resort to the law only when individuals cannot, due to their extreme cannabis use, exercise their "distinct and assignable obligations" to themselves, their family, friends, and society overall, and not when, after a long week, they relax by reaching for a puff instead of a tallboy. And according to current physiological research, occasional cannabis use may even enhance physical health a bit. So, if the US government cannot be consistent enough to label alcohol and tobacco as Schedule I substances along with cannabis, then it should permit pot's realistic use, but only if it wants additional revenue while also decreasing crime.

Returning to Patrick, let's say his nosey neighbor Poindexter suspects that Patrick consumes cannabis. Poindexter phones the police, who in turn get a warrant to search Patrick's house. Upon executing the warrant, the police find a modest amount of cannabis, nascent plants, grow lights, and other incriminating materials and equipment. Patrick is arrested and charged with possession of a controlled substance and drug paraphernalia. Due to the budding plants and growing materials, Patrick is also charged with intent to distribute and his assets are seized.

Before arrest, Patrick was a loving father, active citizen, and productive taxpayer. Now, however, he is facing criminal charges and the cost and time of clearing his name. Patrick moves from being a contributing member to society to, depending on the laws of his home jurisdiction, a potential drain on society. All of this for consuming a historically endorsed, but currently banned substance that is no more dangerous than legally permitted alcohol and nicotine.

For Patrick and many, many other adults, the current laws are unjust, unnecessary and hypocritical. They needlessly fill our judicial system with non-violent, otherwise productive individuals, and divert already overburdened police officers from preventing more important violent crimes. Cannabis decriminalization/legalization leads to a greater social good than the status quo. Morally speaking, therefore, we may even be prompted, if not compelled, to support these measures.

Ending on a high note, folks do not need to consume cannabis to support changing the government's position on its reasonable, adult use. Rather, one just needs to value personal liberty, empirical health data on the neutral (if not mildly positive) effects of cannabis use, be in favor of reducing crime while focusing law enforcement efforts on violent felonies, hate prohibition's increased bloodshed, support additional government revenue, and value the many benefits of commercial hemp.

NOTES

1 Nicholas Graham, "Michael Phelps Bong Picture: Olympic Champion Caught Smoking Marijuana: UPDATED," *Huffington Post*, January 31, 2009, available online at www.huffingtonpost.com/2009/01/31/michael-phelps-bong-pictu_n_162842.html (accessed June 18, 2009).
2 Isaac Fitzgerald, "Kellogg's Donates Michael Phelps Cereal to Food Bank; Stoner Boxes End Up on Ebay," *AlterNet*, March 12, 2009, at www.alternet.

org/blogs/peek/131305/kellogg%27s_donates_michael_phelps_cereal_to_food_bank%3B_stoner_boxes_end_up_on_ebay/ (accessed June 18, 2009).

3   Erich Goode in his 1970 text cites older studies suggesting Patrick is representative. See Erich Goode, "Profile of the Marijuana Smoker," *The Marijuana Smokers*, *DRCNet Online Library of Drug Policy* (1970), at www.druglibrary.org/special/goode/mjsmokers2.htm (accessed July 22, 2009). More recent studies suggest something in the ballpark. One 2005 study of 18–24-year-olds suggests older, so-called rare users – perhaps like Patrick, those smoking pot fewer than three times a month – are more likely than younger, so-called heavier users to claim they have college degrees, be financially independent, and date romantically. See John E. Schulenberg, Alicia C. Merline, Lloyd D. Johnston, Patrick M. O'Malley, Jerald G. Bachman, and Virginia B. Laetz, "Trajectories of Marijuana Use During the Transition to Adulthood: The Big Picture Based on National Panel Data," *Journal of Drug Issues* 35, 2 (2005): 265. A 2007 study of New York City neighborhood income, income distribution, and drug use found that higher "neighborhood median income and maldistributed neighborhood income" were both "significantly associated with a greater likelihood of alcohol and marijuana use but not of cigarette use," and in the target study about 36 percent of the sample were 35–54 years old, 35 percent white, 46 percent had incomes of $40,000 or greater, and 48 percent had finished some college or had college or graduate degrees. See Sandro Galea, Jennifer Ahern, Melissa Tracy, and David Vlahow, "Neighborhood Income and Income Distribution and the Use of Cigarettes, Alcohol, and Marijuana," *American Journal of Preventive Medicine* 32 6S (2007): S195 and S198. Government data from 2007 suggests that between 16 and 25 years of age, nearly 11–19 percent of respondents (peaking around ages 19–21) claim they have used marijuana once in the last month, while those from 26–39 years of age, 5–10 percent of respondents (decreasing with age) claim they have done so. See US Department of Health and Human Services, "Table 1.12B – Marijuana Use in Lifetime, Past Year, and Last Month, by Detailed Age Category: Percentages, 2006 and 2007" (December 30, 2008–June 18 2009), at www.oas.samhsa.gov/NSDUH/2k7NSDUH/tabs/Sect1peTabs1to46.htm#Tab1.8B (accessed June 18, 2009). To provide some national context, one 1995 report for Congress found that 4.7 percent of Americans – just over 12 million people that year – reported they were currently using marijuana. See Jennifer A. Neisner, "Health Care Fact Sheet: Illicit Drug Use in the US," *CRS Report for Congress* 96-781 EPW (September 17, 1996).

4   John Stuart Mill, *On Liberty*, ed. Elizabeth Rapaport (Indianapolis: Hackett, 1978), p. 4.

5   Ibid., p. 74.

6   Ibid., p. 75.

7   Ibid., p. 74.

8   Ibid., p. 79.

9   Ibid., p. 80.

10 In chapter two of *Utilitarianism* Mill argues that the intellectual pleasures are inherently better than the physical ones because the former are preferred by most people who have completely acquainted themselves with both kinds of pleasure, and the intellectual pleasures are also more clearly associated with the sense of dignity inherent to human existence.

11 G. F. Kauert, J. G. Ramaekers, E. Schneider, M. R. Moeller, and S. W. Toennes, "Pharmacokinetic Properties of Delta9-tetrahydrocannabinol in Serum and Oral Fluid," *Journal of Analytical Toxicology* 32 (2007): 470–7.

12 US Department of Health and Human Services (CDC), "Morbidity and Mortality Weekly Report" 51 (2002): 300–3. See also US Department of Health and Human Services, "The Health Benefits of Smoking Cessation: A Report of the Surgeon General. US Department of Health and Human Services, Public Health Service, Centers for Disease Control, Center for Chronic Disease Prevention and Health Promotion, Office on Smoking and Health" (1989).

13 M. Hashibe, K. Straif, D. P. Tashkin, H. Morgenstern, S. Greenland, and Z. F. Zhang, "Epidemiologic Review of Marijuana Use and Cancer Risk," *Alcohol* 35 (2005): 265–75.

14 A. E. Munson, L. S. Harris, M. A. Friedman, W. L. Dewey, and R. A. Carchman, "Antineoplastic Activity of Cannabinoids," *Journal of the National Cancer Institute* 55 (1975): 597–602.

15 B. G. Ramirez, C. Blazquez, T. Gomez del Pulgar, M. Guzman, and M. L. de Ceballos, "Prevention of Alzheimer's Disease Pathology by Cannabinoids: Neuroprotection Mediated by Blockade of Microglial Activation," *Journal of Neuroscience* 25 (2005): 1904–13.

16 M. Perez-Reyes, "Marijuana Smoking: Factors that Influence the Bioavailability of Tetrahydrocannabinol," in C. N. Chiang and P. L. Hawks (eds.) *Research Findings on Smoking of Abused Substances* (Rockville: NIDA Research Monograph 99), pp. 42–62.

17 R. S. Niedbala, K. W. Kardso, D. F. Fritch, K. P. Kunsman, K. A. Blum, G. A. Newland, J. Waga, L. Kurtz, M. Bronsgeest, and E. J. Cone, "Passive Cannabis Smoke Exposure and Oral Fluid Testing. II. Two Studies of Extreme Cannabis Smoke Exposure in a Motor Vehicle," *Journal of Analytical Toxicology* 29 (2005): 607–15.

    Some definitions of mainstream smoke include both inhaled and exhaled smoke. In this study, the levels were detectable but below that for standard drug tests.

18 D. W. Nebert and F. J. Gonzalez, "P450 Genes: Structure, Evolution, and Regulation," *Annual Review of Biochemistry* 56 (1987): 945–93. See also S. S. Hecht, G. Carmella, S. E. Murphy, P. G. Foiles, and F. L. Chung, "Carcinogen Biomarkers Related to Smoking and Upper Aerodigestive

Tract Cancer," *Journal of Cellular Biochemistry – Supplement* 17F (1993): 27–35.

19 M. D. Roth, J. A. Marques-Magallanes, M. Yuan, W. Sun, D. P. Tashkin, and O. Hankinson, "Induction and Regulation of the Carcinogen-Metabolizing Enzyme CYP1A1 by Marijuana Smoke and Delta (9)-tetrahydrocannabi- nol," *American Journal of Respiratory Cell and Molecular Biology* 24 (2001): 339–44.

20 R. J. Price, A. B. Renwick, D. G. Walters, P. J. Young, and B. G. Lake, "Metabolism of Nicotine and Induction of CYP1A Forms in Precision-Cut Rat Liver and Lung Slices," *Toxicology In Vitro* 18 (2004): 179–85.

21 R. Melamede, "Cannabis and Tobacco Smoke are Not Equally Carcinogenic," *Harm Reduction Journal* 2 (2005): 21.

22 R. A. Sewell, J. Poling, and M. Sofuoglu, "The Effect of Cannabis Compared with Alcohol on Driving," *American Journal on Addictions* 18 (2009): 185–93.

23 D. Gieringer, J. St Laqurent, and S. Goodrich, "Cannabis Vaporizer Combines Efficient Delivery of THC with Effective Suppression of Pyrolytic Compounds," *Journal of Cannabis Therapeutics*, 4th edn., ed. Ethan Russo (Binghamton: Haworth Press): 7–27.

24 US Drug Enforcement Administration, *The DEA Position On Marijuana* (May 2006), at www.usdoj.gov/dea/marijuana_position.html (accessed July 22, 2009).

25 *Controlled Substances Act*, 21 USC Sec. 812, Schedules of controlled sub- stances (2002).

26 US National Institutes of Health, "The National Institute on Drug Abuse, Research Report Series, Tobacco Addiction," NIH Publication Number 09-4342, (2009), at www.nida.nih.gov/PDF/TobaccoRRS_v16.pdf (accessed October 23, 2009).

27 US Department of Health and Human Services, Division of Adult and Community Health, National Center for Chronic Disease Prevention and Health Promotion, "Alcohol and Public Health" (2008), at www.cdc.gov/ alcohol/ (accessed October 23, 2009).

28 Jon Gettman, "Marijuana Production in the United States," *Bulletin of Cannabis Reform* (December 2006), at www.drugscience.org/bcr/index.html (accessed April 7, 2009).

29 American Law and Legal Information, "Wickhersham Commission," at www.law.jrank.org/pages/11309/Wickersham-Commission.html (accessed May 17, 2009). The Commission's final report, "Report on the Enforcement of the Prohibition Laws of the United States: National Commission on Law Observance and Enforcement," is archived at the Schaffer Library of Drug Policy at www.druglibrary.org/schaffer/Library/studies/wick/index. html (accessed October 23, 2009).

30 Jon B. Gettman, "Crimes of Indiscretion," *NORML* (March 7, 2005), at www.norml.org/index.cfm?group_id=6411 (accessed July 22, 2009). Though

published by advocacy group NORML, this was based on FBI, Uniform Crime Reports, Arrests by Age, Sex and Race (2002); US Census Bureau, Population Estimates – State Characteristics (2002).

31 Adam Liptak, "Inmate Count in US Dwarfs Other Nations," *New York Times* (April 23, 2008), at www.nytimes.com/2008/04/23/us/23prison.html (accessed March 17, 2009).

32 Common Sense for Drug Policy, "Dutch Drug Policy *Even* More Effective Than Previously Thought" (2009), at www.csdp.org/ads/dutch2.htm (accessed May 1, 2009). This research was based on National Survey on Drug Use & Health, 1997, US Department of Health and Human Services, Substance Abuse and Mental Health Services Administration, Office of Applied Studies, Washington, DC; and M. Abraham, P. Cohen, and M. DeWinter, *Licit and Illicit Drug Use in the Netherlands*, Center for Drug Research, University of Amsterdam, at www.cedro-uva.org/lib/abraham.npo97.pdf (accessed October 23, 2009).

33 Greg Greenwald, *Drug Decriminalization in Portugal: Lessons for Creating Fair and Successful Drug Policies* (Washington, DC: Cato Institute, 2009).

34 Maia Szalavitz, "Drugs in Portugal: Did Decriminalization Work?" *Time* (April 26, 2009), at www.time.com/time/health/article/0,8599,1893946,00.html (accessed October 23, 2009).

35 Ethan Russo, Mary Lynn Mathre, Al Byrne, Robert Velin, Paul Bach, Juan Sanchez-Ramos, and Kristin Kirlin, "Chronic Cannabis Use in the Compassionate Investigational New Drug Program: An Examination of Benefits and Adverse Effects of Legal Clinical Cannabis," *Journal of Cannabis Therapeutics* 2, 1 (2002): 3–57; available online at www.drugpolicy.org/doc Uploads/Chronic_Cannabis.pdf (accessed October 23, 2009).

36 Jeffrey A. Miron, *The Budgetary Implications of Marijuana Prohibition* (Washington, DC: Marijuana Policy Project, June 2005), at www.prohibitioncosts.org/mironreport.html (accessed October 23, 2009).

37 Wyatt Buchanan, "Governor Says He's Open to Debate on Legal Pot," *San Francisco Chronicle* (May 6, 2009), at www.sfgate.com/cgibin/article.cgi?f=/c/a/2009/05/05/MNO617F929.DTL#ixzz0LMZNDwIq&D (accessed May 6, 2009).

38 Jack Herer, "A Brief Summary of the Uses of Hemp" (2009), at www.jack herer.com/chapter02.html (accessed October 23, 2009).

CHAPTER 14

POT POLITICS

Prohibition and Morality

 Activist Jack Herer, legendary author of the underground classic *The Emperor Wears No Clothes*, tells a dramatic tale of the first time he used cannabis. It ends with him wondering, "How could this be illegal?" This same thought has become more common the world over. Citizens provide their governments with the power and ability to punish them. This power obviously must apply only in specific and extreme circumstances. The brief history of marijuana prohibition suggests that use of this power requires considerable thought. Designating the possession of a plant as a crime requires a clear rationale before a government can apply sanctions to citizens.

In truth, the plant has been illegal for less than a century in most places in the world. Local ordinances against possession passed in various spots in the United States just as laborers from other countries entered the area, or when evangelists returned with the plant in their pockets. Mormon missionaries returning to Utah from Mexico upset their fathers with the green weed they'd discovered there. Federal sanctions took years to develop, even in the United States. Their coincidental appearance so soon after the end of alcohol prohibition has generated a lot of speculation about the policy serving as a strategy for keeping members of law enforcement on the payroll. Hearings from the discussion of the first Federal law in the United States reveal that few people even knew what cannabis was at the time. "I believe it is some sort of narcotic," one member of the committee piped. The law was proposed with little science to explain any rationale. Nevertheless, many anecdotes about miscegenation, murder, and mayhem appeared.[1] The Marijuana Tax Act in the United States, which essentially established federal prohibition, passed in 1937. Sanctions have been around long enough to frame the debate. Though many people ask why marijuana should be decriminalized or legalized, no one asks why the plant is illegal in the first place. It seems as if the only way to answer why the legal status of the plant should change would require an understanding of the rationale for its current legal status. In short, it's impossible to argue against the criminalization of cannabis possession until we know why possession is criminalized.

Practical? Moral?

Proponents and opponents of current cannabis prohibition make arguments that they view as either moral or practical. The distinction can be artificial, but practical arguments tend to point to empirical investigation and estimates of cash saved or harm done. There is something potentially moral underlying these arguments, of course, but the general focus is on predictions about what would and would not happen under various scenarios, including decriminalization of possession. Maintaining criminal penalties based on speculation of horrors if they are removed is probably a bad idea. I should emphasize here that social scientists are notoriously bad at these kinds of predictions, myself included. It's not that social scientists are all dumb (though some certainly are). The problem is essentially intractable. We can gather all sorts of data in hope of predicting the future under various policy scenarios, but the unforeseen implications of any law are often larger than all of those we can see. (Listen to the four opinions of any three economists, for an example.)

Moral arguments often attempt to sidestep these issues based on conceptualizations of what is or isn't Right with a capital R. Recent efforts to decriminalize the plant, increase availability of medical cannabis, or create a taxed and regulated market, have fueled debates about the implications of alternatives to prohibition. Some people view current punishments as inappropriate and base their view on data. Their practical arguments focus on the limited negative consequences associated with marijuana use. They explain data on respiratory symptoms or gateway theory or whatever fear seems to be the latest big fear of the plant, and they point out that the impact is markedly less severe than the negative consequences of arrest and imprisonment. Smart ones emphasize that penalties have little impact on rates of use, even among our beloved teens. Anti-prohibitionists have suggested a variety of plans – removal of criminal penalties, an unregulated free market, or a highly taxed, controlled, and licensed arrangement. Proponents of decriminalization and legalization suggest that changes in current laws could save taxpayers money, decrease the potential for violations of civil rights, and still keep marijuana-induced harm to a minimum. In contrast, prohibitionists assert that changes in policy would convey tacit approval of drug use, increase consumption of marijuana and other illicit substances, and exacerbate negative consequences.

Note that these arguments tend to focus on estimates of consequences of the various policies. Many concentrate on estimates of expenses. Social scientists attempt to guess about the unknowable: the amount of law enforcement time saved if cannabis were legal, the potential increase in use, any changes in use of licit and illicit drugs, etc. They then try to boil down drug-induced harm to a financial number. Reducing human experience to a cash amount is never easy and always odd. The arguments usually attempt to estimate the advantages and disadvantages of the current laws relative to alternative proposals. Ideal policy would cost little in terms of every form of expense. Enforcing the laws should be simple and efficient; any negative consequences of use of the plant should also be cheap. Most of these arguments are internally consistent given a specific set of assumptions. Debates between proponents and opponents of prohibition often arise because they cannot agree on the same values for their underlying assumptions. They are also quite good at splitting hairs about ways to reduce all of these to an amount of cash. In fact, opinions on the practicalities of ending cannabis prohibition may rest on assumptions about each of these estimates.

The Moral Alternative

Alternative approaches at least pretend to leave money aside. These arguments sooner or later boil down to something about ethics, principles, or morality. Assertions related to morals and rights can reflect perceptions of good and evil that purportedly transcend simple assessments of expenses or harm. That is, there may be a way to sidestep empirical investigation and the assumptions inherent in practical arguments if we had principles that superseded these issues. Surely economic, psychological, and sociological data would have a hard time convincing citizens to legalize murder, for example. A sense for right and wrong could prove quite valuable. Plenty of folks on both sides of the debate have grown weary collecting more and more data and trying to explain research to people who will never understand it. Others truly believe the moral issues are more important than the empirical ones, though their moral rationales touch on research from time to time.

The problem arises, of course, when we try to explain why something is right or wrong. These can easily slip back to practical, empirical questions if we rely on defining what is wrong by an estimate of negative consequences. Utilitarian arguments sometimes appear to weight costs and benefits in an objective manner. They assign these weights based on underlying perceptions of right and wrong that often reflect a sense of morals or rights. Moral arguments in support of prohibition focus on the perception of ethical behavior. Some proponents of these moral arguments claim that their rationales are independent of the consequences of actions. That is, some behaviors may be wrong even if they do not necessarily lead to harm. Thus, these arguments do not rely directly on estimates of the damage marijuana causes. According to some legal moralists who support prohibition, cannabis remains outlawed because it is wrong – independent of its impact on humans. That is, even if any documented negative consequences of use could be counteracted immediately by a medication or therapy, use would still be wrong and should remain prohibited. (Technically, use is not prohibited, but possession is, creating a comparable effect.) If I understand some of these people correctly, if a person could get high and then take a pill that would counteract any possible ill from doing so, the act would still be wrong, and cannabis should still be prohibited. When pressed, these prohibitionists point to gruesome crimes that we would never legalize even if their negative consequences could essentially disappear through some sort of treatment. (Choices are usually alarmist. Pedophilia is always a favorite.)

Punishing Immorality

A key question behind these rationales often remains unasked: Should criminal law punish people who behave immorally? Is something a crime simply because it is immoral? We have seen this approach create many problems. Back when criminal laws against extramarital affairs and same-sex contact still led to arrests, issues about privacy and civil rights undermined their rationale. Many legal scholars view this legal moralism with considerable distaste. They see morality as completely constructed – a set of standards that may have universal agreement but little confirmable existence in reality. Morals, then, are essentially fairy tales about perceptions of right and wrong. This constructivist argument is a hard sell when we get to the heinous crimes. Many find this argument hard to stomach. They have some inner feeling that morality somehow makes sense, but they may still question the justice in punishing people for acts that are immoral and only immoral. That is, they feel that immorality is not enough to justify a criminal penalty. It may be neither necessary nor sufficient.

Theorists often emphasize that our criminal justice system is inconsistent on this count. We do not provide a criminal punishment for every immoral act, which suggests that immorality alone does not justify government sanction. Husak artfully describes breach of contract as an example.[2] Deliberately breaking a solemn, written, signed, and notarized promise will not land most Westerners in jail. Though the court can order these promise breakers to pay damages, the court cannot assign prison time. No one doubts that breaking such a contract is immoral, yet it carries no criminal penalty. Various forms of lying (cheating on exams, plagiarism, and fibs) fall in the same category of immoral acts with no criminal sanctions. We also punish behaviors that few would find immoral. Traffic violations come to mind. I am hard pressed to say that exceeding the speed limit is immoral, but it certainly generates plenty of penalties. Thus, if we choose to punish the possession of marijuana, proving the act immoral would not seem to be enough. In addition, proving possession moral would not guarantee that it should not be punished, either.

Morality Regardless

Former United States drug czar William Bennett always liked moral arguments. "The simple fact is that drug use is wrong. And the moral argument, in the end, is the most compelling argument."[3] Push this too far and circularity rears its ugly head. The assertion is essentially unfalsifiable. What incontestable ethical insight leads to the conclusion that drug use is wrong? Answering this question often leads prohibitionists to string synonyms together (it's wrong because it's evil and it's evil because it's unethical, etc.). James Q. Wilson's "drug use is wrong because it's immoral" typifies this shell game.[4] Alternatively, these purportedly moral arguments for prohibition fall back on utilitarian estimates of harm. Another former United States drug czar, Barry MacCaffrey, said that drugs are wrong because they are "destructive of a person's physical, emotional, and moral strength."[5] Obviously, a precise estimate of one's moral strength is hard to come by, making it difficult to guess marijuana's impact on it, but note how this statement leads back to an estimate of harm.

The underpinnings of these arguments are hard to identify. It's also unclear how they compare to the morality of jailing citizens for owning a plant. The moral arguments in support of prohibition may stem from attitudes about pleasure, productivity, intoxication, and self-control. An unstated assumption in a lot of Western countries is pleasure should only reward contribution to society. Concerted, responsible productivity, especially when it is devoted to what people perceive is the public good, should bring pleasure of its own. Receiving a humanitarian award should create the flood of neurotransmitters we all would enjoy, and it should be the only sort of thing available to do so. Prayer might be a close second. Consuming a drug is therefore morally wrong because it creates pleasures that some people do not believe are properly earned. Those who point to psychoactive pharmaceutical drugs as a counterargument are told that antidepressants and the like do not create pleasure on their own – they simply allow people to function so they can work to achieve various delights. This sort of statement would make my Ritalin-abusing clients laugh, but prohibitionists would emphasize that orally administered Ritalin taken at the proper dosage should create no euphoria. Indeed, some of the efforts at developing cannabis-based medications emphasize a keen desire to remove any psychoactive effects of the plant, as if those with AIDS and cancer should stay away from anything that might lighten their moods without work.

Attitudes about intoxication and its link to productivity may also underlie these arguments. Any state of impaired thought might hinder productivity, which violates the work ethic many people view as intrinsically good, or Good, as the case may be. It's not that they're not supposed to feel pleasure without work; it's just that intoxication interferes with work and that's why it's evil. Although large studies find no links between cannabis use and various measures of productivity – college grades, salary, sick days, and job turnover[6] – the inherent immorality in the unproductive times associated with intoxication seems self-evident to prohibitionists. It's unclear how these periods differ from watching our beloved television, which certainly makes productivity a hard achievement, but this argument is often brushed aside as a false analogy for reasons I don't quite follow. If I dare mention that time spent in houses of worship generates few goods or services, most prohibitionists recommend my exorcism. This attachment to productivity might also grow quite slippery when applied to illicit use of cognitive enhancers – drugs that claim to increase mental efficiency in some way. I somehow doubt that those who want cannabis prohibition to continue would gladly welcome over-the-counter distribution of modafinil, the narcolepsy drug that keeps soldiers and freshmen awake the world over, even if it does squeeze more work out of its users. Perhaps there is some baby-bear "just right" way to produce enough work without any drugs, though the measurement of how much is enough seems a moving target.

Others suggest that intoxication makes behavior too varied and unpredictable to be safe. That is, using cannabis might lead to ill-advised or troublesome actions that would decrease if cannabis would disappear. This is essentially drawing a wall around the law in hopes that enforcements against minor violations will minimize major violations. Crime and aggression often top the list of behaviors that should decrease if cannabis were wiped from the planet. This argument gets quite convoluted. Links between cannabis use and crime are actually quite tenuous. Since sale requires contact with an underground market, the crimes directly related to this contact would certainly disappear if cannabis disappeared. (Though decriminalizing would arguably have a comparable effect. If possession were not a crime, the crime of possession would certainly drop.)

But crime, by definition, is already illegal. The most efficient way to deter these crimes via law enforcement likely requires enforcing whatever laws forbid these crimes. If you think that cannabis use leads to theft in a subset of users (it does not, by the way), enforcing the laws against theft would be a more direct way to decrease stealing than eliminating cannabis. If a new drug, Stealsalot, appeared, and it immediately made all users steal every time they used it, a rationale like this for its prohibition might follow. In fact, links between serious felonies and cannabis consumption are often specious or non-existent.[7] In addition, time spent enforcing laws against cannabis possession appears to take away from time battling serious crime.[8] Hours spent fingerprinting someone with a dime bag mean fewer police officers on the streets preventing acts of violence. More importantly, since not everyone who uses cannabis commits these crimes, it's unclear why they are not allowed to possess the plant. Surely we cannot punish everyone for the acts of a few.

The idea that cannabis increases aggression has been roundly disputed in laboratory experiments.[9] Even provocation cannot get those who have

❦ MITCH EARLEYWINE

smoked it recently to be more hostile than those who smoked a placebo. This argument that a drug that can increase aggression should be prohibited makes alcohol a tough sell, too. This legendary elixir of life, lubricant of all things social, has increased hostility not only against provocateurs but also against innocent bystanders, even in my own laboratory.[10] Obviously, a return to alcohol prohibition is out of the question. Intoxicated driving is usually next on the list of crimes that should drop with cannabis prohibition. Thankfully, although the impact of cannabis use alone on driving seems comparable to that of antihistamines, which we are unlikely to prohibit any time soon,[11] this act is already a crime. Strict enforcement of laws against intoxicated driving may be a more efficient way to decrease intoxicated driving than prohibiting all intoxicants. It's true that eliminating intoxicants is bound to decrease intoxicated driving. Punishing all people who possess intoxicants because some people drive intoxicated, however, loses its sense of justice. The idea that one citizen is sanctioned for the behavior of another has never been popular. This argument essentially asserts that those who never drive intoxicated must lose their right to own intoxicants for one reason: because some people drive while intoxicated. Note how we would balk at comparable reasoning with other possessions or activities. No one should own guns because some people who own guns commit crimes. No one should listen to rock music because some people who listen to rock music commit crimes. Punishing the many in hope of catching a few seems quite unjust.

As a last resort, legal moralists who support prohibition assert that any change in drug policy would be immoral because it sends the wrong message to citizens. Some authors assert that moralists think that the plant should remain illegal at any expense.[12] Note that these arguments eventually resort to utilitarian assessments of some potential harm. Explanations for the morals often lead to evaluations of costs and benefits. They often cite emergency room admissions, the number of people in treatment for marijuana problems, or other societal ills purportedly linked to the plant. My libertarian friends emphasize that many of these problems actually arise from socialized medicine, not cannabis. That is, if those who use cannabis end up in an emergency room or treatment program and they have to pay for the care themselves, the natural contingencies at work should get them to behave better. Alternatively, if that's how they want to spend their own money, so be it. In fact, the emergency room data are woefully weak, with cannabis-related admissions dwarfed by accidents related to American football.[13] Anyone who wants to prohibit American football based on emergency room data is in for a long fight.

The treatment admissions are also confounded by judicial mandates. Many arrested for possession are given the choice of jail time or treatment, which seems like little choice at all. Suggesting that these people are dependent on cannabis or suffering from some cannabis-related ill confounds the impact of the plant with the impact of prohibition. In fact, over half of those in treatment for marijuana problems are court referred.[14] Clinically, these people are hard to work with. It's not that they're not willing to play the game. They'll gladly attend meetings and talk about their troubles. But there are few things more odd than the casual cannabis user who was busted for possession sitting in a group of meth smokers and alcoholics. Some are homeless and broke, bereft of family and friends, and suffering from serious health complications. And one has a possession bust and eats too much cookie dough. The magnitude of the problems is so disparate that it's hard to create the group cohesiveness essential for good therapy. Clients and therapists can't help but wonder if that seat in the group might be put to better use.

This "wrong message to citizens" argument implies that eliminating penalties will increase use in dramatic and negative ways. Somehow, the right message will keep people away from cannabis. The logic generally goes as follows: if we lift a prohibition, we are condoning the behavior, therefore it will increase, and therefore negative consequences will increase. This line ends up being utilitarian rather than inherently only moral. Alternatively, the logic might go: if we lift a prohibition, we are condoning the behavior, and the behavior is wrong. Keep legal sanctions in an effort to keep use to a minimum, which will keep negative consequences down, too. It seems like a great idea. The problem, of course, is that prohibition has had little impact on use. The fact that use of cannabis and any negative consequences from use seem essentially unrelated to policy seems unbelievable. Surely enthusiastic enforcement of prohibition must alter people's behavior, but the data suggest otherwise. Large samples from San Francisco and Amsterdam reveal that rates of use, use of hard drugs, and negative consequences of use were higher in the locale that had the stricter prohibition.[15] Comparisons across countries and different domains within countries also suggest little impact of legal sanctions. For example, the number of heroin users per capita in the US (308 per 100,000 residents), where laws against possession remain, dramatically exceeds the number in the Netherlands (160 per 100,000 residents), where possession is essentially decriminalized,[16] despite frequent cries of marijuana as a gateway to hard drugs. Fewer teens try cocaine in the Netherlands than in the US.[17] Perhaps the decriminalization of marijuana

❦ MITCH EARLEYWINE

has weakened its connection with these other substances. Given that people can obtain cannabis in shops where cocaine and heroin are forbidden, purchasing marijuana no longer must lead to exposure to harder drugs. Increased availability of cannabis may have decreased interest in other intoxicants, too.

For those who view comparisons from one country to the next as difficult, comparisons within a country produce comparable results. Two of Australia's eight territories also decriminalized possession of less than 25 grams of marijuana. Consumption of cannabis in a public place and sales of the drug remain illegal. People in South Australia and Australian Capital Territory face fines for possession. Offenders receive a Cannabis Expiation Notice, much like a traffic ticket, and must pay their penalties within 60 days. They also have their cannabis confiscated. Law enforcement officers find these notices easier to issue and sustain than a full arrest. Thus, the number of offenses has increased dramatically. In a sense, this approach has increased the likelihood of penalties despite decreasing their severity. Rates of marijuana consumption in the decriminalized areas remain comparable to the rates in Australian territories with harsher penalties.[18]

A comparable comparison within the US may also be relevant. Eleven states essentially removed criminal penalties for possessing small amounts of marijuana by 1979: Alaska, California, Colorado, Maine, Minnesota, Mississippi, Nebraska, New York, North Carolina, Ohio, and Oregon. Decriminalization in America has led to little change in marijuana use, much like the experience in the Netherlands and Australia. Use by high school seniors in decriminalizing states did not differ from use in other states where sanctions remained.[19] Oregon, Maine, and California showed little change in use by adults after decriminalization.[20] Other states have had comparable experiences.

In truth, illegality is rarely the rationale for abstinence. Few people claim that they would change the amount they used if marijuana were legal.[21] A poll of 1,400 adults found that over 80 percent claimed that they would not try the drug even if it were legal.[22] These data require cautious interpretation. People are notoriously poor at explaining why they behave in certain ways, or how they would act if conditions were dramatically different. A long period of legalization may alter these attitudes dramatically, making people more likely to try the drug if sanctions disappeared. Nevertheless, few report that fear of arrest changes their marijuana consumption. It does leave an idea open; maybe prohibition isn't having much impact. Of course, we assume that more people trying cannabis will lead to all kinds of ills that seem unlikely, too. In fact, few people who try the plant go on to become regular users, and fewer still develop any problems.

The impact of marijuana laws on availability of the drug also appears small. For over three decades now, about 80 percent of high school seniors have reported that marijuana is fairly easy or very easy to purchase.[23] Buying beer is actually considered more difficult.[24] The price of marijuana undoubtedly increases because of its illegal status, but users appear relatively insensitive to price, at least to the extent that it can be manipulated by legal sanctions.[25] There always seems to be small amounts available for a little cash. The drug is actually cheap compared to other intoxicants, particularly given the number of hours of altered consciousness it provides. Cannabis intoxication may be less expensive than seeing a movie in a theatre, hour for hour. Thus, these data suggest that the current laws may have little impact on use because they fail to create fear of legal sanctions, decrease availability, or raise prices enough to eliminate demand. Our look at Amsterdam, Australia, and the US suggests that use and policy covary little.

Recent data from the World Health Organization also confirm that policy and use are essentially orthogonal except for outliers with extreme penalties.[26] The United States, with its penalties for possession, has 42.4 percent of citizens reporting lifetime use of cannabis. The Netherlands, which has decriminalized possession of small amounts, has a rate of 19.8 percent. Portugal's experience with decriminalization also supports the idea that policy actually has little impact on the use of illicit drugs. Portugal decriminalized drug possession in 2001. By 2007, cannabis use was essentially unchanged. In fact, key age groups, particularly young teens, showed drops in use.[27]

What About the Children?

Even all of these arguments do not convince folks who view the primary goal of prohibition as a deterrent to use in youth. In essence, we fight the war on marijuana to protect children. Who doesn't love babies? As mentioned above, the current policies have actually done little to keep cannabis out of the hands of youth. As I often ask my undergraduate classes, when was the last time your dealer carded you? But note how slippery the terms "youth" and "children" become. Toddlers aren't passing the bong, and despite disquieting stories to the contrary, grade school students rarely see cannabis either. The real concern is teens. An underground market has little incentive to sell exclusively to adults. A taxed, regulated one could sanction such behavior and provide important incentives for genuinely keeping cannabis away from kids, and by kids I mean teens. But this approach has serious flaws, as our markets on alcohol and tobacco reveal. Despite age restrictions on these drugs, teens frequently get them. Punishing adult users for possession of cannabis appears to do little to keep the plant from teens, and taxed, regulated, age-restricted markets in alcohol and tobacco do not succeed perfectly either.

The tacit assumption behind this argument is that when teens use cannabis it is a disaster. Earlier, heavier involvement with the plant does predict a higher likelihood of problem use.[28] Some data suggest that heavy use before age 18 can lead to deviant brain structure, decreases in IQ, and other complications.[29] These effects aren't particularly large, but they do reach statistical significance. Though it's taboo to say so, quite a few people try cannabis early in life and appear to have functioning brains, above average IQs, and no symptoms of dependence. Several are tenured professors at research universities, mental health professionals, and prominent members of the business community. Still, keeping cannabis away from teens just feels right to adults. Perhaps the way to do it isn't through criminal sanctions. Imprisoning a teen's parents for possession certainly seems an inefficient way to reach this goal. Other criminal penalties have not worked well, either. Prevention programs that have little to do with legal sanctions have shown some success,[30] much the way anti-tobacco programs have worked despite the legality of cigarettes. What would it take to guarantee that no teens will get cannabis? It's hard to say, but the efforts would likely have to be severe. A high probability of an extremely harsh punishment for teens who possess the plant and those who provide it to them seems to resonate with some prohibitionists. This "getting tough" approach has some curious problems, however.

Getting Tough

Prohibitionists reason that stiffer penalties should deter any behavior. Proposals include extremes like "If you try, you die." In 1990, when he was Chief of Police in Los Angeles, Daryl Gates suggested that occasional marijuana smokers should be "taken out and shot."[31] A 2009 email from a representative from Georgia in the US House of Representatives suggests caning for possession and execution for distribution would be appropriate.[32] This approach would likely inhibit many users. Malaysia and Singapore impose the death penalty on drug trafficking. Casual users in these countries are imprisoned in centers purportedly designed for rehabilitation, but the techniques do not parallel most stereotypes of therapy. They often include solitary confinement and hard labor. Both countries have arrest rates for drug possession that are 30 percent lower than those in most Western countries.[33] For obvious reasons, reports of use are probably extremely low. Who would confess to a crime on a survey when punishments are so severe?

It seems hard to justify a moral argument for prohibition if enforcement requires such flagrant violations of civil rights. In addition, the severity of penalties may have little impact without increases in the probability of arrest.[34] Even the harshest of penalties may not deter behavior if the chance of getting caught is slim to none. Currently, fewer than 3 percent of cannabis users in the United States are arrested per year.[35] Appreciable increases in the probability of arrest could prove extremely expensive. More law enforcement personnel, court time, and prison facilities could cost billions. In addition, many users may turn to alcohol or prescription drugs in an effort to substitute for marijuana. The health impact of these changes could prove quite expensive because the negative consequences associated with problem use of these drugs are more severe than those related to cannabis. Moralists in support of prohibition, particularly those who appreciate these policies, suggest that the decrease in drug use is worth the price of increased enforcement. Unfortunately, the data do not support this idea.

Moral Arguments for Prohibition

So, what is so inherently immoral about cannabis consumption? Those who murder, rape, and rob violate the rights of others. But cannabis users need not violate the rights of anyone. Despite long, tangential, and circuitous arguments about how buying from the underground market supports terrorism, it is quite possible for a cannabis user to have no

MITCH EARLEYWINE

impact on anyone else. Prohibitionists might point to public opinion on this one – a bit of a concession to the idea that morality is socially constructed – and polls might support them. Perhaps 51 percent or more of people believe cannabis use is wrong. Is this proof? If 49 percent of the world said cannabis use is okay would they all be wrong? Surely the percentages are not so close for murder, rape, and robbery. A comparable survey 150 years ago might suggest that slavery was moral. And further, does this popularity contest of morality mean that an immoral behavior deserves sanction?

Proponents of cannabis prohibition often claim that the plant's current legal status is designed to protect people from the negative consequences of use. The list of these negative consequences usually begins with concerns about cannabis dependence, progression to hard drug use, respiratory problems, and some sort of long-term loss of motivation, mental health, or brain function. Note that none of these, even if they were true (and data suggest that they may not be), directly involve one citizen harming another. The occasional prohibitionist will make arguments for indirect harms, often mentioning something about how smoking cannabis could increase medical costs for one citizen that are subsequently passed along to others. This slope grows slippery very quickly. If we are going to prohibit behaviors in an effort to lower everyone's medical bills, eating meat, drinking alcohol, smoking cigarettes, and failing to exercise would probably be better targets than cannabis use. Legal sanctions against these actions would not be popular; most citizens would view them as a violation of personal freedom. These examples should reveal the absurdity of this argument. If moves toward socialized medicine lead to micromanaging everyone's habits, we're all in very real trouble.

Thus, if we turn from empirical, consequentialist arguments to purely ethical ones (if that's possible), we find that the immorality of cannabis seems to rest in its inherent immorality. The idea that it should be prohibited simply because it is immoral is inconsistent with other prohibitions and permissions. As far as more utilitarian arguments are concerned, the negative impact of the plant does not appear in all users, making punishing all for possession a bit odd. Current prohibitions designed to increase productivity, prevent crime and aggression, send the correct message to citizens, or protect children appear to do little on these fronts. Except in extreme cases, policy seems unrelated to use of the plant, further undermining arguments for prohibition.

Moral Arguments Against Prohibition

Anti-prohibitionists often take two approaches in their moral arguments. Some argue that prohibition violates human rights guaranteed by laws in various countries. Some focus on the idea of proportionality – that the severity of a punishment should parallel the severity of the crime as measured by the amount of harm it causes others. Perceptions of human rights often rely on perceived links between human freedom and morality. Like the moral arguments to support prohibition, these arguments against prohibition purportedly do not rely on estimates of harm. Most focus on the guarantees of a country's key legal documents, including the rights to freedom of religion, privacy, and property. Alas, many countries do not provide these guarantees. Moralists against prohibition argue that current drug laws infringe on these rights.

Arguments in support of religious rights related to drug use combine two of the most controversial topics in human behavior. The quest for freedom of religion drove many from one land to the next in an attempt to worship as they wished. Atheists who long for civil rights comparable to those religious people continue with a comparable quest. At least two religions have formal histories of using marijuana as a sacrament: the Brahmakrishna sect of Hinduism and the Ethiopian Zion Coptic Church. Rituals involving cannabis are inherent to each. Moralists against prohibition argue that members of these churches should continue their practices as part of their religious freedom. In the United States, most draw parallels between cannabis rituals and the religious use of wine by Jews and Christians. Weighing these benefits of religious freedom against the costs of marijuana consumption has become quite tricky. Religions that have started more recently, many with cannabis-related names (e.g., The Church of 420; Marijuana Church), have popped up with some frequency. They make the same argument for religious freedom.

The US courts do not support these religious arguments against prohibition.[36] Prohibitionists emphasize that wine is not consumed to the point of intoxication in most religious rituals. Moralists against prohibition often point to the Jewish practice of drinking to intoxication on the holiday of Purim. They also emphasize the sacramental use of peyote in the Native American Church, which was protected by the American Indian Religious Freedom Act Amendments of 1994. Peyote clearly causes intoxication. Prohibitionists argue that peyote is used less widely than marijuana and may prove easier to keep under control. The Native

American Peyote ritual also specifies limited, infrequent times for ingesting the substance. In contrast, sacramental consumption of cannabis often occurs frequently, sometimes many times per day. Moralists against prohibition emphasize the right to freedom of religion over any aspects of controlling the drug. (Note that these arguments eventually resort to utilitarian assessments. Thus, moralists against prohibition may see threats to religious freedom as more harmful than any negative consequences of peyote or cannabis consumption.)

Despite protest, the court continues to support prohibition, and religious use of cannabis remains illegal. In the United States, the hallmark Supreme Court case related to this issue, *Employment Division v. Smith 1990*, concerned sacramental peyote use.[37] The case has generated commentaries that could fill a library. Like all Supreme Court cases, this one does not lend itself to an easy summary. A private organization fired two substance abuse counselors for their sacramental use of peyote. When the men applied for unemployment, the state turned them down because they had lost their jobs due to misconduct. The Court ruled that the Free Exercise of Religion Clause of the First Amendment does not bar the "application of a neutral, generally applicable law to religiously motivated action." The ruling allowed the state to deny unemployment payments. The case suggests that people cannot claim exception from cannabis laws for religious reasons unless the laws unconstitutionally attempt to regulate religious practice. This is a difficult argument. If the religion expressly mandates using cannabis ceremonially, the law would seem to regulate the practice. Nevertheless, the religious argument, at least in the United States, has failed to justify changes in cannabis laws.

Moralists against prohibition also view the ingestion of marijuana as a personal act protected by their interpretation of rights to privacy. The legal literature on the right to privacy is vast and convoluted. Moralists against prohibition assert that, although many governments do not guarantee a right to privacy directly, any activity conducted alone or among intimates should be protected against government interference so long as it does not harm others. This interpretation of the right rests on a few previous cases, at least in the United States. For example, the right to use birth control has been protected under the right to privacy. Laws that prohibit sexual acts among consenting adults have been struck down for this reason. Moralists against prohibition assert that cannabis consumption should qualify under this right just as these other actions do. But counterarguments suggest that a right to privacy should only apply in important, fundamental life decisions, like the choice to have children.

These interpretations imply that using cannabis is not comparable in importance and should not fall under a right to privacy. Court rulings in the US seem to support this idea.

The right to privacy became particularly relevant in a classic state case in Alaska, *Ravin v. State*.[38] Attorney Irwin Ravin arranged for his own arrest for possession in 1972. State judges determined that the right to privacy did apply in this case. They emphasized that the non-commercial, individual aspects of this situation made the ingestion of marijuana consistent with the right to privacy. After this decision in 1975, the Alaska legislature removed criminal penalties for possession of up to 4 ounces of marijuana for personal use. Nevertheless, in 1990, new laws restored cannabis prohibition in Alaska. Enforcement of the new law may be rare.[39] A subsequent Federal case, *NORML v. Bell* (1980) was unsuccessful in arguing that the right to privacy applied to marijuana possession.[40] The court asserted that using marijuana was not a fundamental right important enough to qualify for privacy protection. Thus, moralists against prohibition who rely on arguments related to the right of privacy currently have no support from the Federal courts in the United States. Subsequent cases in the United States related to cannabis have not focused on this approach.

Another moral argument against prohibition focuses on the right to property. Ideally, governments should not interfere with an individual's right to own personal effects, particularly those that will not cause harm to others. Thomas Szasz, the psychiatrist who gained notoriety for his debates about conceptualizations of mental illness, emphasized that cannabis, and indeed all drugs, are personal property. Given this fact, they therefore qualify for legal protection. The argument suggests that any state interference with drugs violates this right to property. Szasz and other libertarians do not advocate drug consumption, of course, but feel that interfering with property rights is worse than leaving drugs free. They view the decision to use drugs as part of an individual's liberty and responsibility – a moral issue outside the realm of legislation.

The United States Supreme Court rejected this argument before cannabis was even prohibited.[41] In this case, an individual asserted that the state's prohibition against possession of alcohol conflicted with the Fourteenth Amendment's declaration that no state shall "deprive any person of life, liberty, or property without due process of law." The court did not see the right to possess liquor as a fundamental privilege that no state could violate. The generalization to cannabis possession seems obvious.

❀ MITCH EARLEYWINE

Another argument suggests that drug use relates to the right to self-determination. Countries vary in the explicitness of their legal support for this right, but many world citizens like to think that their own lives are their own to lead. Self-determination may fall under the Ninth Amendment in the United States. This amendment emphasizes that citizens have rights that are not specifically listed in the United States Constitution. Anti-prohibition moralists reason that the right to determine what enters one's own body qualifies as this sort of self-determination. Legal scholars opposed to prohibition argue that this amendment applies to the possession and ingestion of drugs. Some point to United States history to emphasize their reasoning. Drugs were freely available to everyone at the time the United States was founded. These scholars reason that citizens drafting laws at the time would not have considered choosing what one ingests as a right because it was such an obvious right at the time. Szasz and others suggest that the originators of the US Constitution likely viewed the freedom to ingest whatever one chooses as too intuitively obvious to mention as a specific right.[42] Other students of history deny this suggestion vehemently. Marijuana cases related to the right to self-determination have not appeared in US courts. Most arguments that rely on interpretations of the Ninth Amendment do not fare well.

Proportionality of Punishment

A final moral argument against prohibition relies on the principle of proportionality – the notion that the severity of a punishment should correlate with the severity of the harm that the crime causes others. Most citizens like to believe that punishments fit the crime. We cherish the idea that the government would only punish in an effort to keep one citizen from harming another. This arrangement allows for an optimal combination of freedom and protection for all of the citizens. The hope is that people will behave freely in a way that does not hurt others. If they cause harm to someone else, they sacrifice some freedom as a result. Ideally, the magnitude of the punishment should vary with the magnitude of the harm caused. Manslaughter has a worse penalty than double parking because it creates more harm. The idea of this balance between severity of crimes and severity of punishment is often called proportionality, in the sense that reasonable punishments are proportional to the harm caused.[43]

With this idea in mind, we have to ask: How much should a government sanction its citizens for the possession of a dried weed? What is a reasonable punishment for owning a plant? Obviously, owning a plant causes no harm to others. The penalty for causing no harm should be nothing.[44]

NOTES

1   Richard J. Bonnie and Charles H. Whitebread, *The Marijuana Conviction: A History of Marihuana Prohibition in the United States* (Charlottesville: University Press of Virginia, 1974).

2   Douglas Husak, *Legalize This! The Case for Decriminalizing Drugs* (London: Verso, 2002).

3   William J. Bennett, "The Plea to Legalize Drugs is a Siren Call to Surrender," in Michael Lyman and Gary Potter, *Drugs in Society: Causes, Concepts and Control* (Cincinnati: Anderson, 1991), p. 339.

4   William J. Bennett, John J. Dilulio, Jr., and John P. Walters, *Body Count* (New York: Simon and Schuster, 1996).

5   William Raspberry, "Prevention and the Power of Persuasion," *Washington Post National Weekly Edition*, July 15–21, 1996, p. 29.

6   Joel S. Hochman and Norman Q. Brill, "Chronic Marijuana Use and Psychosocial Adaptation," *American Journal of Psychiatry* 130 (1973): 132–9; Robert Kaestner, "The Effects of Drug Use on the Wages of Young Adults," *Journal of Labor Economics* 9 (1991): 381–412; Robert Kaestner, "The Effect of Illicit Drug Use on the Labor Supply of Young Adults," *Journal of Human Resources* 29 (1994): 123–36; Robert Kaestner, "New Estimates of the Effect of Marijuana and Cocaine on Wages; Accounting for Unobserved Person Specific Effects," *Industrial and Labor Relations Review* 47 (1994): 454–70.

7   Mitch Earleywine, *Understanding Marijuana* (New York: Oxford University Press, 2005).

8   Bernard E. Harcourt and Jens Ludwig, "Reefer Madness: Broken Windows Policing and Misdemeanor Marijuana Arrests in New York City," *Criminology and Public Policy* 6 (2007): 165–81.

9   Rodney Myerscough and Stuart Taylor, "The Effects of Marijuana on Human Physical Aggression," *Journal of Personality and Social Psychology* 49 (1985): 1541–6; Stuart Taylor et al., "The Effects of Marijuana on Human Physical Aggression," *Aggressive Behavior* 2 (1976): 153–61.

10 Fredy Aviles et al., "Alcohol's Effect on Triggered Displaced Aggression," *Psychology of Addictive Behaviors* 19 (2005): 108–11.

11 Anthony Liguori, "Marijuana and Driving: Trends, Design Issues, and Future Directions," in Mitch Earleywine (ed.) *Pot Politics: The Cost of Prohibition* (New York: Oxford University Press, 2007); Joris C. Verster and

Edmund R. Volkerts, "Antihistamines and Driving Ability: Evidence from On-the-road Driving Studies During Normal Traffic," *Annals of Allergy, Asthma, and Immunology* 92 (2004): 294–304.

12 Douglas Husak, *Drugs and Rights* (Cambridge: Cambridge University Press, 1992).

13 Charles Roberts, "Data Quality of the Drug Warning Network," *American Journal of Drug and Alcohol Abuse* 22 (1996): 389–401; National Center for Catastrophic Sport Injury Research, Annual Survey of Football Injury (2007); available online at www.unc.edu/depts/nccsi/FootballInjuryData.htm.

14 Substance Abuse and Mental Health Services Administration, Office of Applied Studies (2009) *Treatment Episode Data Set (TEDS) Highlights – 2007 National Admissions to Substance Abuse Treatment Services*. OAS Series #S-45, HHS Publication No. (SMA) 09–4360, Rockville, MD; available online at www.oas.samhsa.gov/TEDS2k7highlights/TEDSHighl2k7Tbl4.htm.

15 Craig Reinarman and Peter Cohen, "Law, Culture, and Cannabis: Comparing Use Patterns in Amsterdam and San Francisco," in Mitch Earleywine (ed.) *Pot Politics: The Cost of Prohibition* (New York: Oxford University Press, 2007).

16 Dutch Ministry of Health, Welfare, and Sport, "Drug Policy in the Netherlands – Continuity and Change" (1995).

17 Lynn Zimmer and John Morgan, *Marijuana Myths Marijuana Facts* (New York: Lindesmith Center Press, 1997).

18 Robert Ali et al., *The Social Impacts of the Cannabis Expiation Notice Scheme in South Australia* (Canberra: Department of Health and Family Services, 1998); Joseph McGeorge and Charles K. Aitken, "Effects of Cannabis Decriminalization in the Australian Capital Territory on University Students' Patterns of Use," *Journal of Drug Issues* 27 (1997): 785–93; Australian Government Department of Health and Ageing, "National Drug Strategy Survey" (1995).

19 Lloyd D. Johnston et al., "The Aims and Objectives of Monitoring the Future Study and Progress Toward Fulfilling them as of 2006," Monitoring the Future Occasional Paper No. 65 (Ann Arbor: Institute for Social Research, 2006).

20 Donald Maloff, "A Review of the Effects of the Decriminalization of Marijuana," *Contemporary Drug Problems* 10 (1981): 306–40.

21 Johnston et al., "The Aims and Objectives of the Monitoring the Future Study."

22 Robert J. Dennis, "The American People are Starting to Question the Drug War," in Arnold S. Trebach and Kevin B. Zeese (eds.) *The Great Issues in Drug Policy* (Washington, DC: Drug Policy Foundation, 1990), pp. 141–86.

23 Johnston et al., "The Aims and Objectives of the Monitoring the Future Study."

24 Center on Addiction and Substance Abuse (CASA), "National Survey of American Attitudes on Substance Abuse II: Teens and Their Parents" (New York: CASA at Columbia University, 2006).

25 Robert J. MacCoun, "Drugs and the Law: A Psychological Analysis of Drug Prohibition," *Psychological Bulletin* 113 (1993): 497–512.

26 Louisa Degenhardt et al., "Toward a Global View of Alcohol, Cannabis, and Cocaine Use: Findings from the WHO World Mental Health Surveys," *PLoS Medicine* 5 (2008): e141.

27 Glenn Greenwald, *Drug Decriminalization in Portugal: Lessons for Creating Fair and Successful Drug Policies* (Washington, DC: CATO Institute, 2009), available online at www.cato.org/pub_display.php?pub_id=10080 (accessed August 13, 2009).

28 Wayne D. Hall and Rosalie L. Pacula, *Cannabis Use and Dependence: Public Health and Public Policy* (Cambridge: Cambridge University Press, 2003).

29 William Wilson, Robert Mathew, Thomas Turkington, Theodore Hawk, Robert E. Coleman, and Joseph Provenzale, "Brain Morphological Changes and Early Marijuana Use: A Magnetic Resonance and Positron Emission Tomography Study," *Journal of Addictive Diseases* 19 (2000): 1–22; Peter A. Fried, Barry Watkinson, and Robert Gray, "A Follow-Up Study of Attentional Behavior in 6-year-old Children Exposed Prenatally to Marijuana, Cigarettes, and Alcohol," *Neurotoxicology and Teratology* 14 (1992): 299–311.

30 Mary Anne Pentz and Steve Sussman, "Marijuana Abuse and Preventions," in Mitch Earleywine (ed.) *Pot Politics: The Cost of Prohibition* (New York: Oxford University Press, 2007).

31 Diana R. Gordon, *The Return of the Dangerous Classes: Drug Prohibition and Policy Politics* (New York: W. W. Norton, 1994).

32 See www.stash.norml.org/georgia-rep-tommy-benton-favors-caning-and-exe cutions-for-marijuana-crimes/.

33 Daniel K. Benjamin and Roger LeRoy Miller, *Undoing Drugs* (New York: Basic Books, 1991).

34 Robert J. MacCoun, "Drugs and the Law: A Psychological Analysis of Drug Prohibition," *Psychological Bulletin* 113 (1993): 497–512.

35 Hall and Pacula, *Cannabis Use and Dependence.*

36 *Leary v. United States* (1967) 5th cir. 383 F .2d 851; *Olsen v. DEA* (1967) 878 F.2d 1458 DCC.

37 *Employment Division v. Smith* (1990) 494 US 872.

38 *Ravin v. State* (1975) 537 P.2d 494 (Alaska).

39 Gordon, *The Return of the Dangerous Classes.*

40 *NORML v. Bell* (1980) 878 F.2d 1458 DCC.

41 *Crane v. Campbell* (1917) 245 US 304; 38S. Ct. 98.

42 Thomas Szasz, *Our Right to Drugs* (New York: Praeger, 1992).

43 See Doug Husak's splendid work on links between this idea and the prohibition of all drugs: Husak, "Drugs and Rights"; Husak, "Legalize This!"; Husak, *Overcriminalization* (New York: Cambridge University Press, 2007).

44 My hearty thanks to Brad Armour-Garb and Doug Husak for discussions relevant to this chapter. Extra thanks to Stacey Farmer for assistance with references.

CHAPTER 15

CANNABIS AND THE GOOD LIFE

Needs, Capabilities, and Human Flourishing

Many people want to get high – much to the chagrin of various law enforcement agencies. But do they need to? Surprisingly, a number of doctors, psychologists, and psychopharmacologists say, "Yes." They maintain that the need to alter our consciousness is just as basic as the need to eat and sleep.

One of the first to make such a claim was physician and alternative medicine guru Andrew Weil. In his 1972 book, *The Natural Mind*, he writes: "It is my belief that the desire to alter consciousness is an innate, normal drive analogous to hunger or the sexual drive."[1] Harvard psychologist Lester Grinspoon concurs: "I have come to the view that humans have a need – perhaps even a drive – to alter their states of consciousness from time to time."[2] Psychopharmacologist Ronald Siegel claims that this need is rooted deep in our evolutionary past. "There is a natural force that motivates the pursuit of intoxication," he writes. "This biological force has found expression throughout history. It pushed all the animals from Noah's Ark into patterns of drug-seeking and drug-using behavior."[3] This alleged need, if real, would have important implications for our drug control policies. If it really is as basic as our need to eat or sleep, the attempt to regulate it would be as futile as the attempt to regulate them. Recognizing this, the city of Vancouver, Canada recently cited this need as partial justification for their proposal to decriminalize marijuana.[4]

Those who claim that we have a need to alter our consciousness are not necessarily claiming that we have a need to take drugs. They realize that taking drugs is only one among many ways of altering our consciousness. Meditation, sensory deprivation, hypnosis, trance inducing music, amusement park rides – all produce altered states of consciousness. These researchers are claiming, however, that a life without altered states of consciousness would be an impoverished one, if not an unhealthy one.

Is this a credible claim? Do we have a need to alter our consciousness? If so, is it wrong to prevent people from doing so? Is a society that prevents its citizens from taking mind-altering substances unjust? To answer these questions, let's examine the evidence.

Human Needs

"Have you ever spun yourself around until you became dizzy?" asks psychologist D. F. Duncan. "Of course you have," he answers. This sort of mind-altering behavior is not only socially sanctioned but also institutionally encouraged. Every playground with a merry-go-round encourages this type of behavior. Less socially acceptable but still ubiquitous is the practice of holding one's breath or squeezing another's chest, which can also produce altered states of consciousness. The universality of this sort of behavior among children, Duncan claims, points toward a basic human need:

> Now imagine that this motivation or drive to experience this non-ordinary consciousness was a basic need, as in Maslow's hierarchy. It seems possible, then, that children engage in certain specific activities to satisfy one of the basic needs of growth and maturation – the need to alter consciousness or to experience non-ordinary consciousness.[5]

Duncan is referring here to the theory of needs developed by Abraham Maslow and suggesting that the need to alter consciousness should be included in it. Abraham Maslow (1908–76) was an American psychologist who attempted to explain human behavior by identifying the needs that motivate it. The attempt to meet these needs, he claimed, lies behind everything we do. Failure to meet them can lead to physical or psychological harm. Maslow thought that these needs are organized hierarchically. The needs at the lower levels must be met before the needs at the higher levels.

Originally, Maslow identified five categories of need:

1. *Physiological:* food, water, sleep, etc.
2. *Safety and security:* shelter, clothing, protection, etc.
3. *Love and belongingness:* family relationships, friendship, sexual intimacy, etc.
4. *Esteem:* confidence, achievement, respect, etc.
5. *Self-actualization:* developing one's capacities, problem solving, creativity, etc.[6]

Later in his life, Maslow identified a sixth category – self-transcendence – which seeks out "plateau" experiences like those achieved through serene contemplation or meditation, as well as "peak" experiences like those achieved through ecstatic or mystical awareness.[7]

Animal Desires

Besides the fact that mind-altering behavior can be found in all cultures at all times, some scientists point to the fact that animals alter their consciousness as evidence for the claim that there is an innate need to do so. Ethnobotanists have documented many cases of animals intentionally seeking out psychoactive drugs. Georgio Samorini, for example, chronicles such behavior in numerous species of animals – everything from flies to elephants.

"Fly agaric" mushrooms (commonly called "toadstools" in Europe) are a particularly potent source of the neurotoxin ibotenic acid. When flies "lick" the mushroom, they appear to fall down dead. A closer examination of the flies, however, reveals that many of them are just immobilized, for they often get up and fly away. Samorini attributes this lack of movement to a high level of intoxication which, he claims, the flies intentionally seek out.[8]

A less equivocal example of animals intentionally trying to alter their consciousness involves fly agaric and Siberian reindeer. "After they have eaten it," Samorini informs us," they run around aimlessly, make strange noises, twitch their heads, and isolate themselves from the rest of the herd."[9] The fact that they find this experience desirable becomes most

❀ THEODORE SCHICK, JR.

evident when you consider another behavior they engage in. Not all of the mushroom's ibotenic acid is absorbed by the system, so some of this psychoactive substance is passed out through the urine. The reindeer apparently know this because "Anytime these creatures scent fungus-rich urine in the vicinity, they make a mad dash for it, engaging in real battles among themselves as they vie for the position closest to the 'golden shower.'"[10]

Elephants' drug of choice is alcohol. Many of the palm trees that grow in their habitat bear fruits that ferment as they ripen. The elephants eat these fruits, often competing to consume as many as possible in the shortest amount of time. Once drunk, these elephants pose a serious danger to humans. According to Samorini, "Dumbo, the imaginary flying elephant of cartoon fame who sees dancing pink elephants himself after drinking alcohol, originated from the knowledge of his real, wild prototypes' fondness for drink."[11]

Marijuana is also sought out by various animals. In Hawaii, cannabis farmers must protect their crops from horses and cows. In Eastern Europe, the most voracious cannabis eaters are lambs. And in North America, deer are the greatest threat to marijuana crops.[12]

Many types of birds are attracted to hemp seeds. Sparrows are known to feed on them and parrot owners often add them to their diet to make them more talkative. "In Italy," Samorini tells us, "many canary owners do the same thing to stimulate their birds to sweeter song."[13]

Although the foregoing data may indicate that animals have a *desire* for psychoactive substances, it doesn't show that they have a *need* for them. Remember, to have a need for something is to be such that if you don't get that thing, you will suffer physical or psychological harm. The evidence presented by Weil, Duncan, and Siegel does not indicate that you (or any other animal) will be harmed by *not* getting high. On the contrary, Siegel provides examples of animals that have put themselves in mortal danger by altering their state of consciousness. In Maui, Siegel witnessed rats that were stripping hemp plants for their seeds. "At sunrise," he recounts, "a few stragglers, still feeding or perhaps slowed by intoxication, were quickly dispatched by the stealthy mongooses on their morning patrols."[14] These rats paid for their altered state of consciousness with their lives.

We may not have a need to alter our consciousness, but that doesn't mean that we can't benefit from doing so. Many argue that altering our consciousness can improve the quality of our lives. For example, Alexander Shulgin, the psycholpharmacologist who popularized MDMA (the psychoactive ingredient in Extasy), claims:

> Chemistry is an art form – like music is an art form. Are psychedelic drugs necessary for humankind? Is art necessary for humankind? Is music necessary for humankind? Is literature necessary? No. Of course not. We could deal without any of this, but life would be much more shallow, much more uninteresting, and less exciting.[15]

Like art, music, and literature, which enrich our lives by altering our consciousness, psychedelic drugs may do so as well. Used in moderation and in the appropriate settings, mind-altering drugs may lead to human flourishing.

The Good Life

According to Nobel prizewinning economist Amartya Sen and philosopher Martha Nussbaum, the quality of our lives is determined by the capabilities we have. To lead a good life, we must have the freedom and ability to perform certain functions like engaging in economic transactions, participating in political activities, and evaluating the courses of action available to us. Those with the freedom and ability to perform such functions are said to have the "capability" to do so. Sen and Nussbaum's theory of the good life, then, is often referred to as "capability theory." In their view, the more capabilities one possesses, the more fulfilling one's life can be.

Capabilities can also be used to measure the economic, political, and moral health of various social arrangements. For example, average per capita income is a notoriously unreliable way of evaluating the quality of life in a society, especially when a great deal of wealth is concentrated in the hands of a few. Properly understood, say the capability theorists, poverty is capability deprivation. People living in a society with a low per capita income may still enjoy a high quality of life provided that their society is arranged in a way that ensures they have the capabilities necessary for human flourishing.

Nussbaum identifies ten types of capabilities that are essential to leading a fully human life, no matter what society one lives in.

1. *Life.* Being able to live to the end of a human life of normal length.
2. *Bodily health.* Being able to have good health, including reproductive health.
3. *Bodily integrity.* Being able to move freely from place to place.

4. *Senses, imagination, thought.* Being able to use the senses; being able to imagine, to think, and to reason – and to do these things in a "truly human" way, a way informed and cultivated by an adequate education, including, but by no means limited to, literacy and basic mathematical and scientific training. Being able to use imagination and thought in connection with experiencing, and producing self-expressive works and events of one's own choice, religious, literary, musical, and so forth. Being able to use one's mind in ways protected by guarantees of freedom of expression with respect to both political and artistic speech and freedom of religious exercise. Being able to search for the ultimate meaning of life in one's own way. Being able to have pleasurable experiences and to avoid non-necessary pain.

5. *Emotions.* Being able to have attachments to things and persons outside ourselves.

6. *Practical reason.* Being able to form a conception of the good and to engage in critical reflection about the planning of one's own life.

7. *Affiliation.* (a) Being able to live for and in relation to others; (b) having the social bases of self-respect and non-humiliation.

8. *Other species.* Being able to live with concern for and in relation to animals, plants, and the world of nature.

9. *Play.* Being able to laugh, to play, to enjoy recreational activities.

10. *Control over one's environment.* (a) *Political.* Being able to participate effectively in political choices that govern one's life. (b) *Material.* Being able to hold property.[16]

Like Maslow, Nussbaum considers the best life to be one in which all your capabilities are fully realized. In such a case, you have become the best that you can be. Unlike Maslow, however, she doesn't believe these capabilities can be arranged hierarchically. All are important to a well-lived life.

The use of cannabis is relevant to the second and fourth types of capabilities identified by Nussbaum because it can improve one's health and enhance one's experiences. Roger Nicoll and Bradley Alger sum up the benefits of medical marijuana:

> Marijuana alleviates pain and anxiety. It can prevent the death of injured neurons. It suppresses vomiting and enhances appetite – useful features for patients suffering the severe weight loss that can result from chemotherapy.[17]

Marijuana can do all these things because it binds to receptors in our brains. We have cannabis receptors because our brains make their own form of cannabis – neurotransmitters known as "endocannabinoids" (short for endogenous cannabinoids). Scientists are just beginning to understand what these neurotransmitters do, but they already know that endocannabinoids form part of a backward-propagating or retrograde signaling system in the brain. A nerve cell that has received a message from another nerve cell can use endocannabinoids to signal the sender to stop transmitting. This function has a number of behavioral and psychological effects. Nicoll and Alger explain:

> Endocannabinoids are important in extinguishing the bad feelings and pain triggered by reminders of past experiences. The discoveries raise the possibility that abnormally low numbers of cannabinoid receptors or the faulty release of endogenous cannabinoids are involved in post-traumatic stress syndrome, phobias and certain forms of chronic pain.[18]

There is a sense, then, in which we do have a need for marijuana. Endocannabinoids are a necessary component of a normally functioning brain. Those whose endocannabinoid system is malfunctioning will experience physical or psychological harm. What's more, as Nicoll and Alger indicate, supplementing the endogenous cannabinoid system with exogenous cannabis may help alleviate physical and mental suffering. Those with the capability of using this substance, then, will enjoy a better quality of life than those without.

Not only can cannabis improve our bodily health, it can also enrich our senses, imagination, and thought. In his contribution to this volume, for example, Lester Grinspoon recounts how marijuana opened up new musical vistas for him. After listening to *Sgt. Pepper's Lonely Hearts Club Band* while under the influence, he remarks that it was as if he heard the music for the first time. Lindsey Buckingham, singer and guitar player for Fleetwood Mac, agrees:

> If you've been working on something for a few hours and you smoke a joint it's like hearing it again for the first time. You walk away for ten minutes and come back, and it allows you to keep coming back in for more and enjoy it.[19]

For many musicians and non-musicians alike, smoking marijuana changes the subjective character or felt quality of the experience of music.

✿ THEODORE SCHICK, JR.

Just how it changes that experience is hard to describe, but the fact that it does, and the fact that many people find this change enjoyable, is hard to deny.

Scientists have recently begun to identify changes in the brain that are associated with the altered perception of music produced by cannabis. Using a mobile EEG machine, Jorg Fachner, of the University of Witten/Herdecke in Germany, measured the brain wave patterns of cannabis users listening to music in the comfort of their own homes. He found an increase in Alpha-signal strength in the parietal cortex and significant Theta band changes in the temporal and occipital areas of the brain. The subjects in the studies, he says, experienced "altered music perception by hyperfocusing on acoustic space and broadened insight into the 'space between the notes.'"[20] He concludes that "THC has a measurable influence on cerebral music processing and seems to enhance acoustic perception temporarily."[21] As one would expect, the subjective effect of listening to music under the influence of cannabis is accompanied by objective effects in the brain.

Some believe that cannabis can improve the creative process as well as the listening experience. Eric Clapton, for example, says of cannabis, "A lot of my creative things came out first of all through marijuana. I started smoking when I was about eighteen or nineteen, and that would let out a whole string of humorous things as well as music."[22]

Jazz band leader Frank Foster echoes those sentiments: "I find that marijuana seems to particularly inspire me to want to create. I've found that some of my most meaningful or deepest ideas have come through inspiration gleaned from marijuana."[23]

Marijuana may seem to heighten one's creativity, but whether it actually does is open to question. Science has so far been unable to conclusively confirm or deny the effect of cannabis on creativity. A major research project in this area is currently being conducted by the Beckley Foundation, however. In their Autumn 2008 newsletter they report:

> The most recent addition to our cannabis research program is a large-scale naturalistic study into cannabis and creativity. This will involve several hundred participants smoking their own cannabis, and testing the effects of that on the propensity to enhance creativity. In this study we will also be looking at the subjects' genetic and personality types to test how these factors might influence the cannabis-creativity relationship. A second stage of the research will use neuroimaging to examine the neurological changes associated with creativity whilst under the influence of different ratios of THC and CBD.[24]

Hopefully, this study will determine whether the subjective sense of enhanced creativity associated with cannabis has a basis in objective reality.

There is a consensus, however, even among musicians, that drug *abuse* can stifle creativity. Ian Wallace, former drummer for King Crimson, describes his experience with hashish:

> Hashish was so powerful at first; it opened up all kinds of things I'd just lie there and fly. Listening to music was just absolutely amazing. You could get into the music so much – every note became a shape – it was really incredible, very influential. It enabled total concentration; it cut off all external influences. You would just get so totally into the sound that nothing else existed. But on the other hand, it took away the desire to do anything about it. After having stopped taking drugs completely, I've realized that for me being under the influence closed many of my creative doors.[25]

Roseanne Cash (oldest daughter of Johnny Cash) agrees:

> I used to think [drugs and alcohol] enhanced [the creative process] but now I think they blocked it. Once I got straight, which has been six years ago, I had a fear that I couldn't write, that being straight would numb out my work. I found that, in fact, drugs and alcohol blocked the access, made it far more elusive. It's not that it can never happen through that, but it makes it more difficult.[26]

Used to excess, any kind of drug can impair one's ability to create.

It has long been known that too much or too little of something can be bad for you. This insight has led a number of philosophers – including Aristotle and the Buddha – to claim that the best life follows the golden mean – the middle path between excess (too much) and defect (too little). According to Aristotle, what makes a person virtuous is that he or she has cultivated certain habits or patterns of behavior (known as virtues) that keep him or her on the path. The virtues help prevent one from losing one's balance and going overboard, so to speak. We may agree with Aristotle and the Buddha, then, that whatever benefits may be derived from cannabis, they can only be achieved through moderation.

Although we don't know whether or how cannabis improves creativity, a number of hypotheses about its effects have been proposed. Edward de Bono, for example, suggests that consciousness-altering substances affect creativity by helping us to break out of old patterns of thinking. He refers to this aspect of mind-altering substances as the "Provocative Operation" (PO) or the "depatterning factor." He describes it this way:

🍁 THEODORE SCHICK, JR.

PO gives a person permission to use ideas that are not coherent with experience. With PO, rather than rejecting these ideas, a person can use them as springboards toward other ideas. PO therefore allows for the use of "intermediate impossibilities." Since these "impossible ideas" do not fit established modes, they render possible a certain distance from existential experience. PO is a liberating device that frees [the mind] of the rigidity of established ideas, schemes, divisions, categories and classifications. PO is an instrument for insight.[27]

Neuroethicist Wrye Sontontia puts the point this way:

Mental diversity is where thinking and creativity comes from. That's where our greatest ideas, our greatest thinkers are mavericks – in how they approach the world. By limiting what states of cognition are legal or not, we're cutting off a vast potential for creative thought.[28]

Whether or not the change in our thoughts produced by mind-altering substances actually improves our creativity, there is no doubt that it enhances our sensory experiences. Those with the freedom to enjoy those experiences have a greater capability to live fulfilling lives than those without. As Nussbaum indicates, "Being able to use imagination and thought in connection with experiencing, and producing self-expressive works and events of one's own choice, religious, literary, musical, and so forth" is an important capability that all humans should possess. The fact that the substances needed to produce these enriched experiences are often illegal and thus difficult to obtain means that many people do not fully possess this capability. As a result, the quality of their lives may suffer.

The rejoinder often made to such a claim is that the legal restrictions are needed to prevent people from doing harm to themselves or others. In the case of those substances that do irreparable harm to the brain and body, such an argument might be compelling. But cannabis doesn't fall into that category. Unlike tobacco or alcohol, whose deleterious physical effects linger long after one has stopped using them, cannabis seems to cause no long-term damage to the brain or mind. In a systematic review of 66 studies of the effects of cannabis on brain structure, an international team of investigators led by R. Martin-Santos found: "Functional neuroimaging studies suggest a modulation of global and prefrontal metabolism during the resting state and after the administration of THC/marijuana cigarettes. Minimal evidence of major effects of cannabis on brain structure has been reported."[29]

Not only does cannabis use have no long-term effect on brain structure, it has no long-term effect on brain function. Harrison Pope, Jr. and his colleagues studied 108 people who had smoked marijuana over 5,000 times during their lives. After stopping cannabis use for a period of 28 days (monitored by urine tests) the subjects and a control group of 72 people (who had smoked no more than 50 times in their lives) were given a battery of psychological tests. The study showed that "By day 28, however, there were virtually no significant differences among the groups on any of the test results, and no significant associations between cumulative lifetime cannabis use and test scores."[30] Whatever psychological effects cannabis use has, they appear to be completely reversible.

Paternalism is the practice of restricting one's freedom for one's own good. Laws against marijuana use are paternalistic laws. Many find paternalistic laws immoral because they deprive people of their most fundamental right: the right to do with their bodies what they want. In the case of cannabis, however, such laws are not only immoral, but unnecessary as well. People do not need to be protected from the deleterious effects of marijuana because marijuana doesn't seem to have any significant long-term deleterious effects. From a moral point of view, then, the current laws restricting the use of cannabis are unjustified. They prevent people from living their lives in conformity with their own conception of the good and from exercising those capabilities needed to live a truly human life. A reform of such laws could lead to a better life for all.

NOTES

1 Andrew Weil, *The Natural Mind: An Investigation of Drugs and the Higher Consciousness* (Boston: Houghton-Mifflin, 1986), p. 19.
2 Lester Grinspoon, quoted in Jonathan Beaty, "Do Humans Need to Get High?" *Time* (August 21, 1989).
3 Ronald K. Siegel, *Intoxication: Life in Pursuit of Artificial Paradise* (New York: E. P. Dutton, 1989), p. 207.
4 City of Vancouver, "Preventing Harm from Psychoactive Substance Use," available online at www.csdp.org/research/preventingharm_report.pdf (accessed July 15, 2009).
5 D. F. Duncan and R. S. God, *Drugs and the Whole Person* (New York: John Wiley and Sons, 1982), ch. 18.
6 A. H. Maslow, "A Theory of Human Motivation," *Psychological Review* 50 (1943): 370–96.
7 A. H. Maslow, *"Theory Z:" The Farther Reaches of Human Nature* (New York: Viking, 1972).

8   Georgio Samorini, *Animals and Psychedelics: The Natural World and the Instinct to Alter Consciousness* (Rochester: Park Street Press, 2002), p. 73.

9   Ibid., p. 39.

10 Ibid., p. 40.

11 Ibid., p. 30.

12 Ibid., pp. 59–60.

13 Ibid., p. 54.

14 Siegel, *Intoxication*, pp. 153–4.

15 Alexander Shulgin, quoted in the trailer for "The Shulgin Project," available online at www.youtube.com/watch?v=46AcrskAmYE&feature=email (accessed September 20, 2009).

16 Martha Nussbaum, *Women and Human Development: The Capabilities Approach* (Cambridge: Cambridge University Press, 2000), pp. 78–80.

17 Roger Nicoll and Bradley Alger, "The Brain's Own Marijuana," *Scientific American* 291 (2004): 69.

18 Ibid., p. 75.

19 Lindsey Buckingham quoted in Jenny Boyd, *Musicians in Tune* (New York: Simon and Schuster, 1992), p. 201.

20 Jorg Fachner, "An Ethno-Methodological Approach to Cannabis and Music Perception with EEG Brain Mapping in a Naturalistic Setting," *Anthropology of Consciousness* 17 (2008): 78–103.

21 Ibid.

22 Eric Clapton quoted in Boyd, *Musicians in Tune*, p. 199.

23 Ibid., p. 204.

24 The Beckley Foundation, at www.beckleyfoundation.org/events/newsletter2.html (accessed September 10, 2009).

25 Ian Wallace quoted in Boyd, *Musicians in Tune*, p. 217.

26 Roseanne Cash quoted in Boyd, *Musicians in Tune*, p. 220.

27 Edward de Bono, *The Mechanism of Mind* (New York: Penguin, 1969), p. 265.

28 Wrye Sontontia, quoted in the trailer for "The Shulgin Project," available online at www.youtube.com/watch?v=46AcrskAmYE&feature=email (accessed September 20, 2009).

29 R. Martin-Santos et. al., "Neuroimaging in Cannabis Use: A Systematic Review of the Literature," *Psychological Medicine* (July 23, 2009): 1–17.

30 Harrison G. Pope, Jr. et al., "Neuropsychological Performance in Long-term Cannabis Users," *Archives of General Psychiatry* 58 (2001): 909–15.

CHAPTER 16

WEAKNESS OF WILL

The Cannabis Connection

 Most people agree that cannabis itself is no more harmful than cigarettes or alcohol, and many maintain that cannabis is significantly less harmful. Yet, in most places, cigarettes and alcohol are legal, while cannabis is not. The most serious contemporary argument in favor of marijuana prohibition is the claim that marijuana acts as a "gateway" drug. The gateway drug argument maintains that the consumption of marijuana increases the chances of consumption of more dangerous drugs, like cocaine and heroin, and therefore marijuana should be prohibited. The aim of this essay is not to challenge the gateway argument; rather, I am most interested in how the argument is supposed to work. My view is that the gateway argument, when adequately understood, does not present a powerful reason for cannabis prohibition.

The gateway argument against cannabis consumption relies on the notion that the use of cannabis weakens our resolve to avoid other more dangerous drugs. So how does cannabis weaken the will? I describe two ways that weakness of will can occur, one based on external motivation, the other on internal motivation. Motivational externalism posits that situations motivate us to behave independently of our own judgment, and sometimes against our better judgment. On this account, using cannabis weakens resolve because of the situations cannabis consumption requires, not because the drug itself weakens resolve. For instance, the criminal connections required for obtaining cannabis are often the same connections required for obtaining more dangerous drugs. By placing oneself in a situation where cannabis is available, the precipice of more dangerous drugs nears. Thus, taking cannabis is a form of moral brinksmanship and is made especially dangerous through prohibition.

The other way that weakness of will develops is when our own evaluations fail us by inappropriately weighing our convictions in competition with our desires; here something internal motivates us to act against our better judgment. For instance, the cannabis user may be relatively inactive – couch locked – while engaging in robust imaginative exercise about the world or her place in it. Here the normative results of imagination may conflict with an agent's desires to act. The worry is that moral imagination may produce such an elaborate story that it cannot be integrated into real life. The result of the epiphany while high simply may not translate into sober life. Still, without imaginative activity our generation of values would suffer and we would have a reduced capacity to critique our desires. I argue that the moment of weak will is occasionally the price we pay for imaginatively assessing our values.

Motivational Externalism

One way to answer the question "how does marijuana use lead to using hard drugs?" is to suggest that marijuana use alters the user's environmental circumstances and the new environment makes hard drug use more likely. This answer relies on a philosophical position known as *motivational externalism*. Motivational externalism is the thesis that one's behavior can be motivated from outside of a person's own value set. On this view, it is possible that people behave as they do not exclusively because of their own beliefs or desires, but because of situational forces to which they are exposed. In effect this means that sometimes we are directly motivated by our circumstances in spite of our better judgment.

If you are skeptical that the environment can really motivate actions with which you are uncomfortable, consider the results of Stanley Milgram's infamous research on deference to authority. Milgram arranged for test subjects to be brought into the control booth of a research laboratory along with a man dressed in a white lab coat and told that they would be helping the researcher by being a "teacher" in today's experiment. The subjects were then instructed to ask questions of a "learner" situated on the opposite side of a glass window and to administer an electric shock for wrong answers. The subjects administered shocks through a control dial labeled from a 15 volt "Slight shock" to a 195 volt "Very strong shock" to a final 450 volt setting labeled simply "XXX." In fact the "learners" in Milgram's experiment were confederates of the researchers and intentionally answered questions incorrectly.[1]

Of the test subject "teachers," 65 percent administered shocks all the way to an almost certainly fatal 450 volts, and beyond the 350 volt point at which "learners" became entirely unresponsive. In order to reach this point subjects had to shock another human being a total of 30 times, hearing responses like "Ugh! Let me out!" (165 volts), "Ugh! Let me out of here. Let me out of here, my heart's bothering me!" (195 volts), "Ugh! Get me out of here. I've had enough. I won't be in this experiment any more" (210 volts), and "Aaargh! I absolutely refuse to answer any more. Get me out of here" (300 volts). Throughout this screaming, subjects expressed extreme distress at shocking another human being, but were calmly told by the experimenter "Please continue" or "The experiment requires that you continue."

It should be noted that the subjects of Milgram's studies were not monsters, they were teachers, salesmen, engineers, and laborers – common members of the community helping with an experiment. They were never coerced or forced to continue. Yet, the situation in which they found themselves, an experiment, a lab at Yale, being told by a man in a white coat to turn the dial, led most of them to administer fatal shocks to other human beings. This result is not unique. The Milgram studies have been through numerous permutations and in each one a staggering number of normal people demonstrate the capacity to shock other human beings to death. In one follow-up, puppies were actually shocked to be sure that test subjects were not subconsciously identifying false cries from the "learners;" the result was 70 percent obedience, only 5 percent higher than the study on human beings.

The discussion of the Milgram studies is intended to make it clear that situational pressures can lead us to do things we don't want to do. Milgram's test subjects didn't want to shock others; indeed, many of them sobbed and were visibly shaken by the experience, so much so that similarly stressful experiments are no longer allowed by institutional review boards. Yet, the situational pressures led most people, 65 percent, to act in ways they believed to be misguided. Similarly, the situational pressures often referred to as "peer pressure" can lead cannabis users toward hard drugs, despite their own better judgment. Consider the common situation of the cannabis consumer under prohibition.

The cannabis consumer meets with her connection in a private setting, perhaps samples the product, negotiates a price, and makes a purchase.

During this encounter others are likely to be present who are engaged in a similar activity, only their focus may be hard drugs like heroin. Perhaps the cannabis connection and the heroin connection are roommates, maybe they are the same person, or are just friends. Just knowing a heroin user/dealer makes it much more likely that the cannabis consumer will try the harder drug. The point is not that the heroin user will intentionally pressure the cannabis user, it is simply that the situation can create pressure to conform. Just as the experimental context led subjects to administer fatal shocks, the demands of a situation often lead the cannabis user to try harder drugs with which she is uncomfortable.

Avoiding Brinksmanship

We often think of ourselves as strong willed people, able to resist temptation and stick with our decision not to use hard drugs in spite of situational pressures. Unfortunately, we often overestimate our efficacy or perhaps underestimate the potency of situational pressures. The problem with unrealistically high evaluations of our own will power is that they can lead us to accept very dangerous situations. The solution to this sort of weakness of will is to stay away from situations which might lead to results with which we are uncomfortable. If you do not want to use hard drugs, it may be best to avoid the sort of situations in which hard drugs are available.

It may be tempting to suppose that the dangers of cannabis use are not dangers that the reader faces. After all, the reader is now informed about the motivational power of situational pressures and with foresight may be able to resist those pressures. Unfortunately, empirical studies suggest that foresight only marginally improves resistance to situational pressures. In a follow-up on the Milgram obedience studies, researchers explained the results of Milgram's experiments to test subjects and then asked them to watch a video of the experiment and predict the behavior of a number of participants. The subjects in this follow-up predicted an average shock of 240 volts, better than the uniformed guess of 209 volts, but nowhere near the actual average of 375 volts. The point is that even armed with this new awareness of situational pressure the reader is still likely to be swayed by the environment in which cannabis is available.

It may be that harmless flirtation with illegal drugs is simply not as likely as was once thought. Moral philosopher John Doris writes, "The joys of ethical brinksmanship are, it seems to me, substantially reserved for the fortunate."[2] Although some cases of harmless experimentation surely exist, experimental results indicate that situational forces are likely to lead the cannabis consumer toward other illegal and significantly more dangerous activities. Illegal cannabis consumption is almost certainly a form of moral brinksmanship, a way of walking near the line and trying not to step over. But as we have seen, walking near the line makes it quite likely that one will step over.

Doris offers this advice: "Given the practical risks, there seems to be little reason for favoring strategies of steadfast exercise of the will over strategies of skilled self-manipulation."[3] He suggests that we should not expect will power alone to keep us from hard drugs; rather, we should be sure that we are not in situations likely to lead to hard drug use – presumably this includes hanging out with friends or cannabis connections with access to hard drugs. I am inclined to agree with this advice. It seems wise to avoid ever having to "Just say no." One never knows what will happen in the heat of the moment. Avoiding the situation is the surest way to avoid the problem.

However, it should be noted that the relationship between cannabis users and hard drug users, between cannabis connections and hard drug dealers, is not merely coincidental. There is a strong causal link bringing the communities of hard drug users and cannabis users into contact; specifically, the fact that they both trade on the illicit market. Producers and distributors of illicit drugs are often required to smuggle their products and the same mechanisms are often used to transport heroin as cannabis. Similarly, vendors and distributers often diversify their stock by selling multiple drugs, in the same way a convenience store sells both cigarettes and beer. Much of the situational relationship between cannabis and hard drugs is created because they both must be produced and distributed by the same market.

One way to effectively reduce the brinksmanship involved in cannabis consumption would be to end prohibition and legalize cannabis use. While cigarettes, coffee, chocolate, and alcohol all contain psychoactive ingredients, none is condemned by the gateway argument. Presumably the key to the switch from cannabis to other harder drugs is not the environment of psychoactive substances, but the environment of illicit trade. So long as cannabis prohibition continues, cannabis consumption will be a more dangerous activity and will be more likely to lead to hard drug use. Thus, the externalist version of the gateway argument indicates the need for cannabis legalization, not its prohibition.

❧ MICHAEL FUNKE

Motivational Internalism

A second way to answer the question "how does marijuana use lead to using hard drugs?" is to suggest that marijuana use alters the user's brain chemistry and the "brain on drugs" is more susceptible to the allure of other drugs. This second answer relies on a philosophical position known as *motivational internalism*. Motivational internalism is the thesis that behavior is motivated by one's evaluations, not one's situations. On this view, internal attitudes such as beliefs or desires motivate people to behave as they do. Weakness of will occurs when a conflict exists between what one believes one should do and what one desires to do. For instance, the cannabis user may believe that she should only smoke marijuana occasionally, but may find herself motivated to smoke much more often.

It is of course quite plausible to suppose that smoking cannabis can lead to smoking cannabis when one thinks it unwise to do so. Consider the parallel of watching TV. Who among us has not watched TV when we really thought we should be doing something else? Participating in an activity makes it more likely that we will participate again. The brain is a neural network and as you engage in an activity the neural pathway to that activity is strengthened, making it easier to follow that path again. This is why we tend to fall into habits and why using cannabis once makes it more likely that you will do so again, but the gateway argument goes a step further. According to the gateway argument, consuming cannabis makes it more likely that you will try harder drugs.

If the psychoactive effects of cannabis consumption can lead to using hard drugs it must be by altering the user's beliefs and desires. It is uncontroversial to suggest that indeed cannabis does alter the user's state of mind – that is the point after all. But can cannabis consumption really make the user believe that hard drugs are less dangerous or make the user want to take them more? Advocates of the gateway argument maintain that cannabis alters the user's mental attitude toward hard drugs in a number of ways. Perhaps the most common defense of this view is the notion that users who experiment with cannabis eventually find the high to be insufficient and then seeking a stronger high move on to harder drugs.

Interestingly, cannabis has a highly specific sort of reaction with the human brain and one quite unlike other drugs. Cocaine, amphetamines, and heroin all work by affecting the dopamine system. Dopamine is the neurotransmitter most closely associated with the pleasure and reward center of the brain. When dopamine is released it connects with dopamine receptors, closing a circuit and causing a pleasurable sensation. Cocaine and amphetamines work by blocking the reabsorbtion of dopamine and allowing the chemical to linger. Heroin and other opiates stimulate the production of dopamine by blocking inhibitory releases of gamma-aminobutyric acid. Cannabis, on the other hand, works by an entirely different mechanism.

The primary active element in cannabis, THC, stimulates the brain's cannabinoid receptors. Cannabinoid receptors are located throughout the brain, not just in the limbic system and not only around dopamine receptors. The result is that the high associated with cannabis shares some of the pleasures associated with other highs, but is substantially distinct. The point is that cannabis consumption does not lead to the sort of high that is pursued through the use of heroin or cocaine. Thus, the gateway argument cannot depend on neuropharmacology to support the claim that cannabis users will ultimately need a stronger high found in hard drugs. If the high from cannabis is physiologically distinct from the high of hard drugs it is hard to see how the desire for one leads to the other.

It is of course possible that the same psychological features that lead people to experiment with cannabis lead those same people to experiment with hard drugs. If, for instance, a desire for an altered perception of reality leads one to try cannabis, it is quite likely that the same desire could lead one to try opiates. Further, since cannabis is markedly safer than opiates it seems highly plausible that one would try cannabis prior to trying opiates. It might then appear that experience with cannabis led one to try opiates, but this would be a mistake. There is correlation between cannabis use and opiates, but not necessarily causation. If the same internal motivation leads one to take cannabis and hard drugs, then cannabis is not the gateway, it is merely on the same path.

A Creative High

For the internalist version of the gateway argument to work it must be that cannabis puts the user in a state of mind that makes hard drug use either more appealing or more difficult to resist. Perhaps the most compelling account of how this change can come about is through the creative associations that often come with cannabis intoxication. Users of cannabis often find themselves laughing at nothing, or at least next to

MICHAEL FUNKE

nothing. Very small features of ordinary life are often magnified while on cannabis. This magnification leads the user to notice the absurdity, beauty, comedy, disorder, etc. common to our daily lives. The high of cannabis can also lead the user to draw unusual connections between the particulars of daily life; grand theories and intricate plots are not an uncommon product of cannabis consumption. The worry is that these creative flights may undermine the cannabis user's active participation in life.

Consider the plot of a recent public service announcement on US television. A thirty-something alone in a basement is pictured smoking a joint. He is startled when asked, "What are you doing down there?" His answer: "Nothing, ma!" Then a voiceover says, "You can do nothing, too." The point is, for all of the imaginative energy created by cannabis, there is a strong suspicion that much more is being imagined than is being done. Of course, some will dispute this characterization and it is certainly true that a good sativa can produce quite an active high. However, it seems to me that there is a good point being made here, specifically, when we allow our creative or imaginative side space to operate, there is a real risk of losing productivity and of descending into more dangerous drug use.

Moral psychologist Michael Smith describes weakness of will as the product of two competing forces on the individual psyche, "normative reasons" and "motivational reasons."[4] Motivational reasons are best understood as psychological states capable of describing why we behave as we do – they are basic desires. Normative reasons are the product of moral imagination and represent our attempts to confer meaning on human behavior; they are not so much states as evaluations of our desires. It may be helpful to think of normative reasons as second order desires about what motivations we find to be worthwhile. On Smith's view we often fail ourselves because base desires generate action almost immediately, while the evaluation of desires often leads to more evaluation. One way to understand this point is to think of evaluation as leading to "analysis paralysis."

To see how cannabis can lead to analysis paralysis all one has to do is recall the anguish that sometimes occurs when deciding how to satisfy the cravings of midnight munchies. The relative merits of various food options can swirl in the brain and it is often very difficult to decide between them. The problem is bad enough when it only involves choosing between immediately available options, but it becomes seemingly intractable when it reaches a higher level of abstraction. If, for instance, you decide that only Mexican food will do, it doesn't take long before a

2,000 mile road trip seems like the only way to satisfy the urge. Then, since a 2,000 mile road trip cannot be had, it becomes quite tempting to just eat whatever is handy – even if it is crusty left-over Chinese takeout. In a case like this the creative high seemingly takes over and results in a perfect choice that is utterly out of reach, and the overall result is that the worst option is chosen.

Of course, the gateway argument has nothing to do with food choices, but the point is that creative normative judgment can be a form of idealizing (ah! that perfect burrito) and the real world usually does not match our normative ideals (ugh! stuck with leftover fried rice.) This leads advocates of the gateway argument to argue that cannabis can leave users disappointed with the world, depressed about the real options that they face, and can thus lead to hard drugs. I think that this sort of thing has probably happened. Cannabis very likely has led some people to see the wide disconnect between the world as it is and as it ought to be. This realization is disturbing, depressing even, and has likely led some people to seek escape in hard drugs. However, it must be remembered that looking beyond the world as it is and to the world as it could be is what makes the human experience special.

Surely cannabis consumption can lead to unhealthy levels of idealization, but stimulating the creative faculty is a necessary component of value in the human life. Beauty and joy are not things that we find in the world, and there is not one molecule of justice that appears anywhere. These concepts are human creations and it is the imaginative faculty that allows us access to them. Of course, imaginative concepts can lead to despair at our failure to realize them fully, but without them we would be adrift in a sea of possibilities with no way to navigate. It is imagination and creativity that provide us with a moral compass.

Taking cannabis can enhance and stimulate human creativity and can propel moral imagination, but we must be very careful to keep our dreams in perspective. Dreams exist to help shape the real world; they are not an end in themselves. Escaping the confines of sober existence in order to stretch our imaginative faculty is useful only to the extent that we can translate the results of our imaginative exercise into actions in real life. The fact that cannabis can over-stimulate the imagination is reason to treat its use seriously, but not a reason for all-out prohibition. In this respect, cannabis is much like religion; they can both help to stimulate moral development, but they both risk minimizing the importance of real life. Like religion, there is enough value in cannabis to offset the risk that comes with the active creation of values.

MICHAEL FUNKE

Shall We Close the Gateway?

In conclusion, it is possible that the consumption of cannabis can lead to the use of hard drugs, both because of the situations involved in cannabis consumption and the psychoactive affects of cannabis consumption on human imagination. However, I do not believe that cannabis consumption ought to be prohibited simply because it can act as a gateway to other, more dangerous drugs. In fact, the prohibition of cannabis is a large factor in the situational pressure on cannabis consumers to use hard drugs and ending prohibition would likely ease situational pressures to advance to hard drugs. Further, the psychoactive potential of cannabis to stimulate imagination is, much like religion, worth the risk of over-idealizing because the imaginative assignment of values is at the root of living the good life. In the end, creatively determining what is worthwhile in your own life and following that path is much more likely to lead away from hard drugs than toward them.

NOTES

1 Stanley Milgram, *Obedience to Authority* (New York: Harper and Row, 1974).
2 John Doris, *Lack of Character* (New York: Cambridge University Press, 2002), p. 149.
3 Ibid.
4 Michael Smith, *Ethics and the A Priori* (New York: Cambridge University Press, 2004), pp. 56–72.

NOTES ON CONTRIBUTORS

BRIAN R. CLACK, PhD, is Assistant Professor of Philosophy at the University of San Diego. He is the author of *Wittgenstein, Frazer and Religion* (1999) and *An Introduction to Wittgenstein's Philosophy of Religion* (1999), and co-author (with Beverley Clack) of *The Philosophy of Religion: A Critical Introduction* (2008).

RICHARD CUSICK is the Associate Publisher of *High Times* magazine and HIGHTIMES.com and the founder of REEFERDADNESS. com, a non-profit resource for pot-smoking parents. He was coeditor of *High Times* from 2005 to 2006 and Director of Advertising from 1999 to 2004. During the 1990s he edited *Gauntlet*, the magazine of Free Expression, wrote and published the indie comic book *Something Different*, and wrote "The Pot Page" for the New Jersey alternative newsweekly, the *Aquarian*. During the 1980s he was Vice President of Operations for the ICI Mortgage Bank. He has been a freelance writer since 1968 and has published over 200 articles. In 1969, when he was fifteen, he was assigned by *Life* magazine to interview the President of the United States, Richard Nixon. H. R. Haldeman said no. In 2007, when he was fifty-three, he was arrested with Keith Stroup, the founder of the National Organization for the Reform of Marijuana Laws, for smoking a single joint at the Boston Freedom Rally on Boston Commons and subsequently challenged the constitutionality of marijuana law and the concept of jury nullification in the Commonwealth of Massachusetts. Their 2008 conviction is currently under consideration by the Massachusetts Appeal Court. He is the single father of a beautiful daughter, Dylan.

MITCH EARLEYWINE, PhD, is Associate Professor of Clinical Psychology at the University at Albany, State University of New York, where he teaches drugs and human behavior, substance abuse treatment and clinical research methods. His research funding has come from the National Institute on Alcohol Abuse and Alcoholism, the Alcoholic Beverage Medical Research Foundation, and the Marijuana Policy Project. He serves on the advisory board for the National Organization for the Reform of Marijuana Laws (NORML) and the executive board for the Marijuana Policy Project. He works on the editorial boards of four psychology journals, reviews for over a dozen, and has more than 100 publications on drug use and abuse, including *Understanding Marijuana* (2005).

RUSS FROHARDT, PhD, is Associate Professor and Chair of the Department of Psychology at St. Edward's University in Austin, Texas. His doctorate is from the University of Vermont, where he studied the contextual effects of learning and memory and models of relapse behavior. He studied spatial navigation during a postdoctoral fellowship at Dartmouth College and currently focuses on the effects of neural and pharmacological manipulations on female sexual behavior in collaboration with his wife, Fay Guarraci, PhD, at Southwestern University in Georgetown, Texas. In his spare time he plays basketball and hangs out with his family, friends, and two boxers.

MICHAEL FUNKE, ABD, is completing a dissertation on weakness of will and addiction at the University of South Florida and holds teaching positions in the departments of philosophy and management. His research interests are primarily in moral psychology and practical ethics, with a special interest in the effects of drug use on human motivation. Despite extensive personal experimentation with weakness of will, Michael has published essays on environmental ethics, Confucian thought, and corporate social responsibility. His favorite external motivators include his toddling son, Quinn, and supportive wife, Rhiannon.

LESTER GRINSPOON, MD, Associate Professor Emeritus of Psychiatry at Harvard Medical School, served for 40 years as Senior Psychiatrist at the Massachusetts Mental Health Center in Boston. A Fellow of both the American Association for the Advancement of Science and the American Psychiatric Association, he was the founding editor of both the *Annual Review of Psychiatry* and the *Harvard Mental Health Letter*. He is the author or co-author of over 180 journal articles or chapters and ten books. A major area of interest has been "illicit" drugs. In 1990 he won the Alfred R. Lindesmith Award of the Drug Policy Foundation for "achievement in the field of drug scholarship." His first book, *Marihuana Reconsidered*, originally published in 1971, was recently republished as a classic. His latest book, *Marihuana, the Forbidden Medicine*, co-authored with James B. Bakalar, was published in 1993 (revised and expanded edition, 1997), and has now been translated into 14 languages.

ANDREW HATHAWAY, PhD, is a sociologist who teaches in the area of crime and criminal justice at the University of Guelph, Ontario. His research on cannabis, spanning over a decade, examines use patterns, benefits, problems and their implications for social policy development. He is principal investigator on two Federal grants exploring the use of marijuana for medical conditions and broader normalizing trends of cannabis consumption.

RYAN E. HOLT, BA, is a psychology graduate student at California State University at San Bernardino. His research interests and pursuits are learning and creativity. He has performed in improvisational Playback Theatre in the US and Germany. In his spare time Ryan enjoys painting, drawing, and watching *The Venture Bros.* and *Adult Swim*.

DALE JACQUETTE, PhD, is Senior Professorial Chair in Theoretical Philosophy at the University of Bern, Switzerland. His research is primarily in philosophical logic and metaphysics, including philosophy of mind, although his recent book-length forays into applied ethics include *Journalistic Ethics: Moral Responsibility in the Media* (2007) and *Dialogues on the Ethics of Capital Punishment* (2009, in the series New Dialogues in Philosophy that he edits). He admits to absolutely nothing concerning the purchase or consumption of any illegal substances, and attributes some of his most vivid, nearly cinematographic and apparently autobiographical descriptions of the subjective psychoactive effects of cannabis entirely to his prodigious reading and an overactive imagination.

TOMMI KAKKO, MA, is a postgraduate student in the English Department at the University of Tampere, Finland. He thinks reading philosophy often turns out to be more harmful than cannabis. He currently lives in Surrey, England, where he sometimes works as a translator to finance his philosophy habit.

JAMES C. KAUFMAN, PhD, is an Associate Professor at the California State University at San Bernardino and the Director of the Learning Research Institute. He is the author of *Creativity 101* (2009) and 14 other books, mostly on creativity; he also edits or helps edit three journals on the same topic. His plays have been produced off-Broadway and he was the narrator of the comic book documentary *Independents*. He lives with his wife, two dogs, and a two-year-old son who won't be allowed to read this book for at least another year or two.

MICHEL LE GALL, PhD, has a longstanding interest in things Middle Eastern. He has studied and traveled in Algeria, Tunisia, Libya, Egypt, Turkey, Israel, and Ras al-Khaima (United Emirates). While he has never personally "drunk hashish" (Ar. sharaba al-hashish), he has witnessed both its beneficial and sad effects first hand. A former associate professor of Middle East history at St. Olaf College, he now works in executive communications for a New York-based global professional services firm. His current interest in gourmet cooking has led him to chase around New York in search of all kinds of ingredients – from dried red peppers from Espelette to sea urchins (nothing to do with children in Dickens' novels). His favorite chef is Eric Ripert of Le Bernardin.

D. G. LYNCH, MA, is an epidemiology policy analyst, writer, and anthropologist based in Austin, Texas. He earned a BA in psychology from Miami University in Oxford, Ohio, and an MA in anthropology from the University of Texas at Austin. He has worked in the fields of health and mental health research and policy for nearly twenty years. He has guest lectured at the University of Texas in Austin, and has presented at multi-disciplinary academic conferences in Fez, Morocco, San Antonio, Texas, and Château du Hollenfels, Luxembourg. As a freelance writer his work has been published nationally and internationally for over two decades.

MICHAEL MONTAGNE, PhD, is Professor of Social Pharmacy and Senior Associate Dean at the Massachusetts College of Pharmacy. Educated as a pharmacist/pharmacologist and sociologist, he has researched over the past thirty years the social, cultural, and historical aspects of drug experiences, mostly anti-depressant medications, anesthetics, and psychedelic drugs. He believes cannabis is a model drug for studying the social pharmacology of users' effects and societal perceptions in many cultures over a number of centuries. He wishes that some sativa strains would not be cross-bred with indicas.

JACK GREEN MUSSELMAN, PhD, is the Director of the Center for Ethics and Leadership at St. Edward's University in Austin, Texas. He has a PhD in philosophy from Indiana University and does most of his teaching, consulting, and research in ethics. Since most of his siblings are attorneys, he's been advised to say that he may have smoked marijuana once in international waters but he didn't inhale, it was a youthful indiscretion, and he didn't enjoy it much.

BRIAN PENROSE, PhD, is a Lecturer in Philosophy at the University of the Witwatersrand in Johannesburg and runs the Philosophy Department's "Applied Ethics for Professionals" program. A Canadian expatriate, he received his PhD from Cornell University and has subsequently taught at Santa Clara University, the University of Toronto, and Memorial University of Newfoundland. His philosophical interests lie in ethics, applied ethics, and political philosophy, and he is working on another paper on how to understand recreational drug use. His other passions include walking with his pit bull terrier, exploring the back roads of Southern Africa, and listening to indy/alternative music. For a couple of inspirational years he lived very near the corner of Haight and Ashbury in San Francisco.

G. T. ROCHE, PhD, received his PhD in philosophy from the University of Auckland, writing a thesis on the Marquis de Sade. From 2006 until 2007 he lived in Tokyo, teaching ethics and critical thinking at Lakeland College (Japan Campus) in Shinjuku. He currently lives in Wellington, New Zealand. His philosophical interests include the aesthetics of industrial design, the ethics of neurological technologies, such as psychopharmacology, the psychology of morality, meta-ethics, applied ethics, early modern philosophy, and twentieth-century European philosophy. His papers on the anti-morality of the Marquis de Sade appeared in *Janus Head* and *Angelaki* in 2009 and 2010, respectively.

THEODORE SCHICK, JR., PhD, is Professor of Philosophy and Director of the Muhlenberg Scholars Program at Muhlenberg College. His books include *How to Think about Weird Things*, *Doing Philosophy: An Introduction through Thought Experiments*, and *Readings in the Philosophy of Science*. In addition to contributing to a number of volumes in the Philosophy and Popular Culture Series, including *Seinfeld and Philosophy*, *The Matrix and Philosophy*, *Lord of the Rings and Philosophy*, and *Led Zeppelin and Philosophy*, he has also contributed to Wiley-Blackwell's *Beer and Philosophy*. His friends complain that when he is not thinking about weird things, he is doing them.

JUSTIN SHARPLEY, BA, is a recent graduate from the psychology program at the University of Waterloo, Ontario. His undergraduate thesis research involved determining the relationship between confrontation with one's mirrored reflection and willingness to engage in consciousness-altering activities. He enjoys getting shpongled and can usually be found with his nose in a book, his hands on a PC, his ears pumped full of music, his hands covered in dirt, and his head in the clouds. His pet peeves include sick societies, unconsidered substance use, and winter without snow.

TUOMAS E. TAHKO, PhD, is a Visiting Research Fellow in the Department of Philosophy at Durham University, UK. He specializes in metaphysics and is working on a book provisionally titled *A Study of the Foundations of Metaphysics: The A Priori, Modality, and Essences*, but he occasionally enjoys tackling topics that have a bearing on the real world as well. He has always been fascinated about psychoactive substances and hopes that someday their role in society will be very different from what it is now.

CHARLES TALIAFERRO, PhD, Professor of Philosophy at St. Olaf College, is the author or editor of 11 books, most recently *Evidence and Faith: Philosophy and Religion Since the Seventeenth Century* (2005). He is on the editorial board of *Philosophy Compass, American Philosophical Quarterly*, and elsewhere. The only time Charles was put in jail due to drugs was when, as a 19-year-old passenger on the Magic Bus in 1972 from Istanbul to New Delhi, he laughed at a security guard who was smoking hashish on the Iran-Afghanistan border. He was let out of jail in two hours after he agreed to stop laughing.

MARK THORSBY, MA, teaches in the Philosophy and Religion Department of New Jersey City University and is currently completing his PhD in philosophy at the New School for Social Research, and has also taught at the New York City College of Technology. His research interests focus on environmental ethics, the philosophy of language, and phenomenological philosophy. Avidly addicted to cultural theory, Mark is an armchair Marxist currently writing a book on green philosophy. Coming from Northern California, he loves to drink bourbon, hike, and smoke while sipping Turkish coffee.